AFTER THE DANCE

AFTER THE DANCE

The Story of Le Roux Smith Le Roux

PHILIPPE LE ROUX

Published in 2025 by Unicorn
an imprint of Unicorn Publishing Group
Charleston Studio
Meadow Business Centre
Lewes BN8 5RW
www.unicornpublishing.org

Text © Philippe Le Roux

Philippe Le Roux has asserted his moral right under the Copyright, Designs and Patents Act 1988 to be identified as the author of this work.

All rights reserved. No part of the contents of this book may be reproduced, stored in or introduced into a retrieval system, or transmitted, in any form or by any means (electronic, mechanical, photocopying, recording or otherwise), without the prior written permission of the copyright holder and the above publisher of this book.

Every effort has been made to trace copyright holders and to obtain their permission for the use of copyrighted material. The publisher apologises for any errors or omissions and would be grateful to be notified of any corrections that should be incorporated in future reprints or editions of this book.

ISBN 978-1-917458-43-6
10 9 8 7 6 5 4 3 2 1

Cover designed by Felicity Price-Smith
Insides typeset by Mach 3 Solutions
Edited by Tracey Hawthorne and Elisabeth Ingles
Printed by Fine Tone

In memory of my mother, Philippa

Haven't I always loved the king completely, second only to God? And obeyed him? Haven't I been so fond of him that he almost became my god, and I almost forgot to pray because I was focusing on making him happy? And am I rewarded thus?
Queen Katherine, Henry VIII, Act 3 Scene 1,
William Shakespeare

Author's Note

The news of the death of my father, Le Roux Smith Le Roux, in August 1963, when I was 11 years old, made little impact on me. My parents divorced in 1955, and my mother Philippa – Le Roux's second, or perhaps third, wife[1] – returned with me to her parents' home in Pretoria while Le Roux remained in London. I had met him only twice, as far as I remember. He hardly contributed to my education, and the only present I received from him was a cricket bat on my tenth birthday. So, in my mind, he was simply a friend of my mother's.

When Philippa died in 2017, at the age of 99, I was living in London. Among her belongings forwarded to me from South Africa were the diaries of her marriage to my father and their time together in London when he worked at the Tate Gallery. There was a letter, written six years previously, on her 93rd birthday, in her clear but shaky hand, exhorting me to write the story of the family – 'Otherwise,' she wrote, 'who will know? What will become of everything we have done?'

She continued:

> You have been a wonderful son to me. I could not have asked for more. But I want you to do this last thing when I am gone. It is all there in the books and diaries. I wrote it all down. I thought I would have the strength to tell the story but I never found the time. And when I had the time in my later years I did not have the emotional energy to tramp down that lonely road again.
>
> Do not mistake me: I loved your father more than anything. I would have done anything for him – except destroy myself. So I returned to South Africa with you when you were little and began my life again, a much sadder but wiser woman. You were my salvation, and I could never have lived without you by my side.

---

1 Le Roux claimed that his first marriage ended in tragedy in 1932 when his wife died by drowning at Wilderness in the Eastern Cape during their honeymoon. There is, however, no documentary evidence of this marriage or death.

Author's Note

With my help and love, you must tell our story so that we can live in the future. Don't apologise. Be brave. Tell people.

With such an exhortation, what else could I do but follow the trail? Early in my research, I came across file TG 16/2/1/77/2 in the Tate Gallery Archive. It contained the Chairman of the Trustees file, covering the period during which Le Roux worked at the Tate Gallery. This file was embargoed for 100 years until 1 January 2079 under the Freedom of Information Act exemption s40(2). That is a long time for notes on a scandal to lie dormant.

―――

This biography is inspired by true events. It is essentially history made readable by using invented conversations deduced from public archives, books, and journals, from the biography of Eleanor Esmonde-White, as well as my mother's diaries, my father's letters and weekly broadcasts on the South African Broadcasting Corporation between 1950 and 1960, and my grandfather's account of his role in the Second Boer War. I have taken the literary licence of using fictional conversations between real people where there is evidence that these situations occurred.

All references and sources have been collected at the end, rather than individual quotes being attributed.

Conversations held in other languages (especially Afrikaans) are, by necessity, rendered in this script in English. I have also used some old-fashioned and politically incorrect terms that were used at the time.

Contents

Author's Note		vi
Prologue		xi

I	Courtship	
1	Early Encounters	1
2	Rushed Decisions	8
3	Hiatus	15

II	Le Roux's Background	
1	New Horizons	25
2	Art Classes	34
3	A European Adventure	39
4	The South Africa House Murals	48
5	Success and A Schism	57
6	Back in Cape Town	61
7	War Stories	67

III	The Job at the Tate	
1	Married Life	81
2	Useful Friendships	87
3	Doubts	99
4	Rothenstein's Offer	105
5	Delicate Subjects	111
6	Duties at the Tate	120

IV	The Great Tate Affair	
1	Rumbles About Rothenstein	131
2	Misgivings at the Gallery	137
3	Domestic Dissent	143
4	Scandals and Complaints	147
5	Interrogation	156
6	Royalty and Riches	164

After the Dance

V		The Final Curtain	
	1	The Worst of Times	175
	2	Broken Trusts	181
	3	The Langley Divorce Case	187
	4	The End of the Tate Affair	194
	5	Loose Ends	198

Acknowledgements and Thanks	202
Sources and References	203
Index	205

Prologue

In October 1932, just as spring burst on to the Cape Peninsula, the dean of the newly opened Michaelis School of Fine Art at the University of Cape Town left a short note for his most promising student, 18-year-old Le Roux Smith: 'Please come to see me at 9 a.m. tomorrow. I have news.'

Le Roux wondered what it was about. His work was up to date, and everybody seemed pleased with his progress over the preceding three years.

Thanks in part to his photographic memory, he was a precocious student who received a first-class matriculation from Jan van Riebeeck High School shortly after his 14th birthday and was subsequently offered a scholarship to study painting and fine art at Michaelis. He had loved drawing as a child, and no person or animal that visited the Smith house was immune to a rendering in his sketchbook. His artistic ability was inherited from his father's side: Johannes Anthonie Smith had been drawing and painting from an early age, considering drawing a God-given talent to be nurtured and developed as a private pleasure and meditation on the wonders of God's creation. He spent much of his spare time painting and etching and was appointed to the board of the South African National Gallery, which opened in 1930 in a new building on Queen Victoria Street, where several of his works were displayed.

The following morning, Le Roux stood outside the dean's office. When the secretary smiled at him, he presumed he was not in trouble.

'Come in, Le Roux,' bellowed the dean. 'Coffee? Coffee for both of us, Mrs Blake, and then close the door.' Indicating a chair to his student, the dean continued, 'So, Le Roux, I have some excellent news for you. Have you heard of Sir Herbert Baker?'

'The architect? Yes.'

Although he had returned to England, Baker's legacy loomed large in South Africa.[2]

The dean continued, 'Well, he has donated a scholarship for two of the most promising young South African artists to study mural painting overseas and then paint murals in South Africa House in London.' This building in Trafalgar Square, home to the High Commission of South Africa, had been designed by Herbert Baker and opened in 1932. 'You will be taught the basics. Then, you will travel through Europe studying the Old Masters' frescos and end up at the British School at Rome, where you will meet experts on mural painting who will teach you the art. Can you imagine, Le Roux: you will see the Sistine Chapel in the Vatican with Michelangelo's wonderful ceiling! Oh, I do envy you!'

'My father will not approve, Dean,' Le Roux said in a low voice. 'Does he need to know?'

'Of course he needs to know,' the dean said. 'Your father must give consent for you to travel, as you are under 21. But I am sure he will. It is a very prestigious, well-funded scholarship, an opportunity of a lifetime.'

Le Roux looked sceptical. 'My father does not like the British. My studying in London may be more than he will tolerate.'

The dean scoffed. 'The Boer War ended 30 years ago.'

'Not in my father's house, Dean.'

On Sunday morning, Le Roux, who was living at home with his siblings and parents in their house in Vredehoek, rose early, put on a jacket and tie, and polished his shoes. Then he, his mother, pushing four-year-old Annette in a baby carriage, and Johannes and Anthonie, Le Roux's elder brother, set off on the 20-minute walk to the Dutch Reformed Church, the Groote Kerk,[3] on upper Adderley Street.

---

2   Having arrived in South Africa in 1892 to visit his brother, Lionel, who was a fruit farmer, Baker made his mark almost immediately, and was commissioned to remodel Groote Schuur, the lavish home of Cecil John Rhodes, then prime minister of the Cape Colony, on the slopes of Table Mountain in Cape Town. Rhodes then sponsored the promising young architect's further education in Greece, Italy and Egypt, after which Baker returned to South Africa. Rhodes died in 1902, and Baker then partnered with various architects, before moving to the Transvaal (today's Gauteng) to design and build residences there; he quickly became noted for his work, and was commissioned by several 'Randlords', the wealthy mining magnates of Johannesburg, to design houses. He also designed commercial premises and public buildings, and undertook work in other parts of the country, including Durban, Grahamstown, King William's Town, Bloemfontein, George and Oudtshoorn.

3   Literal translation is Big Church.

Prologue

The service was even longer and drearier than Le Roux had steeled himself for – it was a couple of weeks before Christmas, and the dominee wanted to make the congregation 'earn' the coming festivities.

Le Roux gazed around the brown and white of the typically austere Dutch Reformed church, devoid of all imagery and paintings. As the dominee in the pulpit droned on, he took a pencil and a pad out of his pocket and began to sketch him, until his mother removed the pencil from his hand.

Finally the service ended, and they stood outside the church, talking to the other parishioners. His father commanded respect locally, and many of the congregation came to speak to him.

When they got back home, the house was full of the aroma of the mutton stew that Anna had put in the Esse oven that morning to slow-cook. They ate lunch in silence, broken only by the occasional babble of the little girl in her high chair.

After lunch, the three men went out on to the stoep, where Anna brought them a pot of coffee and mugs, before going back inside to put Annette down for her nap and clean up in the kitchen.

Johannes had not missed his younger son's apprehensive mood, and now he turned to Le Roux. 'Well?' he demanded.

Le Roux plunged right in. 'I have been awarded the Sir Herbert Baker scholarship to study mural painting at the Royal College of Art in London and the British School at Rome.'

Johannes poured himself a cup of coffee. 'You did not tell me that you had entered an art competition.' His tone was not one of approval.

'I didn't enter it,' Le Roux said deferentially. 'The dean put my name forward.'

'So why are you telling me? I am not interested in British prizes; you should know that.'

'You must sign the papers to allow me to travel, as I am under 21.'

Anthonie, who was studying architecture at the University of Cape Town, broke in. 'Sir Herbert Baker is a very famous architect, Pa. He designed the Union Buildings in Pretoria, you know. He has a wonderful sense of proportion.'

'I know who he is.' Johannes did not bother to hide his irritation. 'You boys must understand that Baker is just one more Englishman sent to South Africa to impose colonial culture on our country.'

Anthonie intervened again. 'We should praise God that Le Roux has been selected, Pa. One day he will be a fine South African artist who decorates the churches I build.' Then, smiling, Anthonie added gently, 'This is not politics, Pa.'

Johannes shook his head wearily. 'Anthonie, everything is politics. I'm going inside to speak to your mother. We will pray on it.'

As their father left the stoep, Le Roux looked quizzically at his brother.

'He will agree because it will break Mom's heart if he forbids it. Anyway, he thinks you are already an uitlander,[4] boetie,'[5] Anthonie said teasingly.

'And you, Anthonie? What do you think?'

'We all have something to contribute. I want to build churches so people can talk to God. The idea makes me feel very humble, Le Roux.'

The brothers sat in companionable silence for a while, listening to the sounds of the neighbour's children playing in the garden.

When Johannes and Anna came back out on to the stoep, Le Roux's heart leapt – his mother was smiling.

But his father's tone was dour, as usual. 'Son, I never wanted you to become an artist. You have so much talent that an artist is the least of what you could become. But it is not my place to stop you from going wherever you want. Give me the papers. I will sign them.'

Quickly, before his father could change his mind, Le Roux gave him the documents, and watched as his father signed them in his familiar, almost childlike script.

Handing the papers back to Le Roux, Johannes said, 'Perhaps, when you have seen the world, you will remember your people, and you will come back to practise your God-given talents in South Africa.' He held out his hands. 'Now, son, hold my hand and your brother's, and let us say a simple prayer to wish you well on your journey and ask God to bring you back to us one day.'

---

4   Foreigner.
5   Little brother.

I

Courtship

1

Early Encounters

1943

In October 1943, 23-year-old Philippa Russell attended a performance in Pretoria of Lillian Hellman's play *Watch on the Rhine* put on by African Consolidated Theatres, with Gwen Ffrangcon-Davies[6] in the leading female role. Set in America in 1940, it called for a united international alliance against Hitler. The main male character, a German-born engineer called Kurt Mueller, was played by a local man, Le Roux Smith Le Roux, known for his photographic memory, who had volunteered to step in when the professional actor fell ill.

When the performance was over, the audience gave the cast, and Le Roux in particular, a standing ovation. Philippa clapped until her hands stung.

Philippa's husband, John Russell, was a doctor with Allied forces fighting 'up north' in Africa, and her escort that night was a Frenchman called Jacques de Simon, who made it his business to know a great deal about everybody. 'You must meet Le Roux and his wife Juanita,' he said to Philippa as they walked to his car. 'I did not see her there tonight, but they are an interesting couple. I'll arrange it.'

A couple of weeks later, Jacques organised an intimate dinner party at the Pretoria Club. Among the ten guests were the Le Rouxs. Jacques

---

6   A British actress who worked mainly in TV and theatre, her life partner was the South African-born Margaretha van Hulsteyn, stage name Marda 'Scrappy' Vanne; she had moved to London in 1918 to pursue her acting career, where she had met Ffrangcon-Davies. The couple founded a theatre company in South Africa at the outbreak of the Second World War. Le Roux became friends with Ffrangcon-Davies, and she would play a role in his later life in London.

1

positioned Philippa to his right, and Le Roux on the other side of her. Juanita was seated opposite them.

Before she sat down, Philippa noticed Mrs Le Roux's hourglass figure, black low-cut dress and elbow-length gloves. She had a tiny wisp of flowers and veiling on her high-piled hair, and her mouth was a half-moon, giving a lingering impression of a smile. Philippa, wearing a simple yellow cotton frock with a pair of diamond earrings that her mother, Blanche, had lent her, felt very plain by comparison.

Philippa was instantly captivated by Le Roux, with his deep, guttural voice and a hint of an Afrikaans accent. 'So, what do you do when you're not gallantly stepping in to save the day for theatre productions?' she asked him, flashing a flirtatious smile.

'I run the Pretoria Art Centre during the day, and at night and on the weekends I paint. And you?'

'I write for the *Rand Daily Mail*, for the social pages. I would like to interview you,' she said. Seeing Le Roux's less-than-enthusiastic expression, she added, 'An article might help you recruit students for the art centre and even sell some of your paintings, you never know.'

Le Roux immediately looked more interested. 'That would be very good of you.'

'Oh, that's all right. I just love fitting people into slots.'

'What slot are you going to fit me into?'

'I haven't quite decided, but it will be a bad one if you don't let me interview you,' Philippa said, giggling.

As dinner progressed, Le Roux talked to her casually and engaged her in conversation, interested in her thoughts and feelings. Philippa occasionally glanced at Juanita on the other side of the table, but she was completely engrossed in conversation with the men on either side of her, who seemed to be vying for her attention.

As the dessert was served, Le Roux announced, 'You will not believe what happened to me today. I took the bus from Johannesburg to Pretoria, and it broke down on the Pretoria side of the Jukskei River bridge.' The other guests stopped talking and began to listen to Le Roux's story. 'All the other passengers had experienced bus breakdowns and, in a few minutes, had hitched lifts from passing motor cars. Seeing I was a novice, the bus driver explained that it might be hours before the bus was repaired and suggested I hitch a lift as well. A couple of cars and a truck shot past, but a huge white ambulance stopped, with two nurses in crisp white uniforms. As I hesitated, they laughed, and the driver said, "Get in. We can drop you in the centre of Pretoria." I must say, my staff at the art centre were surprised when I arrived. One wag commented, "Well, as long as you don't leave the same way!"'

Everybody laughed – except Juanita, who looked bored. Perhaps she had heard the story before, Philippa thought.

Later, on the drive back to Philippa's parents' house, where she was staying, Jacques asked how she had liked the couple.

'I hardly spoke to her, but she is certainly very attractive.'

'Indeed,' Jacques agreed.

'Does she paint too?'

'I don't think so. No, she is *charmante*, which is sufficient for this type of man.'

Philippa saw the Le Rouxs again a few weeks later at a Friday-night cocktail party at the Spanish Embassy. She noticed that Juanita was at the centre of a group of very engaged men while Le Roux remained apart from the general crowd.

It was a hot evening, and the place was heaving with people drinking, smoking and talking. Philippa looked across the room and saw that the curtains were drawn back from large glass doors separating the living room from the garden. She slipped outside into the dark.

The evening was very still, but she could hear thunder in the distance and see occasional flashes of lightning in the sky. As she put a cigarette in her mouth and struck a match, she saw Le Roux exit through the sliding doors. He had his hands cupped around something.

'What have you caught?' she asked, stepping closer to him.

'A large moth.' He opened his hands a fraction so she could see the insect. 'Look at its markings. Isn't it splendid?'

She examined the exquisitely patterned creature lying passively in his hands. She also took the opportunity to look more closely at his long, sensitive fingers. 'I wonder why they always fly into the light, where they burn and die,' she murmured.

'One of life's mysteries.'

Philippa, struck by how dark Le Roux's eyes looked in the half-light, said softly, 'May I remind you, Le Roux, that you promised me an interview?'

'I did.' He thought for a moment. 'What about lunch at The Fountains on Thursday next week?'

'Lovely.'

'Until Thursday, then,' he said, briefly holding her hand.

The following day, as usual, Philippa went to the Caledonian Charity Market, where she worked each Saturday with a group of friends manning flower and vegetable stalls laden with choice selections from their own gardens and selling homemade cakes. The market had been so successful in raising funds for the Red Cross war effort that the organisers had extended their offer to include luncheons, which attracted a loyal following.

Juanita Le Roux and Lee Milroy had been roped in to help on this particular summer's day. Lee and her husband Den, originally from England, had newly arrived from the Middle East, where Den had been with Reuters, and he had been appointed to the *Rand Daily Mail* in the Pretoria office. Den, Philippa's boss on the newspaper, was tall, with a ready smile and tanned skin; Lee was slight, with dark hair and pearly teeth, which she showed to advantage when she spoke. Philippa was soon drawn into their group of young married friends, bachelor diplomats and socialites.

Philippa finished her duties as a waitress and joined Juanita and Lee at their table.

'I suppose everybody is going to the Balleaus' New Year's Eve party?' Juanita asked. She cupped her thick white china coffee-cup in both her hands. Philippa noticed they were strong and capable hands, quite at variance with the ditsy overall impression Juanita created.

Philippa and Lee nodded. 'I'm told there will be a Mexican band,' Lee said.

'Really? That will be fun,' Philippa said.

'Yes, I think it will.' Juanita wiped her mouth daintily. 'Will the delicious Robert be taking you, Philippa?'

'He has suggested it,' Philippa said, a little surprised. Robert Benson was an ex-padre who sometimes escorted her to parties. She thought him pleasant enough but colourless. She added, 'He is nice but not particularly special.'

'Oh.' Juanita tossed her head. 'But you see, I think he is very special. I tell you what: I shall take him over from you at the party.'

'Thanks very much,' Philippa said, laughing. 'And who shall I have?'

'Why, Le Roux, of course,' Juanita replied, looking wide-eyed at her. 'Darling, he thinks you're absolutely wonderful, and you think the same of him, so we shall all be happy.'

Philippa, feeling caught out – which was ridiculous, for she had done nothing wrong – stammered, 'Don't be silly. I am happy with Robert, thank you.'

'Nonsense, dear,' Juanita said, and gave her a wide smile, then stood up and wandered off.

Philippa looked at Lee with a shocked expression. 'What did she mean by that?' she asked.

Lee shrugged. 'I expect she's bored with Le Roux. I hear they nearly parted when they were living in Cape Town, and he took the position at the art centre here to give them a fresh start. Perhaps it isn't working.'

Thursday arrived, and Philippa drove to The Fountains, a public park on the outskirts of Pretoria. It was a beautiful day.

Le Roux was already seated at a table, but when he saw her, he rose, took her arm and guided her to her seat.

He attracted the attention of the waitress and ordered drinks. She felt his charm wash over her and was grateful for the distraction of taking out her notebook and pen while she composed herself.

'So, tell me about the art centre,' she said, with forced brightness, as he turned his dark-green eyes on her.

'The aim is to teach practical art to about 150 postgraduate students, and eventually expand the art centre into a national performing and visual arts institution. Unfortunately, as an educational institution, it falls under the auspices of the department of education, which is bureaucratic and blinkered. But I try to be flexible.' He laughed, and she felt mesmerised by his personality and the timbre of his voice. 'You can imagine how much that annoys them!'

There was a hiatus while they went to the buffet. She helped herself to the lamb curry and rice buffet, the chutney and the sliced tomatoes with onion and then watched Le Roux heap his plate.

Once they'd sat down again, she asked, 'What bothers you about the department's rules?'

'Oh, many things, but that is not for your article.'

While she considered that, Philippa chewed on her food, then said, 'Okay, tell me about the murals you did in London, then.'

As Le Roux spoke, Philippa watched him, wordless, until he said, 'Then the war started, and I couldn't join up because of my father's political views. He's the head of the Ossewabrandwag[7] in the Cape, and I didn't want to be asked to spy on him.'

'Oh, my goodness. That's a pro-Nazi organisation. How awful.'

'I've never agreed with his politics. The best light I can put on it is that he fought the British in the Boer War and hates Britain.' He leaned back and sighed. 'Perhaps you should also leave my father out of your article,' he said.

'There is a lot that I cannot write about you, Le Roux. I will need a large picture of yourself to fill my page,' laughed Philippa.

They ordered coffee, and she called for the bill. When Le Roux took out his wallet, she waved him away. 'It's on the newspaper. It's the least I can do. Perhaps you'll invite me to one of your shows at the art centre in return?'

As the pair strolled towards their cars in the shade of the towering plane trees, Le Roux stripped a piece of loose bark from a tree and held it out to Philippa. 'Come, smell it,' he said.

She did – it was deliciously spicy – then smiled and looked up at him.

He leaned forward and kissed her gently. 'Don't you know that I have fallen in love with you?' he said.

Philippa, appalled and delighted, could only shake her head.

'Well, now you know.' He kissed her again.

'For goodness' sake, Le Roux,' she said, softly, and pulled away. 'We are both married.'

On the night of the Balleau party, all was light and music. Candles had been set in brown paper bags filled with sand and placed along the path to the front door of the house so that it looked as if fireflies lighted it. There was no wind, and the lanterns hanging from the trees illuminated the branches eerily.

Inside, there were about 60 people in the large candle-lit room overlooking the city's night lights. A huge fire on the veranda added to the festive atmosphere, and delicious aromas drifted from the kitchen.

---

7   The Ossewabrandwag (literally, 'ox-wagon sentinel') had been founded recently, in 1938, in celebration of the centenary of the Great Trek. Its leader, attorney Johannes van Rensburg, who had previously served as minister of justice in Jan Smuts's cabinet, supported the Nazi government in Germany.

The hostess came hurrying across the room with a dish of hot mushroom patties, which she handed around while welcoming newcomers. 'Enchanting, my dear,' she commented as she greeted Philippa. 'Take off your cloak and let me get you a drink.'

Someone offered Philippa a cigarette and lit it for her. As she stood, smoking and looking around, the front door opened, and Juanita and Le Roux came in. Juanita wore a close-fitting dress in smoky taffeta that showed off her curvaceous figure, and a circle of gardenias on her piled-up hair, with a wisp of veiling that touched the tip of her nose. Within a few minutes, she had drawn a group of men around her.

Philippa moved from circle to circle, making small talk, and avoiding both Juanita and Le Roux, while at the same time being acutely aware of where they were at all times. It was exhausting and she couldn't wait for the evening to end.

Just before midnight, she was rounded up to dance, and within minutes, Le Roux claimed her. 'I want to see the New Year in with you, so I'm afraid you must suffer my dancing for the next few minutes,' he said, his mouth so close to her ear that his breath sent shivers down her spine.

She looked around nervously, but Juanita was otherwise occupied. When they reached the French windows, he took her hand and helped her over the sill into the garden. She thought they would stop on the grass outside the house, but he pulled her along the lawn until they were out of sight.

'We shouldn't be disturbed here.' He put his arm around her as they stood looking at the fireworks.

'This is all very sudden, Le Roux. I will have to think about it.'

2

Rushed Decisions

1943

Two years previously, in 1941, 21-year-old Philippa, the only daughter of Blanche and Adolf Davis, had become a voluntary nurse and gone daily to the Pretoria General Hospital,[8] opened just eight years previously, to learn first aid and how to bandage wounds.

One morning, when she arrived, the sister in charge of the ward had ushered her into a private room. The curtains were drawn, and there was a strange smell. In the dim light, she had seen a man lying in bed. 'Sit here and watch this patient,' she was told. 'If you see any change in his condition, ring the bell.'

The man lying beneath the white sheets was very pale, and his breathing was harsh. He looked old and brittle. His eyes were closed and his lips were blue. There was a tube protruding from under the covers which fed into a bottle hanging at the side of the bed. Philippa had tried not to look at it. Another bottle hung above the bed, from which a tube was attached to the man's arm.

She had sat quietly and watched him. His hand lay on the coverlet, and she reached out to touch it. His skin was cold and clammy, and she had snatched away her hand.

His eyes had opened, and he had tried to speak. Philippa had bent over him, her heart beating with nervousness. She had realised his open eyes were unseeing, and there was a strange noise in his throat. As she pressed the bell, a great rush of wind came out of his throat, and he gave a convulsive shudder. She put her arms around him, afraid he might fall off the bed.

---

8   Today it is the Steve Biko Academic Hospital.

The sister had found her, eyes wide with horror, clutching the dead man. 'You had better go outside, child, and get some air,' she told her.

The next day, Philippa had put in for a transfer to the dental unit at Voortrekkerhoogte,[9] where there was an army hospital.

There, she had met the young Pretoria doctor John Russell. Tall and good-looking, with an easy sense of humour and a lazy grace, John had charmed Philippa. He played tennis 'admirably', danced 'beautifully' and wore his uniform 'with distinction', she confided to her diary.

John's father was a well-known doctor in Pretoria, and Philippa enjoyed going to their house, which was full of laughter and gaiety, unlike the formality of her own home. 'His mother is a dark-haired Scotswoman who plays the piano and is full of dimples. She never worries about her figure and accepts her plumpness with amusement, as do her husband and son,' Philippa wrote in her diary.

The friendship soon turned into a romance. 'When he drives me home in his little car, we sit and embrace, and I find that I do not shrink from him but enjoy the kisses and exploring hands,' she told her diary. 'When I indicate that I have no interest in going further, he does not press me.'

Philippa liked the attention and grew to trust the young doctor.

One evening, when they were sitting in his car after he'd brought her home, he broke off their embrace and gently held her chin in one hand. 'Philippa, I love you,' he told her. 'It would make me so happy if you would agree to be my wife.'

'Oh, John, that would make me happy too!' Philippa said, and the two resumed their passionate embrace.

But when Philippa told her parents the next day that John had proposed, she was unpleasantly surprised by their reaction. 'Oh, darling, don't be silly,' Blanche said, and was backed up by Adolf, who added, 'Why are you in such a rush? You hardly know him.'

'You have never, ever allowed me to do anything that I really wanted,' she told her parents, passionately, 'but you shan't stop me from marrying John!'

It made for awkward living in the Pretoria house, and matters didn't improve a week later when John called her excitedly. 'I've been ordered up north next week,' he said. 'Will you marry me before I leave?'

---

9   Founded around 1905 by the British Army, and called Roberts Heights after Field Marshal Lord Roberts, the area was renamed Voortrekkerhoogte in 1939. It was renamed Thaba Tshwane in 1998.

'Of course!' Philippa said. 'Up north' meant fighting in North Africa, against Erwin Rommel and his Afrika Korps, and it seemed very romantic to Philippa to tie the knot before her brave soldier was deployed.

Her parents, however, weren't moved.

'Don't do this, darling,' Blanche begged.

'I suppose you will do it if you've made up your mind,' said Adolf, philosophically, 'but I think you are very foolish.'

A week later, on the morning of 19 February 1943, Philippa and Blanche made their way alone to Christ Church in Pretorius Street for the wedding. Adolf, a barrister, had been delayed in Cape Town, where he had a case.

John had arrived with another doctor, Reginald Harper, who would be his best man. Without any choice, Blanche – unhappily – gave her daughter away.

For their wedding night, John had booked them into the classy six-storey Carlton Hotel in central Johannesburg. The finest in southern Africa when it first opened in the early 1900s, with the previously unheard-of luxuries of electric lights, elevators, a telephone in every room, and even air-conditioning, it remained a very fine establishment in 1943. However, after months of anticipation in the front seat of John's little car, Philippa felt let down by the consummation of their marriage. 'I never imagined sleeping with someone would be like that, and I was greatly relieved when it was all over,' she wrote in her diary. 'Now I understand why Mother is so disparaging about "having connection", as she calls it.'

It didn't help that at nine o'clock the following morning, there was a knock on the door, and Reggie Harper walked in. Philippa, disconcerted, put on her dressing gown and went into the bathroom to wash, dress and prepare for the day while the two men slapped each other on the back, Reggie congratulating John with an unpleasant kind of nudge-nudging.

John ordered a slap-up breakfast for the three of them but Philippa couldn't enjoy it. 'As I watched the two men laughing and joking, I couldn't eat and suddenly wondered what on earth I had done,' she wrote.

Philippa was saved further deep thought about her marriage, as John left almost immediately for North Africa. Forced to choose between living in the barracks or with one of the newly-weds' two sets of in-laws, Philippa acceded to Adolf's wish that she remain with Blanche and him in their Pretoria house. She wasn't that keen, but she recognised that she'd been hasty rushing into the marriage and felt inclined to do what her parents wanted.

Two months after the Balleaus' party, when Philippa told her parents that Le Roux had asked her to marry him, Adolf was angrier than she had ever seen him.

'How dare you behave like this?' he stormed. 'You disgrace yourself and us by your behaviour. Have you no decency? As for that man – how dare he approach you in this matter while he and you are still married? His behaviour is abominable.'

Blanche intervened. 'She should never have married John —'

'Now, don't go taking the girl's part. You have always spoiled her.' Adolf threw his hands in the air. 'Oh, the whole thing appals me.'

'But I love Le Roux,' Philippa said.

This was true. Since New Year's Eve, she and Le Roux had met frequently, and when she was with him, the future seemed simple. Among the trees and in the long grass, Le Roux talked about their future, and his voice and loving words mesmerised her. She was sure that being with him was all she wanted, that he would make plain her path.

Adolf was, however, wholly unconvinced. 'Love? What do you know of love? Do you love us – your mother and me? Look how you've behaved. I've tried to do everything I can for you – given you a good home, a wonderful education at Wycombe Abbey – and all you've done is fritter your time away. And now —'

Blanche held up a hand. 'Philippa,' she said, forcefully, 'just wait for a little while. Let Le Roux clear up his own affairs before you do anything final. And at least wait until you see John. You owe him that.'

'I've already written to him and asked for a divorce.'

Blanche gritted her teeth in irritation. 'Why must you always rush into things? It's always all or nothing with you.'

'Le Roux loves me, and I love him,' Philippa said, defiantly.

For the next week, Adolf was irritable and Blanche withdrawn. Philippa accepted their disapproval and felt guilty and frightened. Her parents had planted a seed of doubt, and now, even when she reread Le Roux's letters, his patient arguments did not convince her.

John asked for compassionate leave and returned to see Philippa. When they met, at the Carlton Hotel in Johannesburg, her fear left her. How like John to have chosen the place of their disastrous honeymoon night, she thought. They spoke in a bedroom he had booked for the night, sitting awkwardly opposite each other, each on one of the two single beds.

John urged her to take time – to wait. 'We were together for only one week,' he said. 'I think you should give us a chance. I hope to return very shortly, and then we can make up our minds later.'

But Philippa saw now that he was nothing more than a friend she had known and liked. 'I can't go back to you,' she told him gently. 'I don't love you. I'm so sorry – I should never have married you. It's all my fault. Please don't make me feel worse than I already do. Agree to the divorce and do it as quickly as possible. If you ever loved me, do that.'

In May 1944, Le Roux received a short and civil letter from his father.

Mymers
Yeoville Road
Cape Town

Dear Le Roux

Juanita's father has been in touch with me. He understands that you and Juanita are getting a divorce which he wants postponed because of some inheritance matter. He asked for my help. At the same time, Cape Town is humming with rumours about your private life that I am sure are designed to harm you. Obviously, there is an implication for your mother and me, which is unfortunate. Please attend to this matter immediately.

I have told Juanita's father that I will help him in any way I can.

Greetings

Father

By this time, Philippa had divorced John, but Le Roux's divorce from Juanita was delayed, mainly because the financial arrangements between them were complicated. To make matters worse, Le Roux received a worrying visit from the department of education, and he recounted this in a letter to Philippa, who was in Cape Town at the time.

Philippa, my most beloved,

Much as I adore you, I have such ghastly news and am so overwhelmed by it that you must forgive me for not breaking it more gently. The chief inspector of education called on me today to warn me personally that four prominent but unnamed Pretoria women had laid an 'immorality' charge against me with the department. They apparently stated that I was morally unfit to be head of an educational institution, as could be seen from the fact that my wife had left me and was bringing a divorce suit against me on the grounds of my misconduct with the wife of an army medical officer now up north!

Let me relieve your mind at once by telling you that I ultimately succeeded in blowing the charge sky-high – and succeeded also in my main object of keeping your name out of it. I was also given to understand that the department suspected that the allegations were made in malice rather than good faith, and that they would accept a sworn statement from me that the allegations were false, that my wife was away temporarily for completely natural purposes, that she was returning to me within a reasonable space of time, and would then be prepared to support my sworn testimony, and that the divorce suit was just fiction.

I had a kind of nervous storm afterwards, almost like hysteria. So I drank half a tumbler of rum and went for a long walk. I then phoned Juanita in Cape Town as I now have to ask her to return to me, for a while at least. She was terribly upset about what happened and wanted to write to the education department straight away.

Do you know, darling, I feel quite paralysed, so I'll stop now.

Oh, Philippa, my sweet angel, I feel I have been hurled back in the dark. I hardly know what to say and I have cried like a child about all this. Whatever happens, I want you to know this: as long as I live, I shall love you and my heart will remain yours forever.

All my love, darling one.

Your

Le Roux

Juanita duly returned to Le Roux to convince the department of education that she had not left him and to sort out the details of their divorce. In a letter to Philippa, he said, 'I am sorry that Juanita has had to come back, but I need to be sensitive to the department's concerns. You will just have to trust me on this.'

By the time Philippa returned to Pretoria at the end of June 1944, Juanita had gone back to the Cape and she went to see Le Roux. He looked terrible. His skin was grey, he had lost weight, and the smudges under his eyes looked as if they had been drawn in charcoal.

'I have to go into hospital in Cape Town for tests. The doctor thinks I may have cancer, but he isn't sure. It may mean treatment or an operation. I shall have to take leave without pay from the art centre until it is over,' he told her.

'My dearest love, I shall look after you,' Philippa said. She sat down next to him on his bed and took his hand. 'You shall have the best treatment money can buy. I have some jewellery I can sell, and we shall face this together.' She leaned against him and sobbed quietly, 'Oh, Le Roux, please don't die!'

At home, she threw herself on her bed and wept until she could cry no more.

That evening she sat at the dinner table with her parents but could eat nothing.

After the meal was cleared away, Adolf called her to his study and closed the door. 'What has happened?' he asked her.

His look of concern and the kindness in his voice made her break down. She sobbed out what Le Roux had told her.

Adolf agreed it was an unfortunate turn of events but reasoned that all the facts had not yet come to light. 'It's not certain that Le Roux has cancer,' he pointed out, patting his distraught daughter on the shoulder. 'He is an artist and an emotional chap. You should not distress yourself further. Let us wait and see what news the tests give us. Ask your mother for a sedative and get a good night's rest.'

3

Hiatus

1944 & 1945

When Le Roux returned from Cape Town the following week, he phoned Philippa and asked her to go and see him in his office. 'Why, darling?' she asked. 'I can see you at your home tonight.'

'I have something important I want to tell you. I would rather do it in the office.'

Philippa could hear the strain in his voice and she was worried. Perhaps he had to go straight to hospital for the operation. 'All right, darling. I'm on my way.'

When she arrived at his office at the art centre, Le Roux stood up as she entered. Dressed formally in a pinstripe suit, he looked wan and grave.

'Hello, Philippa,' he said. 'I'm sorry to drag you down here like this, but I wanted to tell you something myself – before anyone else did. Please sit down.' He indicated a chair.

Philippa's heart began to thump so loudly that she wondered if he could hear it, and she clutched her bag more tightly. 'No,' she said. 'I'll stand. What's this about?'

'I have asked Juanita to return to me again.' He moved towards Philippa, but she backed away. 'I know this will be a shock to you – but believe me, I am thinking only of you when I do this.'

'What do you mean?'

'In the divorce agreement we drew up, which we haven't finalised yet, I promised to pay her a third of my salary. But as things are, it looks as if I'm going to have to take significant unpaid leave, and then I won't be earning any salary at all. I have bills, you know that, and I feel I can't drag you into all this. Juanita is still my wife, and she must help me at this time. I cannot be out of work and still support her in Cape Town.'

'So you're asking her to return?' Philippa asked quietly, her disbelief clear.

'I have already done so. She arrives tomorrow.'

'Oh, Le Roux.' Philippa's sense betrayal was evident in her devastated expression and her breaking voice. 'You said you loved me. You promised.'

'Darling, I do love you, believe me.'

He took a step forward, but she held up her hand. 'No, no. Don't come near me.' Now anger crept into her voice. 'How could you have done this?'

'It is only for a time, darling.'

She continued as if she had not heard him. 'You never even consulted me.'

'It is only until I am well again. Everything will work out, you'll see.'

Two weeks later, as they were having coffee after lunch, Blanche let slip that Adolf had gone to see Le Roux.

'When?' Philippa asked, putting down her cup and staring at her mother.

Blanche was flustered. 'Well, the truth is that we were so concerned at the turn of events that your father went to see Le Roux several weeks ago.'

Philippa demanded the whole story. When Adolf got back from work, she cornered him in his study. 'What did you see Le Roux about?' she asked.

'Blanche told you?' Adolf asked, then tutted his annoyance.

'So tell me what you spoke to him about.'

Adolf sighed and sank heavily into the large wingback chair behind his big oak desk. 'Perhaps it is better that you know, Bobs. I did go to see him the night you told us he was ill. I went after you had fallen asleep. You must understand how worried I was about you. I had to see for myself what the position was exactly.'

Her father's defensive build-up annoyed Philippa. What had he said to Le Roux?

'He did look ill, I must say,' Adolf continued. 'I told him I understood he wasn't well, and I was sorry, but that he could not make you his nurse – that the correct thing for him to do was to get his wife back to look after him. I thought we had better get things straight before it was too late. Believe me, Bobs, it is for the best.'

Adolf hadn't looked at Philippa once during this confession.

Philippa, her sense of injustice rising with each word her father uttered, now unleashed her anguish and fury. 'So, it was you! You did this to me! How dare you interfere! How dare you!' She stared wild-eyed at Adolf briefly before saying, 'I have to get away. I shall go to Cape Town, and don't try to stop me.'

'What about your job?' he asked.

'I shall take unpaid leave.'

'Well, don't come crying to me for money.'

'I'll never come crying to you for anything again as long as I live,' she told him coldly.

The Cape Town Philippa arrived in towards the end of August 1944 seemed greener and lusher than she remembered, and she immediately found accommodation in a bed-and-breakfast in the upmarket suburb of Claremont, in the shadow of Table Mountain.

Her place of refuge was the beach at Muizenberg. She would catch the train from Claremont and travel the 20-minute journey to the sea, putting her head out of the window to gulp the salty tang of the ocean.

As soon as the train stopped at Muizenberg station, she would jump out and run along the platform, down the steps, and into the main road, turning left at the corner into Beach Road with its bedraggled parade of shops – the chemist, the dry-cleaner, the shoe shop, and the green-grocer on the corner who always put his goods on stalls on the pavement, making it difficult to pass. She would buy a couple of the peaches or figs in season, and saunter across the hot tar onto the white sands, looking along the curving ribbon of the beach into the distance as far as the eye could see.

It was there that she would walk and weep into the wind until she was exhausted, repeatedly asking the waves why Le Roux had left her.

She would swim far beyond the breakers, longing to be swept out to sea, to sink into oblivion. Afterwards, cold and pale, she would walk to the old pavilion, up the steps and across the thick wooden slats, enter the restaurant and order a glass of hot milk. When she was warm again, she would head back to Claremont on the train.

One day, after a swim, Philippa walked towards the little seaside suburb of Kalk Bay, where her grandmother, Rose, lived in a residential hotel. Philippa looked forward to the time they would sit together holding hands. Sometimes, Philippa would read to her, for although

Rose could see people's faces, her eyesight was not good enough to decipher letters on a page.

The old lady was stout. Her corsets creaked as she walked, and her thinning grey hair was pulled tightly into a knot atop her head. Her aged face was lined and furrowed, with sallow skin marked by liver spots on her cheeks. However, her eyes sparkled behind her gold pince-nez glasses, and her smile radiated warmth.

When Philippa returned to Pretoria in September 1945, after a year in Cape Town, she went back to work on the *Rand Daily Mail*. The war had just ended and there was an expectant mood in the capital city.

Her parents were delighted at her return and her father even opened a bottle of wine to celebrate the occasion.

Where Le Roux was concerned, she tried to control her longing for him – the sound of his voice, the feel of his lips on hers, and the physical feelings he aroused in her. Despite his continued and passionate avowals of love and promises that they would still be together, some day, somehow, there was now a doubt in her mind that she could not dispel. Her emotions veered between belief and disbelief – longing and renunciation, pride and lack of it – until her head whirled, and she would sink into the oblivion of sleep or work to dispel her agonies of spirit.

The daily conference at the *Rand Daily Mail* was held at eight each morning, and the small group of journalists gathered round the editor's desk, talking and smoking, until Den Milroy's head lifted and his eyes circled the room to see if anyone was missing. Philippa, seated next to him, loved these sessions.

Den leaned back in his chair and asked, 'So, what suggestions have you today?'

'It's the Spring Festival and they crown the Jacaranda Queen tonight at the city hall,' someone said.

Philippa bit her pencil. 'Oh Lord, I completely forgot. I suppose I have to go?'

Den nodded, then said, 'By the way, there's a new chap at the British High Commission by the name of Morrice James.[10] I'm told he had a

---

10   John Morrice Cairns James, Baron Saint Brides, who was 30 years old when Philippa met him, was a senior British diplomat. He served as British High Commissioner to Pakistan, India and Australia, and was known as a specialist in the affairs of the Indian subcontinent.

good war – corvettes – might be worth a paragraph for your page on Friday.'

Philippa noted the name. Later, back in her office, she checked her diary. She had two more days to find enough material to fill her page, which had to be sent by courier to Johannesburg on Wednesday night for inclusion in Friday's newspaper. She picked up the telephone and dialled.

'British Embassy.'

'Could I please speak to Mr Morrice James?'

She was put through, and a rich voice with a hint of a Scottish accent announced itself.

'Good morning. I am Philippa Russell from the *Rand Daily Mail*, and I wondered if you could spare me a few moments this morning for an interview. I write a page of events in Pretoria – newcomers, people leaving – and as you have just arrived, I wanted to include you – something about your work, your war record, you know the type of thing...'

She heard a snort of laughter at the other end of the line.

'Why me, for heaven's sake?'

'You're new, and nobody knows you. And I have a space to fill, and I have to write about you before tomorrow. Please?' Philippa begged him flirtatiously, enjoying the moment.

They agreed to meet that afternoon at the embassy, where Philippa was thrilled to discover that Morrice James was tall, with laughing eyes and a head of dark, curly hair. He also got straight to the point, handing her a sheet of paper and saying, 'I dislike being interviewed, Miss Russell, so I have written out a few points that might be of interest to fill that gap in your page —'

'But I wanted to ask you about your experience in the war,' Philippa objected. 'People would be interested —'

'I have included a couple of anecdotes,' he said, smilingly, but Philippa could see that his mind was made up.

Back in the office, Philippa read through the notes he'd given her. She learned he had been decorated twice for gallantry and that he was a fine scholar, having graduated from Balliol with honours. He was also a keen mountaineer and rower.

Bright he certainly was; fun also, she would imagine. She remembered those piercing eyes resting on her and smiled to herself.

Within a few weeks, Philippa was seeing Morrice frequently at diplomatic parties, which he had to attend in his official capacity as political attaché. Very often, they would slip away to dine alone. She enjoyed being with him and, to her surprise, he never tried to make their friendship intimate.

One day, Morrice phoned and asked her to dine the following Friday night at High Commission House. As usual, she accepted with pleasure.

She assumed it would be a formal party, and wore a long, plain, scarlet dress. She knew she looked beautiful.

Morrice had invited her for 7.30, and she was surprised to see no cars in the drive when she arrived. She was shown into the drawing room by the butler. Morrice, also in evening dress, joined her.

'Am I early?' she asked.

'No. Punctual as always. There is no party. We are dining alone.'

Over their drinks, Morrice told her of a recent walking trip he had been on with General Smuts.[11] 'I admire the Oubaas tremendously. He's a wealth of information on practically every subject one cares to mention and an expert on wildflowers – did you know that?'

'I had heard it. I have met him a couple of times but find him intimidating.'

Their two places were next to each other at the vast dining table, and after the meal, they returned to the drawing room, where the central lights had been dimmed and only the table lamps lit the space. The butler brought them coffee, and Morrice put on some music while Philippa lit a cigarette and thought how good it was to be there with him.

Then Morrice said, 'Philippa, I have asked you here tonight to tell me what is going on between you and this chap Le Roux.'

He was looking at her intently, and she met his kind but serious eyes. 'So you've heard?'

'I've heard some gossip but I want to hear the story from you.'

Philippa was totally unprepared for this but felt curiously relaxed and at home. She started speaking and found it was a relief to pour out the tale to Morrice – if only to clear her own mind. She told of their meeting and her slow but growing interest, and of Juanita's strange role

---

11 Jan Smuts, whose nickname was 'Oubaas' ('Old Boss'), played leading roles in the creation of the Union of South Africa in 1910, in leading South Africa's troops against the Central Powers (mainly Germany, Austria-Hungary and Turkey) in the First World War, and at the Paris Peace Conference of 1919, advocating for the creation of the League of Nations. He served as the country's prime minister from 1919 to 1924, and returned as prime minister in 1939.

in throwing them together. She spoke about Le Roux's proposal and her divorce, and then of his illness and her flight to Cape Town. Now, she told Morrice, she avoided any intimate contact with him. He still phoned her but she either didn't take his calls or she made their conversations as brief as she could.

When she finished, there was a deep silence, then Morrice kissed her tenderly. 'I want you to marry me,' he said, quietly. 'I will be posted abroad soon. I am very ambitious and mean to get to the top. We can go there together.'

Her immediate reaction was one of amazement and of gratitude. How wonderful: he would take her out of all this turmoil and mess.

Philippa's decisions about Le Roux had now been resolved. She would have a new life and forget her longing and her hurt. She would have money, children, and an interesting way of life. The diplomatic lifestyle had always appealed to her.

She told her parents that Morrice had asked her to marry him, and hurried out of the house before they could comment.

Interviews filled her morning, and she was tired when she sat down to write in the afternoon. She had just put the paper in the typewriter when the phone rang. It was Le Roux.

'Darling, thank God I've managed to reach you. I must see you desperately. Where on earth have you been?'

Philippa's heart began to beat unbearably but she kept her voice even and her tone cool and clipped. 'I've been swamped. As a matter of fact, I'm very busy now. I'll call you later.'

'No, no!' Le Roux's excitement came flooding down the line, and Philippa felt herself being swept up in it, as much as she was trying not to be. 'I have important news to tell you. I must see you. It will only take a few minutes. I'll come to your office.'

Philippa hesitated – she wanted to object, to deny him, but no words would come. By the time she had collected her thoughts, she realised he had hung up.

Some 20 minutes later, she walked out into the sunlight, and there was Le Roux, tall and pale, and looking disorganised in a crumpled, badly cut suit, with his tie awry. Seeing how his dark eyes softened at the sight of her, she felt her resolve melting.

'It's wonderful to see you. You look marvellous,' he said, taking both her hands in his. His fingers, warm and dry, seemed to send little electrical currents up her arms.

'Le Roux, I have decided —' she said, putting a real effort into injecting iron into her voice.

But he held up a hand and gave her a pleading look. 'You can say whatever you wish when you've heard my news,' he said. 'Juanita and I have finalised our divorce agreement, and she will leave for Cape Town at the end of this week. You and I can be married, darling!'

Philippa stared at him, speechless, trying to make sense of the maelstrom of emotions she was experiencing. This was exactly what she had wanted, what she had so longed for – but also what she had worked so hard to put behind her.

'Marry me, darling.' He smiled, pressing her hands. 'You know that we are meant for each other.'

That evening, Philippa told her parents at dinner what had happened that day. She looked neither in the eye until she had finished describing Le Roux's proposal and then added, softly, 'I am going to do it. I am going to marry him.'

There was a silence. Philippa heard Blanche sigh.

Then Adolf said, 'You know it will be a disaster.'

She looked up and met her father's eyes. His expression was tired.

'Perhaps,' she said. 'But I cannot help myself.'

II

Le Roux's Background

1

New Horizons

1933

On a windy day in May 1933, the dean of Michaelis Art School drove young Le Roux Smith to the Cape Town docks to board a Union-Castle mail steamer for the 18-day sea voyage to Southampton. After speaking with the purser, they struggled down the corridor with Le Roux's luggage and made their way to the lowest deck. It was a small cabin with a tiny porthole, but Le Roux was too excited to care.

The ship's horn sounded the warning that it was preparing to weigh anchor, and Le Roux saw the dean back upstairs and on to the gangway.

'Now, Le Roux,' the older man said, 'you are an ambassador for university and country, and we all do so hope that you will enjoy your time abroad and come back a great success.' Smiling, he held out his hand. 'Oh, I nearly forgot. The young lady from the University of Natal who won the other scholarship boarded the ship in Durban. Her name is Eleanor Esmonde-White. Do look out for her.'

It was a clear but gusty afternoon. Le Roux leaned against the ship's railing as the huge liner made its slow way out of Table Bay harbour, nudged this way and that by the tugs. He watched the activity in the busy harbour – the other passenger liners and cargo vessels, the sailing ships, trawlers and yachts.

Finally, when they were out on the open sea, Le Roux braved what had become a steady breeze as he watched the mountains of the Cape Peninsula sinking slowly below the horizon. As the ship was buffeted by the first shuddering heaves from the Cape Rollers – those heavy diagonal swells along the Northern Cape coast – he returned to his cabin and fell asleep.

He woke late the following morning and walked along the gently swaying passage to the washroom. The water pressure was hardly sufficient to wash, but he spent ten minutes doing his best and felt better for it.

On deck, the breeze was fresh, and the sea was full of white foam as the wind took the tops off the waves. He could feel the sun burning his face, so he looked for some shade, finding it on a deck-chair.

At lunchtime, he was shown to a table laid for ten, one of several tables dedicated to the younger passengers. He sat down and was soon joined by several other young men and women, some solo like him and others in small groups. He tried to guess which was Eleanor, but it was not easy, so he forgot about her. They all seemed so jolly and excited about the sea voyage. He smiled and made polite conversation but retreated as soon after eating as he could.

The ship's library was somewhat better than he had expected, so each day he sat on the deck reading.

Near the end of the trip, he was reading on deck when a young, stern-faced girl came up to him and held out her hand. 'I am Eleanor. You must be Le Roux.' She was not particularly pretty but held herself well and had an intensity that Le Roux liked.

'How clever of you. I must say I did try to guess which one you were but gave up. I was looking in the wrong direction.'

'Well, now you know, I hope we can catch up in the next couple of days.' She paused, watching the wind spray the tops of the waves. ' I have no idea what to expect when we arrive.'

'I'm sure it will be wonderful, and we will never want to leave.'

'Oh, but we must go back to South Africa to paint murals in public buildings and teach others,' responded Eleanor. 'That is what the scholarship says.'

'So it does.' Le Roux smiled and looked into her serious face. 'And you will be our conscience on this matter.'

She gave him a quizzical look – was he laughing at her? – but accepted his comment at face value and nodded.

They hardly spoke again until they landed in Southampton and took the train to London. Le Roux and Eleanor sat together but said very little, staring out of the window at the English countryside, each wrapped in their own thoughts.

It was a brilliant early summer's day, so bright that the cool, gigantic cavern of Waterloo Station seemed welcoming.

Eleanor and Le Roux joined the mad scramble of passengers as they searched for their baggage. Then they took a taxi up Grosvenor Place among the red double-decker buses and along the Mall past St James's Park where the flowers were in full bloom, on to the South African High Commission, a formidable building on the east side of Trafalgar Square.

It was after 3 p.m., and the large wooden doors were closed, suggesting that South Africa had done its business for the day.

They rang the bell, and a man responded: 'Ah, you must be the students. Come in. I am afraid the High Commissioner is indisposed, but he will meet you tomorrow at ten o'clock.'

Le Roux looked around the impressive marble lobby and up the stairs towards the domed skylight, and wondered where the murals were planned.

A middle-aged woman who had been sitting in an alcove rushed forward. 'Oh, Eleanor, how lovely to see you.'

They hugged, and Eleanor introduced her. 'Aunt Bunny, this is Le Roux Smith, my colleague who won the scholarship with me.'

She looked the young man up and down, then said to her niece, 'Well, dear, come along. We've booked you some accommodation at the Young Ladies' Residence in Queensberry Place in South Kensington, very near the Royal College of Art.'

'I presume there is no room for me?' asked Le Roux with a straight face.

'Of course not, young man. But I am sure Mr Stevens here will direct you.' As the two women left the building, Aunt Bunny said rather loudly, 'He seems a bit gauche, that young man. I do hope you find him agreeable to work with.'

'We shall see,' replied Eleanor as they moved out of earshot.

Le Roux turned expectantly to Mr Stevens, who said, 'I have the name and address of a reservation in your name, Mr Smith. It is in St John's Wood.'

'Good, but I have no money.'

'The High Commissioner knows that and has paid for the room for a month, while you find long-term accommodation nearer to the college. He also asked me to give you your weekly stipend.'

Feeling newly wealthy with some money in his pocket, Le Roux loaded his trunk into a taxi to go in search of his lodging. He loved the novelty of travelling in a London cab and talking to the driver.

'Over 'ere to study, guv'nor?' the taxi driver asked.

When Le Roux told him he was studying at the Royal College of Art in Kensington, the driver observed, 'Well, blimey, you have certainly chosen a rum spot to live. Swagger neighbourhood and all that, but it's miles from Kensington.'

This cast a slight shadow on Le Roux's mood.

The taxi pulled up outside a vast St John's Wood mansion, rather dilapidated, with the remains of a lovely garden. His landlady escorted him upstairs to a steaming-hot attic room. Fit though he thought he was, climbing five floors was exhausting. His room was quite pretty, though, with a view of Regent's Park through a small dormer window.

The door of the room next to his was open, and he could hear a clear tenor voice of exceptional quality singing an aria from Bizet's opera *Les Pêcheurs de Perles* ('The Pearl Fishers').

Le Roux stopped unpacking to listen. When the singing stopped, the owner of the voice came through his door with his hand outstretched. He was a heavily built but fine-looking fellow who said with a broad, welcoming grin, 'You must be the South African.'

Charles, a tenor from Tasmania, who had a role in *Tosca* at the Royal Opera House, and was perhaps ten years older than Le Roux, was his guide for what remained of his first day in London. He took him for a walk down Avenue Road to Regent's Park, pointing out notable houses on the way. 'Marie Tempest, the soprano,[12] lives there!' he said.

Charles showed Le Roux the ropes as far as the buses and tube were concerned, and the places where he could eat at reasonable prices.

The following day, when Le Roux returned to the High Commission, there was a queue of people applying for South African work permits before travelling to Cape Town to seek employment.[13]

---

12 Mary Susan Etherington, who was born in London in 1864, was known professionally as Marie Tempest. She was about 70 years old at this time and had become active in working for the good of the members of her profession. The following year, 1934, she was instrumental in the founding of the actors' union Equity. She was created a Dame Commander of the Order of the British Empire in 1937, the year in which her third husband, Graham Browne, died. In 1941, her home in London was bombed during the Blitz, and she lost most of her possessions. She died the following year, aged 78. A blue plaque was placed at the site of her home at 24 Park Crescent.
13 There was a recession in the UK in the early 1930s, as the Great Depression bit across the world, while at the same time South Africa was looking for skilled workers and favoured British immigrants.

Mr Stevens saw him and ushered him inside. 'The young lady is waiting for you outside the High Commissioner's office. Please join her, and the High Commissioner will see you shortly.'

Le Roux found Eleanor, and they waited to be called in.

About half an hour later, Charles te Water[14] opened the door. 'Come in. Welcome,' the High Commissioner said. Tall, good-looking and immaculately groomed, he cut an impressive figure. 'We're so pleased to have you with us to breathe life into this beautiful new building. I've arranged for you to have a studio on the top floor. It's a large room with a wonderful view over Trafalgar Square; you can make as much mess as you like up there, and hopefully produce something wonderful.'

'Thank you, sir,' said Le Roux in Afrikaans. 'We will do everything to make the High Commission proud.'

'I know your father, Le Roux. A remarkable man,' te Water said, then chuckled. 'Between you and me, I never imagined he would allow a son of his to study in England.'

Then he turned to Eleanor and switched to English. 'You have accommodation organised by your aunt, I hear. Satisfactory? Good. Well, I won't detain you any longer. Please make yourselves at home upstairs, and let Mr Stevens know if there is anything else we can provide. The Royal College of Art term begins in two months, so I suggest you use the time between now and then to familiarise yourselves with London. There's plenty to occupy you in this wonderful city.'

The studio was as spectacular as the High Commissioner had suggested. Two other South African artists were already working there: 47-year-old Jacob Pierneef, who had recently completed a commission of 32 panels for the interior of the new Johannesburg Railway Station,[15] and 38-year-old Jan Juta, who a decade earlier had illustrated the English writer D.H. Lawrence's[16] travel book *Sea and Sardinia*. These

---

14 Charles Theodore te Water was a South African barrister, diplomat and politician who was appointed as president of the Assembly of the League of Nations. He served as High Commissioner in London between 1929 and 1939.
15 In 1935, J.H. Pierneef would win the Medal of Honour for Visual Arts Painting by the Suid-Afrikaanse Akademie vir Wetenskap en Kuns (the South African Academy of Science and Art) for his Johannesburg Railway Station and South Africa House works. Originally De Zuid-Afrikaansche Akademie voor Taal, Letteren en Kunst, founded in 1909, the intention of the academy was to support the development of the Dutch (including the Afrikaans) language, literature, art, history and antiquities in South Africa.
16 D.H. Lawrence, probably best known as the author of the highly controversial (at the time) *Lady Chatterley's Lover*, was himself a keen painter. He had died of tuberculosis in 1930, aged 44.

two highly respected South African artists were also working on murals for South Africa House, and the two students were told to help them as part of their apprenticeships in the initial months.

Pierneef was mostly away travelling, but Juta demanded more and more of their time to help him with mixing colours for his panels, which irritated Eleanor. And that wasn't all: 'He includes nuns in Catholic outfits in his panels of the landing of Van Riebeeck, when we know all the early settlers were Protestant,' she complained.

One afternoon, Le Roux could see that Eleanor was about to be rude to Juta, so he suggested they take a break and go out for a meal. 'I would like to see where you live. I'm still at the guesthouse in St John's Wood and need to find permanent digs. Perhaps we should move in together. We could get a better place and save some money.'

'Thank you, Le Roux, but I think we see quite enough of each other as it is,' said Eleanor tartly.

They visited Eleanor's residence nonetheless, and Le Roux waited in the hall while she changed. As the other tenants went in and out of the hall, some looked at the handsome young man and giggled with their friends, but most ignored him.

Eleanor came back down, and they went to a restaurant around the corner. After a couple of glasses of wine, their conversation flowed. They laughed about the stuffiness of South Africa House but agreed that the High Commissioner was a very lovely man and Juta was enemy number one.

'So, according to your Aunt Bunny, I'm gauche?' Le Roux said, seriously.

'Oh, she meant nothing.'

'No, tell me the truth,' he urged her. 'I need to learn if I am to become a Londoner.'

Eleanor smiled at Le Roux. Until then, she had felt somewhat intimidated by him, but his question was so honest that she relaxed. 'You are a little rough around the edges,' she conceded.

'For example?'

'Well, look at how you hold your knife and fork. It is as though you are stabbing the poor animal.'

'How should I hold them?'

She showed him, and they laughed as he tried to cut his meat the new way.

'May I ask you a question?' Le Roux said.

'Of course.'

'Do you have a boyfriend?'

Eleanor coloured slightly, but the room was dark, and Le Roux didn't notice. 'I know lots of boys,' she said.

'You know what I mean.'

'No. And if you're offering your services, I will take that on advisement from my aunt.'

They both laughed again.

'So, how did you become involved with art?'

'I loved art at school, where I was a boarder,' said Eleanor, who had been born in Dundee, Natal. 'The woman who was in charge of art gave me keys to the art studio so that I could go in any time, you know, after hours, and paint. It was a very encouraging start.'

Le Roux gazed at her, then reached out a hand towards her face. 'You know, you would be much prettier if you took your fringe off your forehead,' he said.

Brushing his hand away, Eleanor clicked her tongue and said, 'Stop being such a chauvinist, Le Roux. Like most men, you consider a woman's primary purpose is to look beautiful, have sex and make babies.'

'Well, my mother might add making a home and preparing the food.'

'Gosh, you can be extremely irritating, Le Roux.' She took a short sip of her wine, then thunked her glass back down on the table. 'You think you know everything, but you have no idea what women must put up with. Do you know there was an objection to my getting the scholarship because I'm a woman? I had to sign a statement saying that if I accepted the scholarship, I wouldn't marry for seven years. Did you have to sign such a statement?' She shook her head and looked away, her lips drawn together in a tight line.

'I'm so sorry, Eleanor. You're right.' Le Roux was genuinely shocked. He tried to lighten the mood. 'Come, let's go to the pictures,' he suggested. 'I noticed *Hold Your Man* is showing, with Clark Gable and Jean Harlow, just around the corner. It starts in ten minutes.'

Finally, the ice was broken. Gaining insight into her inner world, Le Roux felt more relaxed around Eleanor; in turn, Eleanor viewed Le Roux as a burly Afrikaner who would be useful as the project progressed, particularly as a companion during their upcoming tour through a tense Europe, where threats of war loomed large. Nevertheless, Eleanor had made it clear there were rules of engagement.

Le Roux was very excited to have a letter of introduction from his art teacher at the Michaelis, Barry Craig, to the sculptor Jacob Epstein, who was at the height of his prominence, having recently produced his two figures *Day* and *Night* on the St James's Park Underground Station and his rendering of pregnancy in marble, *Genesis*.

The few bronzes that Le Roux had seen in South Africa were reproduced in illustrated books along with Epstein's meaty drawings. He loved the vigour of the bronzes and the strength of the modelling.

It was a drizzly afternoon, and Le Roux made his way to Epstein's home and studio at 18 Hyde Park Gate. At the top of the road Le Roux got off the bus, with traffic swishing noisily along the wetness of Kensington Gore.

Le Roux found the house and was shown inside to the dining room where, at a crowded long table, Jacob Epstein sat at one end and his wife at the other. After being greeted, he sat down among an assortment of friends, admirers and hangers-on who were tucking into a tea-time spread. After a while, Epstein called to him:

'Le Roux, come and sit next to me,' he said, with a twinge of an American accent. 'I want to hear how Barry is.'

Le Roux was struck by the man's vivacity and blue eyes, but as the tea continued, he was surprised by Epstein's concern about what other artists were saying about him and why critics were against his works. He had come to gather pearls from the master, not to hear him complain about his own treatment.

When he saw Eleanor the following day, she asked him about the encounter.

'I don't know,' Le Roux shrugged, 'I was expecting to learn something, but Epstein spent the time running down other lesser artists.'

'Oh, what a shame; your first meeting with a great artist, and you discover he is human?'

Annoyed, Le Roux didn't look at Eleanor. 'Something like that.'

A few months later, Le Roux and Eleanor went out for dinner together again, choosing a cheap restaurant near the High Commission.

'So tell me,' said Le Roux, after they'd ordered their food and settled in with their first glasses of wine, 'do you have anyone in your life yet? A man, perhaps?'

'It may surprise you that I have many suitors and a hectic social life,' Eleanor said archly.

'I don't doubt it, and I see you have changed your fringe. It looks much better, if I may say so. But my question is, having turned down my offer, who is the lucky chap?'

'Oh, shut up, Le Roux. I know all about the facts of life from the girls at Queensberry Place. I must say they do get up to a lot of mischief, those girls.'

'Well, you must introduce me. Perhaps I could get up to mischief myself,' he said, grinning.

'I'll tell you this. Several girls did ask who you were after they saw you in reception.'

Le Roux laughed. 'What did you say?'

Aware of his rough charm, Eleanor had grown to like Le Roux and certainly admired his talent.

'I said you were nice enough, but sadly have no money.'

2

Art Classes

1933

When lectures started at the Royal College of Art in October, they included life drawing, mural painting, and instruction on architectural interiors. Professor Ernest Dinkel,[17] a college graduate, provided most of the instruction. An artist in the arts and crafts tradition, he worked in many media, including oil, watercolour, pencil, stained glass, sculpture and murals.

Painting a mural is very different from painting on canvas, he told his students. 'The way the paint is applied on a canvas is fundamental because it adds to the feeling of the painting. But a mural is too big to be influenced by brush-strokes: the feeling and personality of a mural come from the whole.'

Dinkel introduced his students to the mural techniques of the Old Masters – Da Vinci and Michelangelo, among others – and explained how a combination of egg yolk, water and coloured powder is layered on to a slaked lime plaster surface to achieve the right depth of colour. 'The egg yolk on the slaked lime dries immediately, so there is no opportunity to correct the drawing,' he noted. Using a trowel to cover a plaster surface in the art room with slaked lime, Dinkel added, 'Do you see how porous it is?'

'What about drawings of figures and plants in the mural?' asked Le Roux. 'How do you go about filling in the detail?'

'You need to map out the surface in a grid format on a large piece of paper with similar dimensions and then trace the figures on to it to create

---

17 Dinkel would go on to be head of the School of Design at Edinburgh College of Art from 1947 to 1961.

a framework for your painting. One labour-intensive method is to use a sharp, hard pencil to make small holes in the paper along the outlines of the objects. You grind the paint colours into powders and fill muslin bags with the different hues. Then, you strike the perforated paper with the muslin bags so that a powder residue penetrates the tiny holes, leaving a clear outline of the drawings on the wall once the paper is removed.'

A month later, Jan Juta's historical panels in the High Commission were unveiled, with Van Riebeeck dressed in peasant costume praying with women under a cross. The Catholic symbolism attracted fierce criticism from the Afrikaans newspapers. As Eleanor opined sourly, 'Everybody knows they were Protestants.'

And that wasn't the end of the students' displeasure with Juta. At the end of 1934, a major row broke out at the High Commission when he was quoted in the South African *Cape Argus* newspaper saying that he was supervising the work of the two scholarship students in London.

Eleanor rushed into the studio the next day and slammed her fist down on a table, startling Le Roux. 'I've just heard what Juta claims in the South African papers – that we're working under his tutelage, and once he has trained us, we will work under him on future projects in South Africa. I'm furious!'

'Oh, Eleanor, it doesn't matter. He's just a windbag.'

'Of course it matters, Le Roux. Don't be so obtuse. When we bid to work on other murals, the clients will read this and say we must have Juta supervising our work.' She went on, with unmistakable purpose, 'You and I are going to write to the editor of the *Cape Argus* and ask for a correction.'

Le Roux carried on drawing. 'If you feel that strongly about it, write a letter from both of us and send it. But I do think it's a storm in a teacup.'

Eleanor's letter was more strongly worded than Le Roux would have liked, but he signed it anyway.

Charles, the tenor from Tasmania, included Le Roux in a fair-sized party at Quaglino's, one of London's smartest night haunts – not a nightclub as such, but a splendid restaurant where you could have a first-class supper after the theatre and dance until the early hours.

They had some debutantes in tow, with their chaperone, a charming society lady who knew everyone. She insisted on a fair amount of attention from the young men, and that night her eye settled on Le Roux. While dancing with him, she suddenly squeezed his hand, raised one eyebrow and then glanced sideways in a manner full of meaning – if Le Roux could only have guessed what that meaning was.

When he looked nonplussed, she leaned forward and said in a low voice, 'That hard-faced woman, my dear, is Mrs Simpson!' She indicated a striking woman dressed in a simple low-cut evening dress of black velvet, backless and with long sleeves.

Le Roux was still none the wiser, so when they sat down, the chaperone enlightened him. 'She's an American, and has already been divorced once,' she told him, in a scandalised whisper. 'Her current marriage is to Ernest Simpson – he isn't here, of course. The Prince is completely infatuated – he's already throwing money and jewellery at her.'[18] Le Roux couldn't help but notice the stupendous bracelet of diamonds and emeralds, at least three inches across, that Mrs Simpson was wearing.

Just then, the American woman was joined by Edward and his entourage. Charming and informal, the Prince of Wales was popular, and fond of sport and parties. Le Roux watched Mrs Simpson, a sparkling conversationalist whose face lit up as she talked, while the chaperone finished her sotto voce gossiping. 'He met her at a house party a few years ago, which she attended with her husband. She and her husband invited him to dine at their London flat, which he did, and now he's besotted with her...'

After another dance, Le Roux excused himself and went to the lavatory. As he opened the door, there was an almighty row going on. One of the men he recognised from the Prince of Wales's party – it was Lord Mountbatten, whom Le Roux had heard referred to as 'Dickie'[19] – and the other was the black band leader.

'I'm telling you, it's not my business, mister,' the band leader was saying.

'It bloody well is! It's your band!'

---

18 Edward, later King Edward VIII, abdicated on 10 December 1936, broadcasting a memorable farewell message by radio, and left the country to live with Wallis Simpson in France. Wallis divorced Ernest in 1937, and married Edward. Edward was made Duke of Windsor and lived abroad, maintaining friendly, if distant, links with his relatives until his death in 1972. Wallis grew increasingly frail, and succumbed to dementia, eventually dying in 1986, aged 89.
19 Louis Mountbatten's nickname among family and friends was 'Dickie', even though 'Richard' was not one of his given names.

'So?'

'So, my wife is somewhere in this building with Hutch.[20] I want her back right now. Do you understand?' The man pushed the band leader against the wall.

Le Roux could see that the situation was getting out of hand, so he intervened. 'Sir, sir, excuse me, sir, but the Prince sent me to find you.'

Without a look at Le Roux, Mountbatten said, 'You'd better control Hutch. Otherwise I will have you black banjo players closed down.' He marched out, leaving Le Roux alone with the band leader, who was laughing.

'Thanks, man. That was about to get ugly. He cannot control his woman, and I am to blame.' He held out his hand. 'I'm Ric, by the way.'

'Le Roux. Nice to meet you.'

'I guess I'd better go and find Hutch.' Ric opened the door and turned to Le Roux. 'Any time you want to pop in for a drink and dance with your girl, tell the front desk you're Ric's guest, okay?'

'Okay. Thank you.'

As Le Roux returned to his table, he glanced at Mrs Simpson and heard the Prince of Wales shouting, 'Dickie, old chap, where's Edwina? Still powdering her nose?' There was a snicker around the table.[21]

Le Roux could not afford many evenings at restaurants with debutantes, but country-house parties had many benefits: food and drink were free, and there was the possibility of getting to know one's fellow house guests more intimately than under the watchful gaze of a chaperone at a London nightclub.

There were, however, standards of decorum to be observed, even at house parties. On one occasion, the mother of his hostess thought that hymns and some fresh air would do her daughter's young guests a world of good after a rather drunken late night, no matter how unenthusiastic the visitors were about the jaunt. Feeling rather fragile and sorry for themselves, the party was gliding along a deep, narrow lane in the family sedan when Le Roux saw an elephant dash across the lane from a gap in the high hedge on one side to a similar gap on the other.

Le Roux, astonished, was about to say something when he was nudged by his hostess, who was driving and keeping one eye on the mirror so

---

20   Leslie 'Hutch' Hutchinson, one of the first popular black entertainers in Britain, was a regular performer at Quaglino's in the 1930s and 1940s.
21   Edwina Mountbatten, described by a journalist in 1944 as 'one of the most beautiful women in England', was known to have affairs throughout her marriage, doing little to hide them from her husband; one of these was with Leslie Hutchinson.

she could see her rear-seat passengers. One of these, a heavy-drinking American, was craning his neck to look through the rear window towards the receding spot where the elephant had materialised momentarily.

'I say, did you see that?' he exclaimed.

Le Roux and his hostess simultaneously said they had seen nothing. Some minutes later, a subdued American entered the church and spent most of the service on his knees, praying earnestly.

'There's a private zoo nearby,' the hostess explained later, 'and the elephant makes the occasional dash for freedom but is soon caught and returned.'

3

A European Adventure[22]

1934

In June, at the end of their first year, Professor Dinkel called Le Roux and Eleanor into his office. 'I'm very pleased with your work, and I've discussed the matter with Sir William Rothenstein,[23] the director of the Royal College of Art, and High Commissioner te Water. We think you should begin planning the murals for a room in South Africa House. Before you begin, however, we suggest you tour Europe and study the Old Masters.'

As they left, Le Roux said to Eleanor, 'A cause for celebration?'

'Let's go back to South Africa House first and look at the room,' his ever-diligent colleague suggested, 'then we can plan our work over dinner.'

The proposed room was on the fourth floor, with huge French windows opening on to a veranda, and plenty of light. It had beautiful red tiles on the floor and blue Dutch tiles along the skirtings. 'The walls are perfectly plain, without wood panelling, so the slaked lime can be applied easily,' Le Roux observed approvingly.

---

22 Much of the information in this chapter and the next two chapters is taken from *Eleanor Esmonde-White* by Leanne Raymond, based on interviews with the artist and published by Main Street Publishing in 2015, as well as Leanne Raymond's unpublished notes of the interviews.

23 William Rothenstein was an English painter, printmaker, draughtsman, lecturer and writer on art. He served as principal at the Royal College of Art from 1920 to 1935. He married Alice Knewstub, with whom he had four children: John, Betty, Rachel and Michael. John Rothenstein gained fame as an art historian and the director of the Tate Gallery from 1938 to 1964, and would play a significant role in Le Roux's later life.

As they were leaving, the High Commissioner came out of his office. 'Ah, you've heard the news! I want you to dine with me at the residency tonight so we can talk about your plans. I'm seeing Sir Herbert Baker next week, and I want to be up to date.'

The dinner was relatively informal, with just the three of them seated at one end of the long, gleaming dining table. It had been a year since Le Roux had eaten South African food, and he tucked into the bobotie[24] with enthusiasm while Eleanor took the lead in the discussion.

'Le Roux and I have a suggestion about the subject matter which we would like to discuss with you, High Commissioner.'

It was an idea that Eleanor had raised briefly with Le Roux, and he was not at all sure it would fly.

'There are no pictures of natives in South Africa House,' Eleanor continued, 'so we thought we would portray the tribal life and customs of the Zulu people before the white settlers arrived. We want to symbolise the traditional native ceremonies that have vanished today.'

Le Roux wiped his mouth and sat back in his chair, studying the face of the High Commissioner, a man of his father's age, and from the same area of the country. Le Roux knew what his father would have said but te Water's reaction was simply to look surprised.

'Well, that's certainly a novel idea,' he said, cheerfully. 'I will discuss it with Sir Herbert.'

In July 1934, Eleanor and Le Roux departed from the North Sea port of Harwich by boat to Bergen in Norway on their European adventure. The High Commission had booked the tickets at the last minute, so they were too late to get a cabin. They sat in the dining car for the night and arrived exhausted at 6.30 the next morning. Bergen was a lovely town, surrounded by mountains and on a fjord.

After drawing a few sketches of the buildings, they made the breathtaking 300-mile train trip from Bergen to the capital city of Oslo. The train climbed steadily up and up, through the mountains and lakes – some at mountain summits – first with a view of the west of Norway. Once they were over the top and heading east, they climbed down again

---

24 A Cape Malay dish of mildly curried mince with lemon juice and dried fruit, topped with a savoury egg custard.

to sea level, through the deserted countryside with its ice-cold lakes and rivers full of timber floating towards the port.

They found Oslo, on the country's southern coast at the head of the Oslofjord, disappointing. It is an industrial city with few notable buildings. So they stayed only one night, then took the evening sleeper train to Stockholm, 'the Venice of the North', another 300 miles eastwards.

This beautiful city sprawled across 14 islands criss-crossed with waterways, dotted with parks, and it boasted simple architectural lines and an impressive museum. It was also half the price of Oslo: two rooms and meals cost six shillings a day, and a bath was included for free, so they stayed a week. Work involved sketching the Engelbrekt Church, with its high nave and art nouveau style, but the rest of the time, they enjoyed sightseeing in Stockholm.

Then they took a sleeper to the coast and a ferry to Copenhagen, arriving at lunchtime the following day. There they visited the Museum of Sculpture, which they did not like because most of the collection was archaic Greek sculptures.

After travelling through Scandinavia, they headed for Berlin. A mix-up with their tickets meant they had to stand for the entire ten-hour journey, and they arrived bone-weary on 8 August, the day after President Paul von Hindenburg's state funeral. The field marshal had led the Imperial German Army during the First World War before becoming president in 1925. He'd played a key role in the Nazis' seizure of power early the previous year when, under pressure from his advisers, he'd appointed Adolf Hitler as chancellor of Germany.

When Hitler had received word that Hindenburg was dying of lung cancer, he'd had the cabinet pass a law stipulating that on the president's death, the office of president would be abolished and its powers merged with those of the chancellor under the title of Führer. This made Hitler both Germany's head of state and its head of government, cementing his status as the absolute dictator.

After viewing the bust of Queen Nefertiti, believed to have been crafted in 1345 BCE, in the Neues Museum in the historic centre of Berlin, and making side trips to Potsdam and Dresden, Le Roux and Eleanor caught the train to Munich. They were unprepared for what they saw on the streets there: portraits of Hitler on every wall, swastika flags hanging from windows, and loudspeakers fixed to public buildings, pouring out propaganda.

'Look at those posters,' cried Eleanor. 'Aren't they terrible? And the flags! This place gives me the creeps. And what is it with everybody greeting us with "Heil Hitler"?'

They stayed in a pension opposite the Academy of Arts, which had loudspeakers attached, blurting out propaganda from 6 a.m. until late at night.

On 19 August, there was a referendum on merging the posts of chancellor and president in order to gain approval for Hitler's assumption of supreme power. On the eve of his victory, as the events in the streets got out of hand, Le Roux insisted they take refuge in a cinema. 'I think we need to move on tomorrow. The atmosphere is volatile, and we will be targeted as foreigners.'

'Well,' said Eleanor, 'I'm going to take some pamphlets and newspapers back to London so we can show people what's happening here. This place has gone mad.'

The following day, with Eleanor's suitcase full of Nazi propaganda materials, they headed for the station to catch a train to Vienna. Three miles from the Austrian border, German police stopped and boarded the train. They discovered Eleanor's bag of propaganda and ordered her off the train. She was stripped and searched, and her suitcase was confiscated before she was allowed back on. The train was delayed for well over an hour, much to the annoyance of the other passengers.

They arrived in Vienna at eight o'clock that evening and booked into the first cheap hotel near the station. As there was only one room, they shared it.

They awoke to a mood much different from that prevailing in Munich: no sign of the propaganda placards and flags here. The previous year, the chancellor of Austria, Engelbert Dollfuss, had banned the Nazi Party, and allied the country with Italy. Austria had, just a few months before, recovered from a short and nasty civil war, a series of skirmishes between the right-wing government and socialist forces that became known as the February Uprising. The result was that the government had also banned the Social Democratic Party, and replaced the democratic constitution with a corporatist one modelled along the lines of Benito Mussolini's fascist Italy, but whose underlying ideology was that of the most conservative elements in the Austrian Catholic clergy.

As Eleanor and Le Roux walked along the run-down, deserted streets, they saw tanks with Italian markings on the Ringstrasse. Despite this show of militarism, cultural institutions ran normally; they managed to visit the main museum and several galleries, and were fortunate enough to buy two standing tickets to *Die Walküre*, one of the four operas in Wagner's *Der Ring des Nibelungen* cycle, at the Vienna State Opera. Le Roux, who had never seen an opera, found the production incredible.

Towards the end of the show, the singer playing the Valkyrie Brünnhilde, who was what boxing promoters generally refer to as a heavyweight, began to spin helplessly on the cable that suspended her. To stop the whirling, she kicked over most of the vast flat scenery representing clouds. Nothing was more wonderful than her look of relief when she slowly spun to a stop. The next moment, however, she began to unwind the other way, faster and faster, despite frantic efforts on her part to grab what little scenery she had left standing. The opera, meanwhile, continued.

Finally, the cable broke, and Brünnhilde's crash to earth was spectacular. In the best Wagnerian style, she was wearing 'Nordic armour' on her bosom – two hollow metal saucepan-lid-like discs – which shot off, rolling noisily down to the footlights, where they spun around with a decreasing whanging sound, stopping just as the curtain came down. Le Roux and Eleanor were in almost uncontrollable spasms of laughter.

In early September, they reached Padua in northern Italy, where they studied the Giotto frescos in the Scrovegni Chapel in a picturesque little garden near the Bacchiglione River. Eleanor wrote later, 'You cannot imagine how beautiful those paintings are. They have been the most prominent influence on my work.'

On 14 October, they reached the Etruscan village of Arezzo, where they intended to copy Piero della Francesca's frescos of the Legends of the True Cross that decorate the choir of San Francesco, telling the story of how the wood of the True Cross was employed in the building of the Palace of Solomon. William Rothenstein had recommended this mural. But it was wet and windy, and too dark in the church to examine the frescos, so they spent their time sketching in cafés and restaurants, waiting for the weather to break.

One evening they were in a restaurant on the main square, having dinner, and Eleanor wasn't eating her food. Concerned, Le Roux asked, 'Is something the matter?'

'Oh, I don't know.' She pushed her plate away. 'I've been thinking about home. The idea of returning to South Africa fills me with dread. It's so insular. I want to live in England.'

'What about our scholarship commitment to return to South Africa to teach? You're our conscience on this matter, remember?'

'I know, I know. I feel awful. But coming overseas has opened my eyes to so many things. Le Roux, I wasn't alive before I came here. I don't think I could return now.'

'My ideal would be to come and go between Europe and South Africa.'

'Easier said than done.'

'So far, we have patronage. Why could it not continue? Murals are in demand everywhere. We just have to ingratiate ourselves with the right people.'

'Le Roux, you are so much better than me at ingratiating yourself,' his companion said, and gave him a teasing smile, 'particularly with women.'

'But you are oblivious!'

Ignoring his joking provocation, she continued: 'I hate all the bowing and scraping that seems to be required.'

'It is a fact of life.' Le Roux poured them both more wine. 'My guess is there will be a war between Britain and Germany, and if there is, our work will dry up in Europe, and we will have to go back to South Africa.'

Eleanor looked worriedly at Le Roux. 'This militarism is getting worse in each village we visit. Perhaps we should travel to Rome earlier than planned.'

'We're not expected there for several weeks, and there is much to see. Also, there is the Palio in Siena, remember?'

'Ah, the Palio!' mimicked Eleanor in a bored tone, making it clear how little the famous twice-yearly horse race interested her.

On 28 October, a holiday commemorating Mussolini's 1922 entrance into Rome and the bloodless coup that gave rise to two decades of fascist rule, they arrived in Siena. They spent their time in the medieval Duomo (the cathedral) and the museums.

The Palio was held on 3 November. It was a bitterly cold day, so they put on layers of clothes and joined the crowds in the main square in Siena, the Piazza del Campo. There were fascist posters everywhere, and the crowd was quite unruly.

The race, in which the jockeys rode bareback around the piazza, where a thick layer of earth had been laid, lasted no more than 90 seconds, but that was long enough to drive the crowd into a frenzy. Eleanor had had enough. 'These Italian men are pigs!' she shouted to Le Roux. 'Come on. I'm going back to the hotel.'

When they finally managed to untangle themselves from the crowd and return to the hotel, she was crying. 'I'm black and blue from being pinched in that crowd. If you were not with me, I would not be able to go outside. I hate this place!'

Later that evening, after supper, Eleanor put her arms around Le Roux. 'Oh, Le Roux, I'm so glad you are here. I would never have been able to make this trip on my own.'

A European Adventure

It was a relief for them to arrive in Rome a week later and register for their studies in the shelter of the British School at Rome, which was housed in a magnificent building, surrounded by lovely gardens with cypress and mimosa trees. The secretary of the school, Mrs Shaw, whose constant companions were her two wire-haired terriers, showed them to their studio, which they had for a month. They decorated it with the copies of the frescos they had made on their long trip south.

Eleanor complained that the regime was like being back at boarding school, with all its do's and don'ts. But Le Roux, who had no such experience, thought it was rather jolly, particularly as they would be there for Christmas and planned to hold a drinks party in their studio.

But their work in Rome proceeded at a slow pace. They had to apply for permits to copy the frescos. No sooner had they received them than the weather turned bad, and they could not see the art in the churches because they were dimly lit. And when the sun finally came out, they were restricted to working for short periods when there were no religious services.

Their first visit to the Vatican was disappointing. 'The Raphael and Michelangelo frescos have none of the charm of the Early Masters, and used such unpleasant colours,' Eleanor said, adding that covering up the genitals of the male nude statues with large plaster-of-Paris fig leaves looked ridiculous.

This censorship had begun in 1563, when the Council of Trent – the northern Italian council of the Catholic Church – launched the 'fig leaf campaign' to camouflage the penises and pubic hair visible in art across Italy. It began with Pope Paul IV (Pope 1555–59), and then Pope Innocent X (1644–55), who preferred metal fig leaves to plaster ones, ordering that the remainder of the Vatican's collection of Greek and Roman statues be covered up. Pope Clement XIII (1758–69) had the Vatican mass-produce fig leaves for statues that still sported penises, and finally, Pope Pius IX (1846–78) did the most damage, ordering any statues that still had uncovered penises to be destroyed.

Socially, however, things were improving for the two itinerant students. Eivert, a Swedish writer, and Victor, a Spanish painter, whom they met in Scandinavia, arrived unexpectedly, which livened things up, and they made friends with a couple of artists from the British School, who took them to nightclubs that played American jazz and sold vodka cheaply.

After the Dance

The director of the British School arranged for Le Roux and Eleanor to visit the American Academy research and art institution in Rome. Le Roux's inkling that accepting the invitation might be a mistake was confirmed when Eleanor insisted on leaving after half an hour.

'Why were you so rude? Those Americans could have helped us with winning commissions,' he shouted as he ran after her down the path to the gate.

'I told you I couldn't do all that. Those young men were flashy and pretentious, with plenty of their bad art to show for it.' Remonstrating with Le Roux, Eleanor was not looking at the traffic as they crossed the Vale Giulia. Suddenly, a very long Hispano-Suiza luxury motor car came around the corner at full speed and missed her by inches.

Eleanor, shaken, fell to the pavement.

'What a car!' said Le Roux excitedly as he offered her a hand. 'And did you see who was driving it?'

Getting to her feet, trembling, Eleanor dusted herself off. 'Bloody fool! He nearly killed us!'

'It was Alfonso XIII, the ex-king of Spain![25] Imagine that!'

'Oh, Le Roux, you are such a boy at times!' cried Eleanor in exasperation.

Outside the British School, they found Eivert and Victor waiting for them. Eleanor ushered them inside as they listened to Le Roux's description of their near-death experience at the hands of one of Europe's least popular monarchs.

'Come on, boys, enough of that,' Eleanor said briskly. 'Let's decorate our studio for our Christmas drinks party while Le Roux prepares dinner.'

'So you're a cook *and* an artist?' Victor said to Le Roux, one eyebrow raised in mock admiration.

'It's self-defence. Eleanor eats very little and won't cook, even when it's her turn. She says cooking is what all chauvinistic men think women should do.'

'Eleanor, how cruel you are!' shouted Eivert.

---

25 Alfonso XIII was the king of Spain from his birth in May 1886 until 14 April 1931, when the monarchy fell and he was forced to flee the country, living in exile first in France and later in Italy. He died of a heart attack in Rome in February 1941. Alfonso is sometimes referred to as 'the playboy king', due in part to his promotion and collection of Spanish pornographic films, as well as his extramarital affairs – he had seven children from his marriage, and a further five known illegitimate children.

On Christmas Eve, Victor, who was Catholic, was keen to attend midnight Mass in the Basilica of Santa Maria Maggiore. They all agreed to go with him and managed to squash into the crowd at the rear of the basilica, just in time to see the Pope being carried in on a throne adorned with large peacock feathers by four men.

'Isn't it rather marvellous?' whispered Eleanor.

Le Roux's Calvinist upbringing came to the fore, and he bent very close to her ear and said, 'Idolatry, in my opinion.'

4

The South Africa House Murals

1935

Le Roux and Eleanor arrived back in London on 15 February after a bumpy trip across the Channel. They were warmly greeted by the High Commissioner and Professor Dinkel, who admired their copies of the frescos and declared they were now ready to begin their work in earnest.

Although the South African High Commissioner approved of their suggested theme of Zulu culture, it was unpopular with many embassy staff members, who preferred murals about the history of white people in South Africa.

'Perhaps we should paint a montage of the Great Trek,' offered Le Roux, goading his partner.

'Absolutely not,' responded Eleanor. 'Our proposal to paint traditional Zulu ceremonies has been accepted. Why change it because some reactionaries have complained?'

'Well, for one, I know little about Zulu ceremonies,' said Le Roux. 'They were not part of my upbringing.'

'No servants?'

'My father did not employ servants. His philosophy was that the races should be kept separate.'

'Don't be irritating,' sniffed Eleanor. 'We will just have to learn about Zulu culture.'

'I had a quick look in the British Museum, and there is very little in the library on Zulu customs,' said Le Roux. 'All I found was that they died out with the defeat of King Cetshwayo by the British in 1879.'

Eleanor gave him a smug look. 'I enlisted the help of the High Commissioner. He contacted the Foreign Office to identify an ethnological expert who knows about Zulu customs. The Foreign Office recommended a Mr Stewart, retired under-secretary of native affairs in Zululand, who lives in Wimbledon.'

Le Roux looked at her respectfully. 'Now, that was a clever idea.'

'It is only a start. There has been a fair amount of to-ing and fro-ing about Mr Stewart's advisory fee of 12 guineas, which is not in our budget. But we do have a meeting scheduled for next week.'

The next problem was finding African models. Placing advertisements in *The Times* yielded no candidates, so Le Roux persuaded Eleanor to accompany him to Quaglino's. He said he knew somebody who might be able to help them.

Eleanor was not well pleased about what she considered a frivolous diversion: 'This escapade is not coming out of our budget, Le Roux.'

When they arrived in their day clothes, Le Roux noticed odd looks from the staff. When he mentioned he was a friend of Ric's, the hostess smiled and showed them to a table near the stage, where they ordered drinks. The restaurant's first sitting had not yet started, and the band was playing a medley of jazz to warm up for the evening. Le Roux could see that Eleanor, although uneasy about the expense, was enjoying the atmosphere.

As the restaurant began to fill, there was a musical interval, and Ric came to the table and greeted them warmly. 'Happy to meet Le Roux's girl,' he said, taking Eleanor's hand.

Eleanor was about to correct him when Le Roux interrupted her and began, somewhat haltingly, to explain the purpose of their visit.

'So, you want some African folks as models?' Ric said, getting right to the point.

'That's right,' Le Roux said.

'And it will be the tribal thing?'

'Exactly.'

'Bare chests and assegais?'

Le Roux smiled.

'Well, it's not my kind of gig but there's a young guy who sometimes plays the piano here who may be available. Emmanuel Roberts. He's from Nigeria. He's lived in Europe and America for several years, working in film and playing piano in jazz orchestras, and now he's teaching tap-dancing at night.'

'Can we meet him?'

'Sure. He always needs cash to keep his woman.'

'We're at the South African High Commission on the east side of Trafalgar Square.'

'Okay, I'll send him along. He may go for it.'

'We also need a female model,' interjected Eleanor.

'Emmanuel's woman is Ghanaian. Her name's Cherrie. Maybe she will do it.' Ric examined Eleanor's rather scrawny frame. 'But I warn you, she has big titties.'

Eleanor rolled her eyes, and Ric roared with laughter.

'We would like both of them to visit us,' Le Roux said. 'Tell Emmanuel to ask for the artists on the fourth floor.'

Mr Stewart arrived at South Africa House for their meeting dressed in a dark pinstriped suit that had seen considerable wear, and he smoked continuously. He was nothing to look at, said Le Roux later. 'That wasn't the brief,' replied Eleanor tartly.

'As I understand it, you aim to represent the ceremonies of Zulu tribal life pre-colonisation?' Stewart asked, glancing around the room designated for decoration. It was small, roughly 800 square feet, rectangular in shape, with three walls featuring two doors and two windows, along with French windows that opened on to a magnificent balcony overlooking Trafalgar Square.

'Yes, that's right.'

'At the request of the Foreign Office, I have come up with several suggestions that are authentic, but you may wish to embellish.' Stewart waved his yellow-stained fingers in the air. 'You have artistic licence, is what I mean.'

'We don't want artistic licence, Mr Stewart. We want historical accuracy as far as possible. This is meant to be a historical record and a work of art,' retorted Eleanor.

'I see.' He lit another cigarette to help his thought process. 'All right, then I would suggest a series of tableaux that capture the main rituals of Zulu life, which, if you are agreeable, I will describe.'

Mr Stewart looked around the room. After some consideration, he said, 'You could devote each wall to one aspect of Zulu custom. For example, on the east wall, which is the largest, you could depict the most important Zulu festival, the Festival of the First Fruits, which, as far as I know, was last performed in 1878. Tradition has it that before the harvest festival, no one could eat the new crops.' He pointed to the centre of the wall and went on. 'On the occasion of the festival, the king is endowed with supernatural powers and is the centre of national life, so he would command the centre of your decoration.' Pointing downwards, he continued, 'Then, here, at his feet, would be his *indunas*, wise old men, and on either side hand-picked warriors with all their plumes, carrying ox-hide war shields. On the king's left would be the snuff-bearer, and a little distance away, his *imbongi*, or praise-singer, clad in leopard skin.'

'Like King Lear's fool?' asked Le Roux, looking up from his notebook, where he'd been scribbling furiously as Stewart talked.

Stewart shook his head seriously. 'No, there is no humour in the *imbongi*'s praises for the king. If there were, he would have a short job tenancy.' Stepping sideways, he continued, 'Further along the wall, you could have three ceremonial oxen, representing the black, white and red royal herds. At the extreme end, I suggest dancing girls, who participate in the celebration's fertility rites.'

'What a wonderful picture. I can visualise it, can't you, Le Roux?' Eleanor's face lit up as she looked at her fellow artist, who nodded as he wrote. 'Go on,' she urged the older man.

'Now that I've seen the site, I will need to go away and think of some other ceremonies for the other walls and come back to you with descriptions.'

'So we are clear, Mr Stewart: there would be six tableaux, one for each space?' Le Roux confirmed.

'Yes, that is how I would do it. It will be a wonderful record of Zulu customs that have all but disappeared.'

'Oh, thank you, Mr Stewart, you have been most helpful. As a first step, we will draw out these tableaux in full size on paper and then invite you back for a further meeting, if we may?'

'I would be delighted.'

After he had gone, Eleanor turned to Le Roux. 'This is so exciting: we now have a plan for our murals. I think we can visualise what we must create, don't you, Le Roux?'

A couple of days later, a rather flustered porter showed a black couple into their studio.

'Hey, man, this place is like Fort Knox!' said a large, athletic man with a cheerful face. 'First, they didn't want to admit us; I guess that's a black-white thing…'

'But here you are! Thank you for coming,' said Le Roux, realising they were Ric's friends. 'You must be Emmanuel?'

'A pleasure, man, and this is Cherrie, like the cherry on top.' He laughed.

After the Dance

But Eleanor interrupted, shaking Cherrie's hand while Le Roux began explaining what they were painting on the room's walls.

'Ric said it was a nude gig?'

'We need to draw Zulus in their tribal dress, so if you could both strip to the waist, we can draw the upper bodies, and later to your underpants so we can do the legs.'

'No problem.' He looked at Cherrie, who nodded. 'And pay?'

'We need you for three days a week for about a month. But not at the same time,' elaborated Eleanor. 'So, let's say 12 days each over a six-week period, and we will pay nine guineas altogether.'

Eleanor and Le Roux enjoyed working with the couple. Emmanuel had a wicked sense of humour, and he caused more than a flutter in the typing pool on the same floor. Whenever he arrived and took off his clothes, there would be whispering outside the door as the girls took turns peering through the keyhole.

'Oh, dear,' said Eleanor, 'they are behaving badly,' and took it upon herself to give a loud lecture to the typing pool while Le Roux and Emmanuel exchanged smiles, and Le Roux continued drawing.

During the summer of 1935, the project began to take shape. They showed their initial sketches to Dinkel and explained the symbolism they would use. Then they showed him their portfolio of drawings of South African botanical plants that they had drawn from exhibits in Kew Gardens. He was delighted.

By October, they had prepared large sheets of paper hanging from the ceiling, on to which they had transposed a grid and the outlines of figures, flora and fauna. These were what are called 'cartoons' of the tableau for each wall.

The next part of the artistic process, painting the murals, was quite tricky and involved some trial and error. The method they would use comprised a combination of egg yolk, water, and powdered colour, known as egg tempera, applied to damp slaked lime plaster – the same technique as that used by the Italian masters. The results lasted for years in warm climates, but in wetter climates like the UK, they could deteriorate quickly.

First, they prepared the walls with a clear preparation of slaked lime – a combination of calcium oxide, or quicklime, and water – and then used egg tempera to apply the colours. The attempt went disastrously wrong, as the mixture of slaked lime was too porous, and the colours ran.

The two people who were meant to guide the artists in this process did not. Pierneef had travelled to Natal, and Juta couldn't or wouldn't help them to prepare the walls. Professor Dinkel suggested visiting the Department of Building Research in Watford, which tested all types of building materials. After several consultations and a visit to South Africa House, the department specified a different lime composition for the slaked lime, which combined well with the paint.

A few weeks later, Eleanor wrote to her parents in Natal that the murals were going splendidly, but 'I am trying to draw a dead leopard hanging upside down. I cannot make up my mind whether to go out and kill a cat!'

The reports of the progress of the murals were, nonetheless, favourable, and the High Commissioner, concerned that the scholarship funds were running low, persuaded the South African government to pay for the remainder of the work through a government commission.

One day, 25 April 1938, on their way from the Royal College of Art to the High Commission, Le Roux and Eleanor saw a large crowd gathered on a triangular plot of ground[26] directly in front of the Victoria and Albert Museum in South Kensington. The National Theatre Movement had collected enough money to buy this piece of land as a site for its new theatre.

Eleanor and Le Roux pushed through the crowd until they saw the Irish playwright George Bernard Shaw.[27]

'What's happening?' asked Eleanor, standing on tiptoes and struggling to see what was going on.

'Shaw is being handed a document, and I think a spade with soil on it.'

'Why?'

'No idea.'

Then Shaw spoke. 'This sod...' He paused for a moment, then continued, 'and this deed should really have been accepted by someone

---

26 This site is occupied by The Ismaili Centre, which was inaugurated in 1985 by Prime Minister Margaret Thatcher in the presence of His Highness the Aga Khan.
27 Bernard Shaw left his native Dublin at the age of 17 and established himself as a respected music and theatre critic in London; he achieved his first big success as a playwright only 20 years later. He had a large appetite for politics and controversy.

else, but as William Shakespeare can't be here, I have been asked to be present as the next best thing.'

Everybody started to laugh at his joke but the merriment was interrupted by a loud hiss of derision from a lanky young man, who obviously did not hold Shaw in the same regard as he held himself.

'Oh my God,' whispered Eleanor, 'that's Noel Langley, a friend who was at university with me in South Africa. He's a writer. I must say hello.'

'Well, I'm going to leave you. And my advice is to wait to see if anyone punches him before rushing to greet him,' Le Roux said, with a grin.

'Aren't you gallant!' she retorted sarcastically.

On 16 May 1938, three years after the artists had returned from the British School at Rome, the murals were unveiled. It was a high-profile event, with the unveiling ceremony itself, plus a lavish cocktail party afterwards, and with a guest-list including many celebrities, ambassadors and royals, including Princess Alice, the wife of Alexander Cambridge, 1st Earl of Athlone, a former Governor-General of the Union of South Africa, who did the official unveiling. Ramsay MacDonald shuffled in, looking like a tramp; afterwards, Eleanor asked Le Roux who he was.[28]

Le Roux made a real effort with his appearance. He hired a morning suit, which suited his tall, slim build, and, sporting a yellow waistcoat, he looked particularly dashing. As Eleanor arrived, he pinned a pink carnation to her lapel, which she felt was rather nice of him but unnecessary.

While Eleanor remained with a circle of her friends, Le Roux worked the room, talking to journalists and important guests. His energy and manner engaged his audience as he explained aspects of the murals and their technique.

Eleanor came over to Le Roux. 'I want you to meet a friend from Natal University.' She indicated a lanky man who was talking to several students. 'Noel, I would like you to meet my collaborator. Le Roux, this is Noel Langley. He's a novelist and playwright who has just completed the script for the film adaptation of L. Frank Baum's *The Wonderful Wizard of Oz*.'

---

28 Ramsay MacDonald was prime minister of the United Kingdom from 1929 to 1935. Aged 72 at the time of the unveiling of the murals, he died in November the following year (1939).

'Delighted,' said Le Roux, who knew the book from his own childhood, and remembered being fascinated by the illustrations of the Scarecrow, the Tin Man, the Cowardly Lion, the Wizard and Dorothy by Baum's collaborator, W.W. Denslow. 'I take it you're an admirer of L. Frank Baum? But not of Bernard Shaw?' This he said in a light-hearted but teasing manner.

'How would you know that?' There was an edge to the question that suggested to Le Roux that Noel was not the confident, opinionated chap he made out.

'Just a hunch,' Le Roux said, taking wicked pleasure in the other man's evident irritation.

'Rubbish,' intervened Eleanor. 'He was with me when you booed Shaw at the theatre sod-turning ceremony.'

Le Roux put a mollifying hand on Langley's forearm. 'Well, I am a fan of yours, Noel. After Eleanor pointed you out, I bought your novel *Cage Me a Peacock* and loved it.'

'And where is the lovely Naomi?' asked Eleanor.

'Over there, talking to the High Commissioner. She has a deadline for a piece on this for the *Rand Daily Mail*.'

'But she should be here, interviewing us, don't you agree, Eleanor?' said Le Roux. He looked in the direction of Naomi. Without thinking, he said: 'My goodness, she is gorgeous.'

'Yes, my wife is beautiful,' replied Noel, flatly, and he made his way to the bar for another drink. His marriage was very recent, and perhaps he was unsure if having a knockout for a wife was a blessing or a curse.

Just then, Naomi walked over to them and, brazenly looking Le Roux up and down, said, 'Eleanor, is this dishy man your painting partner?'

'This is Le Roux,' said Eleanor, tiredly.

'I will have to interview you, Le Roux.' Naomi gave him a ravishing smile.

'Le Roux!' It was the High Commissioner, beckoning him.

'Excuse me, ladies,' Le Roux said.

As he turned to go, Eleanor caught his arm and said under her breath, 'Keep away from Naomi, Le Roux. Noel is one of my oldest friends, a sweet guy, and I feel very protective of him.'

The High Commissioner was surrounded by a group of Afrikaner academics who were demanding to know why he had allowed these young people to paint naked Zulus in the South African High Commission. Indeed, the author's opinion is that Le Roux's father would certainly have been much more outspoken.

After the Dance

Praise from other quarters was abundant, however. The art critic Charles Marriott, writing on 17 May 1938 in *The Times*, called the work 'an example of the right thing in the right place' and stated, 'No praise is too high for the taste and skill and hard work with which it has been executed.'[29]

The *Manchester Guardian* of the same date proclaimed, 'The young artists have done a grand piece of work from every point of view.' The wall paintings were, the article went on, 'full of incident and interest… The colours have a rich earthy warmth, and the designs, meticulous and thorough in detail, are broad and restful.'

---

29 It was an opinion that didn't age well. 60 years later, South African political commentator Justice Malala said that the featureless black characters depicted on the walls were 'a typical manifestation of white racism in South Africa: blacks are inscrutable and alike, unknown and dangerous'. Eleanor was very troubled by this, writing, 'It really hurts me to think that the paintings cannot be taken for what they are – a sincere attempt to present the Zulu tribe in a historical setting, before white settlers' influence. The figures may have lost their features over time but [they] were undoubtedly there once. How can the decorations be seen as typical of white racism?' The South African government proposed to paint over the mural, but the work was protected as the only egg, oil and tempera work in the UK. Although politically offensive to some, the murals are regarded as technically excellent and historically relevant.

5

Success and A Schism

1938

The completion of the South Africa House murals launched Eleanor's and Le Roux's careers, and the commissions began rolling in. Among them was an invitation to paint the main decorative panel in the first-class dining room of the Cunard ship that would become known as the *Queen Elizabeth*. There were also several inquiries from the Public Works Department in South Africa.

The artists hired a studio in Chelsea, which would become their place of work for the next year.

Snow began to fall a few days before Christmas 1938: it would be a white one, a rarity in London.

Noel Langley, whose career had recently taken off with his script for *The Wizard of Oz*, was making final arrangements for the 'best Christmas Eve party ever'. He had rented a big house in South Kensington, an area he described as 'a way of life rather than a place'. He had even hired two balalaika players to play Russian folk songs, which, thanks to a new musical in the West End, had become all the rage. Noel, being thorough in his extravagant way, had taken the balalaika players to Clarkson's, a place specialising in theatre costume, and hired a pair of real Russian costumes, with high fur hats, Cossack coats, embroidered belts and Russian boots.

Eleanor and Le Roux arrived at the Langleys' house in South Kensington a few hours early to help with preliminaries. They were impressed with the giant Christmas tree Noel had set up in the small courtyard beyond the dining-room windows. Covered with real snow, it glistened magnificently when he switched on the decorative lights.

Noel asked Le Roux to look after the balalaika duo when they arrived. They were to be hidden in a bedroom until the party was in full swing, and then were to appear miraculously in full costume on the stairs to strum their instruments.

As there might be some considerable delay before that moment, Noel asked Le Roux to ensure that the musicians had a stiff drink when they came in, and perhaps another nearer the time of their performance. Unfortunately, Noel asked the same favour of another helping friend, and also his butler, so the bemused – although not unwilling – balalaika players, making themselves comfortable in the bedroom, were plied with stiff drinks for the next couple of hours.

When Noel gave him the signal for the players, Le Roux hurried upstairs, where he found the Russians lying in a happy stupor, as useless as two Russian dolls. A hurried council of war followed, and it was decided that they must get them out of the house. While there were no guests in the hall, Noel telephoned for a taxi, and Le Roux and the butler carried the Russian pair to the taxi and tried to prop them up inside. Noel gave their address to the taxi driver, paid him handsomely and went back to his guests.

As Le Roux sat down wearily on the stairs, Naomi appeared from nowhere. 'What on earth were you carrying outside?'

'Bodies!'

Naomi's eyes were as big as saucers.

'Don't ask. It's a long story,' he said.

Naomi knelt next to him and kissed him passionately.

Le Roux, taken by surprise, didn't demur, and she kissed him again.

'I've wanted to do that since I met you, Le Roux,' she whispered, stroking his cheek. 'That's my Christmas present to myself.'

In early 1939, the prospects of war in Europe grew. Hitler's expansionist aims had already become evident three years earlier when his forces entered the Rhineland, a demilitarised zone established by the Treaty of Versailles at the end of the First World War. Hitler's justification for the invasion was the May 1935 treaty of friendship and mutual support signed between France and the then USSR,[30] which Germany claimed was hostile towards them. The occupation of the Rhineland was, however, a gamble on Hitler's part, and his generals were apprehensive about it: German rearmament had not yet progressed to a level where they felt prepared to confront a well-armed nation like France.

The British people felt that the Treaty of Versailles was unfair to Germany and overly restrictive. Consequently, the British government chose to do nothing. Unchallenged, Hitler annexed Austria two years later. Yet again, Britain remained inactive: at the Munich Conference in September 1938, Prime Minister Neville Chamberlain, desperate to avoid war, consented to Germany occupying the Sudetenland, the German-speaking region of what was then Czechoslovakia.[31] Not everyone in Britain supported this: Winston Churchill, then estranged from the government and one of the few to oppose appeasement of Hitler, termed it 'an unmitigated disaster'.

Hitler promised to make no further territorial demands in Europe but then occupied the remainder of Czechoslovakia in March 1939. Conditions seemed dire, so Le Roux planned to return to South Africa. He noted to Eleanor that returning to South Africa was, in any case, part of the scholarship agreement.

Undeterred, Eleanor decided to stay in England to help with the war effort – 'Otherwise, one day, the Germans will take over South Africa,' she told Le Roux.

Shortly afterwards, Eleanor made her way to their studio, where she knew Le Roux was packing up his things. She wanted to chat with him about a letter from the Johannesburg Municipality about a commission to paint murals in the law courts. Turning the corner into the street where the studio was located, she glanced through the window and saw, to her shock, Naomi in Le Roux's arms.

She could not believe it. Had she not said explicitly to Le Roux that Naomi was not somebody he could dally with? She'd thought her bond with Le Roux was strong enough to prevent this from happening – they'd been in the very closest of proximities, advising each other, helping each other through ups and downs. But, clearly, she'd been mistaken. She felt deeply betrayed.

Eleanor waited down the road until Naomi left, and then she stormed into the studio.

---

30 The Russian Federation was only one of 15 republics that made up the USSR
31 Today, the two sovereign states of the Czech Republic and Slovakia.

'Hello!' Le Roux said, looking surprised.

She ignored him and packed her belongings into several boxes that Le Roux had gathered for his own possessions.

'What are you doing?' he asked, although his tone was muted, as he realised that Eleanor must have seen Naomi leaving the studio.

Wordlessly, Eleanor continued packing. Le Roux knew better than to try to force a conversation. Several excruciating minutes later, Eleanor picked up the boxes and left.

She enrolled at the Beaufoy Institute in Lambeth to receive training in the munitions industry.

'Precision to the smallest fraction of a millimetre was needed. It was quite a different approach for a painter who tends to see things on a free and grand scale.'[32]

Although Le Roux and Eleanor had spent six formative years in each other's company, they never spoke again.

---

32 *Eleanor Esmonde-White* by Leanne Raymond, *op. cit.* (see n.22).

6

Back in Cape Town

1939

The liner from Southampton docked in Cape Town early on 22 July, after 18 days at sea. The weather was terrible – typically for the Cape Town winter, there was unrelenting rain.

Nobody met Le Roux because nobody knew he was returning from Europe. He found a porter to carry his trunk off the ship, then set off in a taxi for his digs – rented via correspondence, sight unseen – in Tamboerskloof, a central suburb of Cape Town. As well as being near his new mural commission in the city centre, the accommodation had the advantage of being protected by the mountain from the worst of the weather.

Le Roux's first assignment, secured on the recommendation of High Commissioner Charles te Water, was to paint murals in the assembly room of the newly built Old Mutual headquarters in Darling Street. The art deco edifice was the tallest office building in the country at the time, symbolising the board's confidence in the future of the insurance business.

A few days after his arrival, he discussed his ideas for the murals with the architects and the management of Old Mutual. He envisaged five subjects on the walls of the assembly room that reflected the Old Mutual's role in investing in the country and building its main industries. First, there would a mural of the Great Trek, to set the context of a pioneering nation, followed by tableaux depicting agriculture, industry, mining and travel.

His preliminary sketches were accepted, and the management agreed that painting could begin in a month.

The next evening, Le Roux walked to his parents' house in nearby Vredehoek. As he approached, he saw no lights on, so he guessed the family were at a Friday-night church meeting, and he walked to the Groote Kerk on upper Adderley Street. He stopped outside the rear door and listened to the end of the hymn. Then he heard the shuffle of the congregation sitting down, followed by his father's voice.

'Good evening, my fellow Afrikaners,' Johannes began by reminding his audience that it was the 35th anniversary of the death of Paul Kruger. 'Tonight,' he said, 'we honour him and what he stood for.'

Le Roux stepped through the door, manoeuvring until he could see his father in the pulpit. The older man – he was now in his mid-50s – looked as young and agile as when he had last seen him.

With a change of tack indicated by his change of tone, Johannes continued:

> Tonight, I want to talk to you about the many ways the British undermine our Afrikaans culture. The latest British ploy is to force South Africa to join the British side in the coming war against Germany. Why? We Afrikaners have no quarrel with Germany. And the Sudetenland in Czechoslovakia is too far away to be a South African problem.
>
> It is nearly 40 years since the end of the Boer War, and we still fight for equality in our own country. If the struggle for an Afrikaner nation against Britain means we side with Britain's enemy, Germany, so be it. If they call me a Nazi for siding with Germany, then yes, so be it, and you, my friends, if you as Afrikaners are against Britain, then you too are Nazis.
>
> We must see Britain for what it is: the occupier of our country, the oppressor of our leaders, and the jailer of all those who do not accept allegiance to Britain. As they did in the Boer War, they come – backed by Jewish money – to buy control of the wealth of our country at the expense of our Afrikaner birthright.
>
> Today we are building our Afrikaner nation based on the beliefs and principles of our fathers. That is what we stand for, so let the British understand we will never surrender during the peace as we did in the Boer War.

There was loud applause and the stamping of feet on the wooden floor. People rushed to shake Johannes's hand, and Le Roux realised it was not the time or place to announce his return. He decided to head back to his parents' house to wait for them.

As he turned to cross the road, a car drove slowly towards him. He waited to let it pass, but the car stopped in front of him. The passenger wound down the window, the streetlight illuminating his face, and asked in Afrikaans, 'What is your business here? Are you part of those people in the church?'

Le Roux answered in English that he was just passing by.

'Well, on you go! Those people are trouble, and we are watching them.'

Le Roux watched the car park on the other side of the street, then turned round and walked back the way he'd come, taking a circuitous route to his parents' home to ensure he wasn't followed. When he arrived, the lights were on, and he could see his mother in the kitchen. He did not want to startle them, so he knocked at the front door.

His mother came to the door with her apron on. 'My dear boy, you're back! How wonderful. I have missed you so! Give your old mother a big hug.'

His father appeared and welcomed Le Roux awkwardly, without embracing him. 'Son, we hoped you would return from Europe.'

'Come and eat!' Anna said.

'Where are Anthonie and Annette?'

'Anthonie is at the university, and Annette is staying over with friends. They will be sorry to have missed you.'

The three of them sat at the kitchen table, on which Anna placed a chicken stew and a pot of steaming mashed potato. 'So, tell us. How was it?' she said, as she served. 'It must have been such fun.'

'First, let me give you a present that I bought in Venice,' Le Roux said, and he handed Anna a shoebox with something wrapped inside it.

'So thoughtful!' his mother murmured, beaming from ear to ear, as she extracted the object and carefully unwrapped it. She held it in front of the paraffin lamp. 'Such a pretty jug!'

'It's made of Venetian glass. I got it in Murano, which is an island near Venice, known for its glass-making.'

'The colours are so beautiful,' she smiled, continuing to turn the jug in front of the light. 'You see, Johannes, Le Roux is very thoughtful.'

His father's expression was inscrutable but Le Roux was aware that he would probably not approve of such a frivolous gift.

'Now, I want to hear it all,' said his mother. 'What impressed you most?'

Aware of his father's judgemental presence, Le Roux said, 'As an artist, it was the magnificent frescos of the Old Masters in the churches of the Italian countryside. To me, these great works depict man reaching out to God, so He listens to man's supplication. They inspire us, like supplicants, to believe in something greater than ourselves.'

Anna, nodding, said, 'And it is just as well that God was watching over you. We were afraid that you would stay in Europe until the outbreak of war, and then not be able to come home, weren't we, Johannes?'

His father clearly had other things on his mind. 'I read that you painted naked Zulus in the embassy in London,' he said.

'An artistic record of pre-colonial Zulu life. We did our research and included a lot of detail.' Noticing his father's frozen expression, Le Roux continued, 'It wasn't my idea, by the way, but the High Commissioner and Herbert Baker liked it. Frankly, I was more interested in the process of painting the murals than the subject matter.'

'Painting history is a matter for the people whose history it is. What did the Zulus say about your murals?'

Le Roux laughed. 'I don't know. We never found any Zulus in Europe. Our models were from West Africa.'

His father raised his eyebrows, then changed the subject. 'Now tell me, is war imminent, son?'

'Undoubtedly. The German people's fervour for Hitler is palpable, and he definitely wants war. London is full of stories of Jews fleeing Germany. Everywhere in England, people are preparing for war. Even Eleanor, the painter who shared the scholarship with me, has gone to work as a draughtsman in an armaments factory.'

'Here, there is a movement to enter the war on the side of Britain. Prime Minister Hertzog is resisting it, but Smuts insists that we must fight.'[33] His father's look made it clear what he thought of this plan.

'So, will you fight against the British?'

'Not now. Not yet. We cannot win against the British. But if Germany gets the upper hand, then Germany will support our rebellion.'

Anna, bustling back into the room with a milk tart in her hand, said, 'It is very dangerous for your father. The government is watching him all the time.'

'So, what will you do, Father?'

---

33 J.B.M. Hertzog formed the National Party in early 1914, and served as the third prime minister of the Union of South Africa from 1924 to 1939, advocating for the development of Afrikaner culture and being determined to prevent Afrikaners from being excessively influenced by British culture.

Back in Cape Town

'What I have always done: promote Afrikaner rights, and if Britain wins the war, we must be ready to defeat the English at the ballot box.' His father dug his spoon into his dessert as if he were impaling a khaki.[34]

Le Roux looked from his father to his mother. 'I don't want to worry you, but police stopped me outside the church. Secret Service, I think.'

'What did they say?'

'They wanted to know if I was a congregation member.'

'What did you say?'

'That I was passing by.'

'Good answer, son.'

After dinner, they sat in the living room and drank coffee. Le Roux would have liked a stiff brandy, but alcohol was one of the many things his father disapproved of.

'Mother, your cooking is as good as I remember,' he said warmly to Anna. 'I missed it terribly while I was away.'

She smiled and reached out for his hand. 'It's so lovely to have you back. I have missed you too. Now, Le Roux, I have something to ask. Your father is going on a camping trip in the Eastern Cape for a few days, and it would be so nice if you went with him.'

Le Roux was clearly surprised. Although his elder brother, Anthonie, enjoyed accompanying their father on occasional game-hunting trips, it had never been an option for him. He had been a weak and sickly child, and as he grew older, father and son had become increasingly distant. Le Roux had an instinctive way of annoying his father, even though Anna was sure he did not mean to. On the subject of politics, he questioned Johannes's constant railing against General Smuts as the devil incarnate; to the young man, he was a world-renowned South African statesman and scholar. Then there was religion: this topic always sparked tension between the two because while Le Roux acquiesced to Sunday visits to the Dutch Reformed Church, he never hid his boredom.

Art was one point of intersection between the stern father and his sickly younger son: Le Roux's drawing skills were exceptional, and sometimes, when Johannes was painstakingly sketching a scene, Le Roux would sit near him and, with a few fluent lines of his pencil, draw the same scene. Johannes felt that there was something unnatural about the boy's ability,

---

34 The scarlet woollen tunics typically worn by British soldiers proved extremely uncomfortable for fighting colonial wars in tropical regions, and at the beginning of the Boer War in 1899, a directive from the British War Office stated, 'Khaki is the best colour for the South African campaign as it most approximates the country's general colour.' Hence the nickname given to the British by the Boers, 'the khakis'.

and no good could come of such precocious talent. If the truth be told, life for Johannes had always been about struggle and sacrifice; for Le Roux, he felt, most things came too easily.

After an uncomfortable silence, Johannes said gruffly, 'People who have never fought a war cannot imagine what it is like, and we who have need to remind ourselves of the terror of it all. I will retrace some of my steps in the war, and if you join me perhaps you will understand more about what happened to our people.'

Johannes had joined up at the age of 14, in June 1901, to fight on the side of the Boers in the Anglo–Boer War, which by then had been raging for two years. Then on 31 May 1902, the Boer leaders had signed the Treaty of Vereeniging and the following month Johannes had surrendered to the British. Being from the Cape, he was a British citizen, and he was tried for the crime of high treason and sentenced to death by firing squad. On 10 August 1902, shortly before his 16th birthday, Johannes had been released; his sentence, along with those of many other defeated Boers, had been revoked by King Edward VII. Nonetheless, Johannes had never got over his hatred for the British. Even now, at the age of 50, married and a father of three, a successful painter himself, and the arts editor of *Die Burger* in Cape Town, he spent as much time on politics as he did on the newspaper's business, promoting Afrikaner rights.

Le Roux was scratching around in his mind for an excuse not to go when his mother interjected, 'Oh, please go, Le Roux. It's important.'

Le Roux smiled at her and nodded, and relief flooded her features.

'Good,' his father said. 'Come to church on Sunday, and we will head off after lunch. There are puff adders in that area waiting for nice white legs like yours, so get some knee-high leather boots, and a warm coat for the evening. I'll bring everything else, including a fishing rod and a gun to feed us.'

7

War Stories

1939

Sunday arrived, and Anna was pleased to introduce her son to the congregation after the service.

'We are so grateful to your father,' one woman said fervently to Le Roux. 'Someone has to stand up for us.'

'We appreciate your family's sacrifices,' said another, taking Le Roux's hand, squeezing it and looking earnestly into his eyes.

The situation made him feel uncomfortable, and he was relieved when the congregation began to disperse, with his parents heading towards home and Annette skipping between them. Walking quickly to catch up, Le Roux noticed the motor car that had previously stopped him parked nearby. Inside, two men were watching them.

After lunch, his father loaded his car with a tent, cooking utensils, and other equipment while his mother busied herself preparing *padkos*[35] – tomato sandwiches, hard-boiled eggs, apples, and a flask of hot, strong, sweet coffee.

In the early afternoon, they left Cape Town, heading towards the Hottentots-Holland mountains. They climbed the winding road over Sir Lowry's Pass, recently widened and tarred, and paused briefly at the summit to admire the breathtaking panorama of False Bay below. After enjoying a cup of coffee from Anna's flask, they continued up the coast. Progress was slow – they covered only about 100 miles – and arrived in the fishing village of Gansbaai after sunset. An icy wind blew off the sea, prompting them to book a guesthouse for the night instead of camping.

---

35 Food for the road.

After the Dance

The next day, they left early, driving towards George, over the Outeniqua mountains in the direction of Oudtshoorn, stopping where the old Cradock Kloof Pass and the Montagu Pass separated. They walked to the edge of an outcrop and looked south to the sea.

Johannes said, 'It is hard to imagine our people traversing these mountains a century ago with their ox-wagons, cattle, and families. Many perished during the journey due to the cold and attacks from the Khoisan[36] people who lived here. Your mother's grandfather, Gerhardus Le Roux, travelled from Oudtshoorn to Krugersdorp in ox-wagons with his family and animals. He settled in Krugersdorp, where I met your mother.'

'Did you fight around here?' Le Roux said, scanning their surroundings. To the north he could see the flat plains of the interior.

'No, although it was always our aim to ultimately go south along the coast to Cape Town.'

British troopships arrived in Cape Town in January 1900, bringing reinforcements.[37] Lord Roberts was commander-in-chief,[38] and Lord Kitchener[39] was his chief of staff. They took command of 200,000 British troops in South Africa, travelling from the Cape to relieve Kimberley and Ladysmith, which had been under siege by the Boers. They then marched on Pretoria. Britain annexed the two Boer republics, and the main campaign was over in a matter of months.

What was left of the Boer forces was scattered in commandos[40] over the Transvaal. General Kitchener assembled 50,000 men to systematically scour the republic for these Boer fighters; he ordered all Boer farms

---

36 The Khoikhoi ('men of men'), also known as the Khoi, Khoekhoe or Khoisan, were a group of indigenous people of south-western Africa, primarily in South Africa and Namibia.
37 The Boers who came from the Cape Colony in the Great Trek settled just north of the Orange River, which formed the border between the Cape Colony and the rest of South Africa; they declared the area the Orange Free State Boer republic in 1853. The Zuid-Afrikaansche Republiek (South African Republic), also known as the Transvaal Republic, was established as a result of the 1852 Sand River Convention, in which the British government agreed to formally recognise the independence of the Boers living north of the Vaal River.
38 Frederick Sleigh Roberts, born in India in 1832, was a British field marshal and combat leader, and served as commander-in-chief in South Africa until November 1900, when he was succeeded by Kitchener. He died in France in November 1914.
39 Horatio Herbert Kitchener, 1st Earl Kitchener, born in Ireland in 1850, was a British field marshal and imperial administrator. He died at sea in June 1916.
40 Boer commandos, volunteer military units of guerrilla militia, were the backbone of the Boer forces during the Boer War.

to be burned, and crops and herds destroyed, while women and children were rounded up and put into concentration camps.[41]

The Boer leadership responded by attacking Cape Colony[42] because the large Afrikaans population there might join the fight against the British.

―――

Father and son stopped in Oudtshoorn for lunch, parking next to the road and finishing the food Anna had packed for them. They had covered 250 miles and still had a way to go – Graaff-Reinet was another 200 miles on.

'Why did we leave Graaff-Reinet, Father?' Le Roux asked, biting into an apple, warmed by its hours in the hot car. The family had lived there from when he was born until he was nearly six, and he had only the vaguest memories of it.

'The droughts. Although I was editing the local newspaper, *Ons Koerant*, it was difficult to make ends meet. Nobody had the money to buy a newspaper.'

As they drove through the brown plains of the Little Karoo, Johannes remarked, 'I love this place. It is where I feel at home. It may look desolate, but you can find all kinds of animals, birds and insects here, all looking for the same thing we are – water. When the rains do come, this veld is a magnificent sight, covered with wildflowers.'

The road led them halfway up the Camdeboo mountains, where they parked the car. Johannes turned off the ignition, and the two men sat in silence for a few moments, listening to the ticking of the cooling engine.

'Here is where we were based during the war,' Johannes finally said.

They got out and proceeded on foot, loaded with their tent, food, and other gear. For Le Roux, it didn't prove easy to keep up with his father. Not as fit as he'd thought he was!

Near the top of the mountain, Johannes put down the tent. He straightened up, putting his hands in the small of his back and stretching, and

---

41 There were outbreaks of measles, typhoid and dysentery in these camps, and food was sparse; rations for the families of men who were still fighting were smaller still. By the end of the war, almost 28,000 people – mainly women and children – had died of starvation, disease and exposure in the camps.
42 The Cape became a British colony after the Battle of Blaauwberg between Batavian (Dutch) and British forces in 1806.

looked around. 'From here, we could spot British troop movements in the distance from the dust trail of the horses and infantry.'

Le Roux surveyed the enormous Camdeboo plain, stretching as far as the eye could see, and tried to imagine his father, as a boy, standing on the buttress, watching for signs of the khakis.

Johannes sighed. 'Come, son, we must make our camp before it gets too dark,' he said.

They chose a flat area next to a rocky outcrop that shielded their backs from the wind. Le Roux busied himself with the fire to prepare the evening meal, then heated up a thick soup his mother had made. He did not have the spices he would have liked to add, but there was something invigorating about cooking on an open fire at the top of a mountain.

As the sun went down, the temperature dropped quickly. Le Roux served the soup and the two men sat in companionable silence, the only sound the scrape of spoons against the tin bowls.

'This is good,' Johannes said, and Le Roux felt pleased to have earned this praise from his gruff father. 'Your mother prepares a good soup.'

When they finished eating, Johannes added several pieces of wood to the fire and, watching the flames leap and flicker, began to speak. 'These mountains were our grain store during the war. If you knew the gorges as we did, there were places to rest without being exposed to attack, and there was always plenty of grass for the horses.' He paused for a brief moment of reflection, then continued, 'Actually, in 1901, that wasn't true: spring arrived without the usual rain. The red grass on the mountain plains was still good fodder for the horses, but the Karoo plain was dry, so the horses couldn't venture far from the mountains. Drinking water was scarce, so we drank from the water that had sometimes been polluted by the horses. I contracted dysentery. Oh my goodness, that was awful. I vomited until I prayed for death. Afterwards, I lay under a tree, unable to move, listening to a group of commandos saying evening prayers.

'The night was hot. Heavy, dark clouds were coming from the west, and the rains looked as though they would finally arrive. The air was oppressive, and now and then, the thunder sounded in the distance, and the lightning shot a dull searchlight over the dark earth. Here and there, a campfire was burning, but most of the commando was asleep. It is a moment that has stuck in my memory.'

Johannes fell silent for a few moments. 'I am talking too much,' he said. 'Come, I will make us some coffee, then we must go to bed.'

The following day, over breakfast of *boerebeskuit*[43] and coffee brewed on the rekindled fire from the previous night, with plenty of condensed milk added, Johannes said, 'When I have nightmares, it is about Driefontein, a farm in the Swartberg mountains. It is very special to me because I lost friends there, and nearly lost my life. That's where we will go today.'

Johannes drove for several hours across the bleak Karoo landscape, finally making his way up a narrow valley between high mountains and rocky hills. He then crossed a rickety bridge over a fast-flowing stream. It was immediately evident that the farm had been abandoned: the grounds were overgrown, and there were no animals.

'Let's set up in the shade of those trees, where the ground is level, although tonight it may be more comfortable to sleep on the grass.'

'What about inside the cottage?'

Johannes shook his head. 'I was nearly killed last time I slept in there.' He walked over to the doorway and bent down. 'Look, you can still see the bullet marks.' He looked back at Le Roux as his fingers caressed the bullet holes. Standing up and shaking his head as if to rid himself of the bad memory, Johannes looked around and pointed at the edge of the property, 'Perhaps there are fish in the mountain stream. It should have trout or, better still, *geelvis*.'[44]

They walked through the tangled mess of an orchard, its fruit trees covered with creepers, to the river-bank, which was shaded by a large pepper tree. The river was wide and looked deep in parts. Johannes beat the long grass with the fishing rod to scare off snakes.

Le Roux baited the hook and put a light sinker on the line to catch *geelvis*. He waded into the icy water, which sparkled in the afternoon light. After a couple of minutes, he got his first nibble, then pulled in a two-pounder. 'One of us will eat tonight,' he shouted.

Soon afterwards, he hooked another *geelvis* of similar size. He handed the rod to his father. 'I'm going to swim where the river bends under those large rocks.'

The water was cold enough to snatch the breath from his lungs, and he didn't stay in for long; however, it was wonderfully refreshing. As he walked back through the orchard, he spotted some ripe lemons on a tree.

When he reached Johannes, the fire was lit, and the fish were gutted and cleaned. Le Roux smiled: his father had always been efficient in such matters.

---

43 Rusks.
44 Yellowfish.

As the sun sank in the west, the two men sat side by side, eating the fish with their fingers, saying little. It was delicious. Le Roux felt content and almost at ease with his father.

He took their utensils and plates to the river to wash them, and when he returned, Johannes had put the coffee-pot on the flames.

A short while later, 'Being back at Driefontein after so many years brings back memories,' Johannes said, sipping his coffee slowly. 'It was September 1901, and our fight against the British was going well. There were about 120 of us. We had been forced to retreat to the Swartberg, with the enemy close behind.

'As it grew dark, we met an old farmer who guided us along a short-cut through the mountains. The terrain was very steep, and the rain didn't let up. The horses stumbled and slipped, and one fell. After two hours, we reached this place.' Johannes looked around. 'We were tired and hungry, and the farmer invited us to spend the night. Commandant Scheepers[45] decided to ride ahead with 50 men and ordered me to stay behind to guide the others to the rendezvous the following day as I knew the area.

'I slept in the front room of that cottage, with a wounded commando in another room. The other men slept in the upper house, near the mountain, with Commandant Piet Van der Merwe – he was only 19 years old and hotheaded. There was no intelligence from the scouts that we were being followed, so we didn't post any guards.' Johannes shook his head. 'That wouldn't have happened if Scheepers had been with us,' he said.

'Early the next morning, just after dawn, I went to look for my horse, which had wandered from the house. When I entered the garden, I heard an English command, "Fan out," to my right. I looked but couldn't see anything. Then I heard, "They're in the upper house." That was where Van der Merwe was sleeping.

'I dived back through the cottage doorway to grab my gun just as the khakis opened fire. Bullets clattered against the cottage. I couldn't come back through the front door, so I climbed out of a window.

---

45 Gideon Scheepers was born in 1878 in Middelburg in what was then the Colony of the Transvaal. He trained as a heliographer (a specialist using a mirror and sunlight to transmit messages to other troops). In 1898 he was seconded to the Orange Free State and promoted to sergeant. General Christiaan de Wet used him as a scout and later promoted him to captain in charge of his reconnaissance corps. Scheepers's commando operated in the Cape midlands.

'Our men were running in all directions, some shooting at the enemy and others trying to catch their horses, which were running back and forth as bullets peppered them from both sides.

'Commandant Van der Merwe with some commandos sought higher ground at the back of the upper house, where I was also headed. From there, they shot at the khakis, who were charging up the hill. But another group of khakis stormed from the side of the upper house, using the orchard as cover.

'The commandant tried to untether his horse but he was shot in the thigh and fell on one knee. I crawled to help him. As he straightened up and pointed his revolver at a khaki, a bullet hit him in the heart, and he fell forward on to his face. The khakis screamed at me, "Hands up! Stop, you damn Dutchman!"

'I jumped on to Van der Merwe's horse and rode blindly through several khakis. Son, I am not ashamed to say I was terrified.

'One khaki almost pulled me off the horse, but his hand slipped. I thought I was free until a bullet hit the horse, and it stumbled, throwing me into some low bushes. A group of khakis who had captured six or seven commandos ordered me to stop, but I ran, zigzagging through the bushes, with the bullets hitting the trees around me.

'In a ditch further on, I found a tethered horse that I mounted and rode up the bank to a path leading away from the farm. As I looked back, I saw the khakis had surrounded the whole farm and were shooting at our men. I could do nothing.'

Johannes stood up to put more logs on the fire. 'Driefontein was a disaster for our commando. We lost the commandant, some officers, and 50 men, either dead or captured. Later when I caught up with Scheepers, we found the Khoi spy who had reported us. We executed him on the spot.'

'But wasn't he a prisoner of war?'

Le Roux could see his father was irritated by the question. 'The Khoi were British spies. They were enemies and, frankly, we killed them where we found them. There was no time for *due process*, Le Roux. In the Cape, we were at most 3,000 men on horseback, with no base, fighting 45,000 British troops, and double that if you count all the colonial auxiliary police and officials in the towns. We had nowhere to imprison spies and no time to stop for a court-martial.'

There was silence between the men, as Le Roux absorbed what his father had said.

'You want to know the process? Usually, we found one or two Khoi making smoke signals to the British to warn them that we were in the area. Sometimes, when we searched them, they had notes to say that they were under the protection of the British. Often, they would confess. We would give them time to pray if they wanted to, then we blindfolded them and seated them with their back to the shooter. One of us held the rifle a few feet from the Khoi's head, and on the order of one of the officers, he would be executed. That was the process.'

Catching Le Roux's horrified expression, Johannes said, 'Don't look shocked, son. It was war. What seems terrible now was a regular occurrence in the war. I have no guilt about it. The only rule of war is to win. The winner makes the terms of peace and writes the history of the war.'

If it was affirmation Johannes sought, Le Roux did not offer it.

Johannes put his coffee-cup down and stood up. 'I am tired, and it is getting late. Let's lie under the stars, son, and remember how insignificant we are in His creation.'

―――

The next morning, they began the two-day drive back to Cape Town, each man wrapped in his thoughts.

Eventually, Johannes broke the silence. 'Tell me, as a South African living abroad, how was it?'

Le Roux paused for a moment and then said, 'I loved being a foreigner in England – unnoticed yet observing everything, part of it but not fully integrated. I saw and heard things I had never imagined. Of course, I felt nostalgic about being away from home. However, I don't share your emotional connection with South Africa, perhaps due to numerous unresolved issues.'

'What do you mean?'

'In my view, the British are the least of South Africa's problems.'

'We have to rid South Africa of the British to build Afrikaner nationhood,' his father said emphatically. 'Each step we take brings us nearer to independence.'

'Father, they are such small steps, and by the time Afrikaners take the next step, the previous one is less important. Events like the Battle of Blood River and the Peace Treaty of Vereeniging[46] were, in retrospect,

---

46 Natal (today's KwaZulu-Natal) was proclaimed a British colony on 4 May 1843 after the British government annexed the short-lived Boer Republic of Natalia, founded in 1839 after a Voortrekker victory against the Zulus at the Battle of Blood River. On 31 May 1902 the Boer leaders signed the Treaty of Vereeniging, bringing an end to the Anglo–Boer War. Terms included that all Boer fighters had to give

decisive only in a limited sense, part of a continuum. Tell me what they mean today.' When Johannes didn't say anything, Le Roux continued, 'The goal of Afrikaner control of South Africa and independence from Britain is only one more decisive but small step.'

'We have to free ourselves from the British so that we can fight other battles.'

'Like what?'

'We have to find a solution with the natives so that they live and work separately, otherwise they will overwhelm us.'

'I can't imagine what that solution might be, Father.'

'We don't want to govern the natives, and we certainly don't want to be governed by them. We will divide the country along the lines of the tribal reserves,[47] give them their own schools, their own residential areas and their own governments.'

'Father, the land allocated to the native reserves is already the worst farming land in the country.'

'Because Africans don't understand how to farm.'

Le Roux snapped back, 'Because they are overcrowded, making soil erosion rife. And the fit leave for the cities. Those left behind do what they can to survive. How will you stop that?'

'Restrict their movement,' his father replied with a casualness that made Le Roux grit his teeth. 'We cannot be overrun.'

As they descended the Hottentots-Holland mountains, with the gorgeous tableau of winelands and farmlands laid out below, Le Roux said impatiently, 'Pa, I'm not a politician, but the natives are the largest group in the country, and therefore it seems to me they will always believe they are entitled to the biggest share of the land, if not the whole country. So it will be an endless struggle.'

Johannes replied stoically, 'We have to be ready to fight for our survival.'

'Well, it's not my fight.'

'And that is disappointing to me.'

---

themselves up, everyone had to swear allegiance to the Crown, no death penalties would be dealt out, the two republics would eventually be granted self-government, the Boers would be paid £3 million in reconstruction aid, and the property rights of Boers would be respected.

47 The Natives Land Act of 1913 prohibited Africans from buying or hiring land in 93% of South Africa, confining them to ownership of just 7% of the country's land. (This was increased to 13.5% by the Native and Land Trust Act of 1936.) Africans were permitted to buy and sell land in 'reserves' or 'scheduled areas', while whites were prohibited from owning land in these places.

There was a long silence, with only the sound of the wheels on the road and the wind over the car cushioning both men's thoughts.

Finally, as they passed through the little settlement of Somerset West, Johannes said, 'Will you go back to Europe?'

'When the war is over, yes.'

'And now?'

'I have one commission, in the Old Mutual headquarters in Cape Town, which I will start next month.' He added, 'Why don't you drop by to see what I am doing, Father?'

'I would like that,' Johannes said, and then spoiled the moment with an unwelcome opinion. 'But, you know, son, I have always felt that you should put your talent to more practical use. You are uniquely placed to play a big role in this country. Think on it, my boy.'

There was another long silence and then, as Table Mountain came into view, Johannes tried again: 'We disagree about many things, but you are the apple of your mother's eye. So we would not want anything to happen to you,' he said.

Le Roux looked at his father. 'Like what?'

'In the coming war, if Germany gets the upper hand, I will organise armed resistance in the Cape: we will disrupt the British so they have to send more troops to South Africa, and then Germany will follow. Until then, we will organise and prepare, but quietly.'

'Why tell me this, Father?'

'There will be no neutrality, son, no "passing by", as you told the Secret Service the other day. They will try to use you to spy on me, so it is better we stop contact.'

Both men were quiet again. As Johannes gripped the wheel and stared at the road ahead, Le Roux could see his father's profile, lips pressed together, jaw sticking out. He was the same uncompromising man of his childhood.

They drew up in front of the house.

'Let's say goodbye here. I will contact you when it is safe to do so.'

This was unexpected. 'And Mother?' Le Roux asked, lamely.

'She will understand.'

Britain declared war on Germany on 3 September 1939.

At the outbreak of the Second World War, J.B.M. Hertzog, the prime minister, represented the pro-German Afrikaners and advocated that

South Africa remain neutral. Jan Smuts, the leader of the pro-Britain South African Party, forced a vote in parliament on the matter, which he won by 12 votes. He then replaced Hertzog as prime minister. On 6 September, South Africa entered the war.

In 1941, Le Roux lodged an official application to change his surname from Smith to Le Roux, his mother's maiden name. The reason he gave was that, as an artist, he was known as Le Roux, and that is what he wished to be called. In reality, however, the cartoon published in an English newspaper early that year positioning Johannes as the orchestrator of pro-German support in South Africa aroused Le Roux's worst fears, that he would be associated with his father's anti-British faction, and he decided that the time had come to distance himself permanently.

From then on, he became known as Le Roux Smith Le Roux.

John Dronsfield, a fellow artist, noticed the change of name in the *Government Gazette*, and wrote in the *Cape Argus* in November 1941, under the headline 'Smythology and Logic', 'The name Smith / Is all very well to sign a small water-colour with / But when there's a mural to be done / 2 Le Roux are better than 1.'

Le Roux responded with alacrity, his own piece appearing in the newspaper under the header '1/2 Wit', 'Sir, your wit is but half for two things / I never do: / Paint water-colours or sign murals. / Yours truly, / Le Roux.'

III

The Job at the Tate

1

Married Life

1947

One mild winter afternoon, Le Roux was at a regular meeting with the Pretoria City Council. He was the curator of the Pretoria Art Collection, which was housed in City Hall. The collection consisted mainly of a bequest by Lady Michaelis of 17th-century Dutch artists. Le Roux was attempting to persuade the council to allocate a more generous budget to purchase art by South African artists.

Meanwhile, at his office at the Pretoria Art Centre, a black man in blue overalls asked to see him. Le Roux's secretary recognised Gerard Sekoto,[48] a pioneer of urban black art and social realism, who was a regular visitor.

The secretary motioned him to go through to Le Roux's office and wait for him. 'He's due back any minute,' she assured the visitor.

In the office, Sekoto picked up a beautifully illustrated book on Gauguin and sat down to read. However, he could not concentrate, as he had several pressing matters regarding his overseas trip that he wished to discuss with Le Roux. He couldn't continue living in South Africa, where life was becoming increasingly untenable for black people, and he planned to emigrate to Paris. He had recently held a very successful solo exhibition at Christie's Galleries in Pretoria and had a near sell-out solo

---

48 Born in the Eastern Transvaal, Sekoto had trained as a teacher, but he was also very musical and passionate about art. At the age of 25 he moved to Johannesburg to pursue a career as an artist, holding his first solo exhibition the following year. A year later, in 1940, the Johannesburg Art Gallery bought one of his pictures, the first by a black artist to enter a South African museum collection. Sekoto then lived for a couple of years in Cape Town before moving, in 1945, to Pretoria, where he immersed himself in his art.

exhibition at the Gainsborough Galleries in Johannesburg. He would use the sales from these two shows to fund the trip, travelling by boat from Cape Town and spending three weeks in London en route. His painting *Six pence at the door* was scheduled to go on show at the Tate the following year, as part of a travelling exhibition of South African art.[49]

Sekoto thumbed through the book listlessly and then looked at the trees outside the window.

There was a light knock on the door, and before he could rise from the chair, a tall, grey-haired man stepped into the room. It was Jacobus Lombard, Le Roux's boss from the department of education.

Lombard stared, aghast, at the sight of a black man casually making himself comfortable in a white man's office.

Sekoto, seeing Lombard, jumped up, holding the book behind him.

'What are you doing?' Lombard demanded in Afrikaans, then repeated the question in English.

Sekoto remained silent. He knew Lombard. He had applied to him for a grant to study art overseas and been refused.

Lombard then put out a demanding hand and, as if Sekoto, a 34-year-old man, were a naughty child, gestured with his chin that he should hand over whatever he had behind his back.

Sekoto handed over the book. He was careful not to make eye contact, and he mumbled, 'I was waiting for Mr Le Roux. I came to see him.'

'If you want to see him, you wait at the door!' Lombard blustered. 'You have no right to touch these books, or sit in this office. These are the property of the department of education!'

'Mr Le Roux said —' Sekoto began, only to be cut off by the furious Lombard.

'Out!' he shouted. 'Get out! And don't let me catch you here again!'

There was no point in trying to salvage any dignity. Sekoto picked up his bag and left.

Le Roux arrived 20 minutes later, and was furious when his secretary told him what had happened. 'Mr Lombard went straight into your office, and there was Mr Sekoto. Mr Lombard was very rude to him.'

Le Roux immediately phoned Lombard. 'What business is it of yours who comes to my office?'

'I won't tolerate natives sitting in a department office reading department books!'

---

49 Famously, the Queen Mother visited this exhibition and remarked how much she liked Sekoto's piece.

'Jacobus, I am here to teach art, and that man is a talented artist.'

'Listen, my friend, let me be clear: no blacks are allowed on the premises. It is a point of principle. If you want to resign over this, the department will not stand in your way.' With that, Lombard put down the phone.

Le Roux's heart was racing as he replaced the receiver. How he hated the narrow-mindedness of the people who ran the department of education. They had the same uncompromising attitude as his father, and reminded him of everything he detested about discussions at his parents' home.

He leaned back in his chair and looked out of his office window. The jacaranda trees, although green, had shed their purple blooms. The days were drawing in, and the leaves were beginning to fall, and he wondered if his job at the art centre would last until the spring.

The phone rang, startling him. It was Hugo du Preez, director of the Johannesburg Art Gallery, whom Le Roux liked.

'How are things going?' Du Preez was Dutch, and Afrikaans came easily to him.

They spoke for several minutes, arranging one of their regular meetings to discuss their efforts to expand the collections. Du Preez mentioned that he had heard that the director of the Tate was visiting later in the year, and they needed to arrange a programme for him.

When the call finished, Le Roux looked at his watch. It was Friday, after 4.30 p.m. He decided to go home.

As he drove the 20 miles out of town to the 25-acre smallholding where he and Philippa now lived, he reflected on his new marriage. Philippa had given up her work at the *Rand Daily Mail* and turned her attention to being a full-time wife and homemaker, while he commuted each day to his job at the Pretoria Art Centre. It had been a time of strange magic for him, during which he had felt at peace with himself, his life and his painting.

He turned up the bumpy gravel drive towards the square stone house built by Italian prisoners of war during their internment in South Africa.[50] He parked and walked towards the house.

---

50 During the Second World War, South Africa was a destination of choice for the Allies holding Italian prisoners of war as it was a considerable distance from Europe. About 90,000 Italian prisoners were transported to South Africa, where they worked on construction and house-building projects, mainly in the Transvaal.

Philippa came to the front door with Matt, their wire-haired fox terrier. She threw her arms around Le Roux's neck and exclaimed, 'You're home early. How wonderful!' She kissed him enthusiastically.

'Yes, I thought I would escape.' He embraced his wife lingeringly, then released her and rubbed his hands together. 'We must light a fire tonight. It's quite chilly.'

'That would be lovely, and we can eat in front of the fire.'

While Le Roux lit the dry twigs and wood, laid earlier in the day by the domestic servant, Koos, Philippa fetched a tray of glasses and the ice from the kitchen.

As she laid them on the coffee table, Le Roux asked, 'Do you want anything?'

'Perhaps a small sherry.'

He went to the cupboard where the drinks were kept and said over his shoulder, 'Apparently, John Rothenstein, the director of the Tate Gallery, has accepted the invitation to come to South Africa to judge the art submitted for the exhibition at the Tate later this year.' He poured Philippa's sherry and handed it to her, then helped himself to a brandy, added a little water and ice, and crossed over to his armchair. 'We'll give a reception at the art centre. I'll discuss the details with Hugo and see what he suggests.'

One Saturday, Philippa and Le Roux enjoyed breakfast on the patio outside the living room. Philippa gazed at the miles of veld surrounding them and reflected on how much she loved the sense of space in the Transvaal. She liked this house. The rooms were spacious and airy, and the woven African grass mats used as ceiling boards gave the rooms a distinctive look of rural sophistication. The floors were tiled, and the indented windows in the thick stone walls kept the house cool in the heat. But, goodness, it was chilly in winter.

Later, she sat in the studio with Le Roux, thumbing through a copy of *The Illustrated London News* while he painted. The studio was sited on the east side of the house, with a view of the surrounding hills.

Coming across a portrait of a child by the Welsh painter Augustus John, Philippa crossed the room to show her husband. 'How wonderfully he always catches their special look of questioning innocence! He is a great artist, isn't he?' she said.

They examined the picture, heads together.

'If we had a child, would you like a boy or a girl?' Philippa asked quietly.

'Do you want a child?' Le Roux said in response, as quietly.

'Some day, yes.' She pulled her head away, breaking the intimacy of the moment. 'I realise it's not possible now, but later, when things become easier financially...' When Le Roux said nothing, she added, 'You haven't answered my question.'

He maintained his silence, beginning to clean the paint off his brushes.

'I thought you wanted to paint all day?' She touched his arm and he flinched. 'Was it something I said?'

'I was just surprised that you want a child. I thought we were happy as we are.' She could hear the anger in his voice.

She heard herself answer as if from a long way off. 'Of course I'm happy, darling. I love you —'

'Well, what is it, then?'

'I don't know...' She was regretting bringing it up – she couldn't bear it when Le Roux got into one of his moods. 'It was just an idle question,' she said, in an attempt at mollifying him.

'It must have been on your mind for some time.' His tone remained icy.

'No. I just thought the child in the portrait was so beautiful, and that I should, one day, like to have your beautiful child.'

Le Roux stared at her coldly. 'I had no idea you wanted children.'

'But darling, I don't. At least, not yet.'

'But you do want them?'

'Oh, Le Roux, don't you? I don't mean now or even next year, just one day.' Her voice trailed off.

'I'm going for a walk.'

She stood alone in the studio for a while, wondering what had happened. How could he have been so upset about a child? It must be something else. She searched her mind for something that had occurred that could have provoked his reaction.

Tears rose to her eyes, and, closing the studio door, she walked down the stairs and back into the house. Matt sniffed at her heels, following her into the cool of the living room. The front door was open and she saw that Le Roux had taken his hat, and his rifle off the rack. Perhaps he would bring home a rabbit.

She sat down on a stiff upright chair, curling her feet under her, facing the door. She could see the little hill out of the window, and she decided to wait there for Le Roux's return. Matt lay down in the open doorway to catch the draught and put his head on his paws.

She must have fallen asleep, for the next thing she knew was Matt's frenzied barking. Half-awake, she mumbled, 'No, Matt. Lie down.' Matt continued barking. She sighed, accepting that she would have to get up and throw a ball, when she heard Le Roux's voice.

'Don't move, darling.'

He was standing in the doorway, his rifle pointed at her.

Time seemed to slow as she absorbed the unfolding scene. Her husband was aiming a gun at her. Frozen in place, she watched his finger turn pale as he squeezed the trigger. The sound of the shot echoed painfully in the confined space, and she let out an involuntary scream, covering her ears with her hands.

Then Le Roux was beside her, hooking the dead snake from under the chair with his walking stick. Its head was blown clean off.

Koos came running in, his eyes large and frightened. '*Rinkhals*,' he breathed reverently. The ring-necked spitting-cobra-like snake was known to deliver a painful bite, and could spray its powerful venom into an adversary's eyes.

'Burn it, Koos.' Le Roux turned and threw the dead snake out of the front door. Then he looked at Matt, who seemed to be having a kind of fit. 'Good God! Matt has been bitten!'

Le Roux gathered the dog in his arms and rushed to the car. 'Bring the keys!' he called over his shoulder to Philippa. 'You drive!'

She started the car while Le Roux held the dog tenderly in his arms. Driving as fast as she dared, she glanced sideways at Matt, seeing his head droop and his eyes begin to film. A few moments later, Le Roux said quietly, 'You can slow down. He's gone.'

Philippa pulled over to the side of the road and burst into tears. 'He saved my life,' she sobbed.

The next day, they buried Matt's body in the shade of a milkwood tree on the koppie behind the house.

2

Useful Friendships

1948

In mid-1948, John Rothenstein travelled to South Africa in preparation for the *Exhibition of Contemporary South African Paintings, Drawings, and Sculpture* to be held at the Tate Gallery that September. By then, he had been the director of the Tate for ten years. Rothenstein wore distinguished glasses perched on his nose, and his receding hair was always neatly combed back.

Le Roux and Philippa gave a reception for Rothenstein at the Pretoria Art Gallery, to which they invited artists and diplomats, South African celebrities, business people, and anybody else of note they could think of. Philippa threw herself into its organisation, and it was declared a huge success.

The Department of Education then asked Le Roux if he would take Rothenstein to Kruger National Park.[51] The park, which had opened to visitors 20 years earlier, was an extremely popular tourist destination, featuring furnished huts and tents at Satara, Skukuza and Pretoriuskop. The two men clearly had a wonderful time on the game drives, during which they saw a wide variety of African plains game and wildlife, including lions, giraffes and buffalo. Their visit during the dry winter months was beneficial for them; not only were the daytime temperatures pleasantly warm with deep blue, cloudless skies, but because the deciduous trees had shed their leaves, the bushveld was more open,

---

51 In 1898 Paul Kruger had proclaimed the Sabie Game Reserve between the Crocodile and Sabie rivers, and the Shingwedzi Reserve between the Shingwedzi and Luvuvhu rivers. In 1926, the two reserves were merged, and the 70 privately owned farms between them were bought by the government, to form the Kruger National Park.

allowing for better visibility. Additionally, as water sources began to dry up, animals were drawn to the remaining waterholes and rivers to drink. During their early-morning and evening forays, they encountered large concentrations of wildlife.

And South Africa's flora and fauna weren't the only things that impressed John Rothenstein. He was excited by the vitality of the South African art scene, and suggested to the government that it would be a good idea for Le Roux to attend the exhibition of South African art at the Tate later that year.

It was decided that the exhibition would be accompanied on its tour through Britain, Europe and North America by a representative from South Africa (preferably 'an art authority'). In August, it was announced that the South African Arts Association had appointed Le Roux as cultural attaché for the exhibition. Not only could he speak knowledgeably about South African art, but he also had three pieces in the exhibition, including his work *Deserted Karoo Farm*.

But a snag arose when Jacobus Lombard said Le Roux could not be spared from his duties at the Pretoria Art Centre. There was an outcry in the press, but the department would not budge. Le Roux was bitterly disappointed.

Early in 1949, Le Roux and Philippa moved from the country to a penthouse that had been built above the art centre as part of an expansion. Living on the premises would be convenient for Le Roux, and in addition, there was only a small rent to pay.

One morning, he telephoned Philippa to say he would be up for lunch early as he had some news. He entered their flat with a flourish and gave his wife a bear hug, sweeping her off her feet.

'I hope you have something special to eat because we're celebrating!'

'I'm dying to hear the news.'

'Well, I had a letter this morning from the Holland-Africa shipping line[52] asking me to paint a mural on one of their ships. They say they will pay my air-fare to Holland, put me up while I'm doing the job, and

---

52 Dutch shipping optimism was high in 1920 and resulted in the formation of the United Netherlands Navigation Company (Vereenigde Nederlandsche Scheepvaart, VNS). The Holland-South Africa Line (founded in 1919 with financial support from the Dutch government) was liquidated in 1932, and the VNS took over the fleet of five vessels, operating under the name 'Holland-Africa Line'.

pay a handsome fee! Darling, this will enable us to do a few of the things we've always dreamed of, including making a settlement on Juanita so that I don't have her maintenance to pay every month.'

'How wonderful!'

'And there's another thing. There's an outstanding surgeon in Holland who could have a look at my eye.'

Philippa knew her husband was very worried about an inward pull and cloudiness in his left eye, which had suddenly appeared just a few weeks before and distorted his vision.

'That sounds perfect,' she said. 'What about the department?'

'My contract allows me to take unpaid leave to paint mural commissions. I should think the job will take a couple of months at least, so that will mean being away for a term. They may not like it, but I'm sure it can be managed.'

'Is there,' she said, feeling her way, 'any way I could go too?'

'Oh, darling, I've been trying to think of a way all morning. I wish we had the money. I could show you my London and, of course, to have you with me in Holland would be marvellous.'

After careful thought, Philippa went to speak to her father. Over a cup of tea, she explained about Le Roux's commission in Holland, and also about his eye. 'That is why I am so anxious to go with him, Dad,' she told Adolf. 'He'll probably have an operation there, and I want to be there to care for him.'

'Yes, I understand.' Adolf looked distractedly out over the garden, avoiding his daughter's eyes.

Philippa decided there was nothing to do but plunge in. 'I hate to ask you,' she said, 'but we don't have the money for me to go too, and I wondered if you could see your way clear to letting me go over with him?'

Adolf sighed and put down his teacup. 'No, Bobs,' he said, with what seemed to be genuine regret. 'I can't do it. I haven't the money, and even if I had, I wouldn't pay.'

'But why? Can't you see what this means to me?'

He got up and looked down at Philippa. He spoke gently. 'You chose this bed for yourself, my girl. I did all I could to stop you. If Le Roux can't pay for you to accompany him, you will have to remain here.' He walked to the door. 'I am sorry, Bobs, but I can't help you.'

Philippa saw Le Roux off at the airport, determined not to let on how miserable she was.

'I shall write to you as often as I can, my darling,' Le Roux told her, his arm around her as they stood together, waiting until the last minute before he had to board the plane. 'Just think how wonderful it will be for us to have a little money, for once, and if I do this job to their satisfaction, they might give me another.'

'I shall worry until I know what is being done about your operation. Write about that at once.'

'Of course! Ah! There's the call... Goodbye, my angel, and take care of yourself for me.'

True to her husband's word, for the next few months, Philippa received three or four letters each week.

25 April 1949

Dearest one

I hope that you have received by now my letter posted at Kano airport, quite the most God-awful spot I have yet seen. Temperature is 125° in the shade – huge vultures sitting in the streets, and lizards in grey and yellow the size of a man's forearm running around.

We flew over the Sahara to Tunis, where we had an early dinner. Although we could not see very much, Tunis looked wonderfully green. Having filled up with fuel, we flew over the Mediterranean in the glow of the setting sun.

It was dusk already, and we could only dimly distinguish Sardinia and Corsica. Then we saw the lights of Nice. We flew over the Alps (flying at 23,000 feet) and saw the lights of Lausanne. We arrived in Amsterdam in perfect time, but we were delayed there and only got a plane to London at 1.30 a.m.

London is more marvellous than ever. You can't imagine how green everything is; there are flowers everywhere – in the parks, in window-boxes, on sale in the streets. I walked for miles.

I've seen Gwen Ffrangcon-Davies[53] and John Rothenstein, both looking marvellous. Tomorrow night I'm going to Gwen's play and afterwards to a supper party she has laid on.

---

53 By the time Le Roux saw Ffrangcon-Davies on this trip to London, she would have been in her late 50s, and still enjoying success: she played Lady Macbeth for almost an entire year in 1942 opposite John Gielgud's Macbeth, and in 1958 would win the Evening Standard Award for her performance as Mary Tyrone in *Long Day's Journey Into Night*. She retired in 1970 at the age of 80, but continued working in

I am weekending with John. Tonight, I am going with him to the Art Collection from Munich opening at the National Gallery.

Always yours

Le Roux

27 April 1949

Darling

This trip has already yielded results which are so worthwhile that if I returned today, the whole undertaking would have been justified.

London is quite appallingly expensive but, fortunately, I am being asked out for most meals. Last night, I had a late supper with Gwen, Edith Evans,[54] and others. It was a perfectly uproarious evening. I hate saying it, but Gwen is a different person away from Marda Vanne.[55] I don't think I have ever laughed so much for years. We only ended our session at 1.30 a.m.

I don't think I got the chance to tell you that I went to the very crowded opening the night before of the paintings from the great Alte Pinakothek at Munich[56] at the National Gallery. There I met several fascinating people through John, whose guest I was.

The most fantastic change in Britain is exhibition consciousness. I couldn't get into the National Gallery again yesterday to have another look. Two solid, slow-moving, four-deep queues stretched right down the steps and into Trafalgar Square.

John is still talking about his South African trip and has apparently created quite an effect after his Venice visit by claiming that he had

---

radio and TV, and made her final acting appearance in a teleplay of the Sherlock Holmes mystery *The Master Blackmailer* at the age of 100. She died in 1992, two days after her 101st birthday.

54 A great English actress of a similar age to Ffrangcon-Davies. She was best known for her work on the stage, but also appeared in films, and was nominated for three Academy Awards. A few years before Le Roux socialised with her in London, in 1946, she had been appointed Dame Commander of the Order of the British Empire (DBE) by King George VI. She died in 1976.

55 Le Roux clearly wasn't particularly fond of Gwen's long-time partner, Marda 'Scrappy' Vanne. Born in Pretoria, Marda had moved to London in 1918 to pursue her acting career, where she met Gwen; the two had a relationship that lasted until Marda's death in 1970.

56 The Alte Pinakothek ('Old Picture Gallery') was (and is) one of the most significant art museums in Europe, home to one of the world's largest collections of European paintings from the 14th to the 18th century. Founded by an avid art collector, the Bavarian king Ludwig I, it opened in 1836. It closed in 1939 at the outbreak of the Second World War, and its collection was removed as a safeguard. The building was severely damaged during the war and remained closed until its restoration was finished in 1957.

found Pretoria more interesting! He is just the same breathless, purple-faced, enthusiastic, likeable John. I am slowly meeting all the people I should, but [South African] High Commissioner Leif Egeland's office had mislaid my letter and had done nothing – not even invited me to the reception for the Prime Minister. Mind you, Malan's visit has upset the office terribly.[57] I'll only see Leif tomorrow for the first time.

Gwen got hold of me at one of my appointments to tell me that she has succeeded in getting the flat a month longer, and from Monday onwards, I am to be her guest. Thank God for that.

Darling, I love you so much and miss you terribly – all my love, dearest heart.

I'll write again soon.

Always yours

Le Roux

1 May 1949

Dearest one

Yesterday was full of coincidences. I had hardly been at [the Rothensteins' home] Shillingford an hour when a car stopped outside, and Nicholas and Olga Davenport[58] walked in. John, of course, had no idea that I knew her, and she had no idea that I was in Britain. You could have knocked the two of us over with one feather. Anyway, as I was to drive John to see his mother, brother and sisters at Stroud (near Gloucester), and we had to pass the Davenports' exquisite home on the

---

57 In 1949, British Prime Minister Clement Attlee arranged a conference to discuss India's request to retain its membership of the Commonwealth despite its new status as a republic. The South African Prime Minister D.F. Malan attended. India was given permission to remain within the Commonwealth, and as a result, Malan released a press statement that South Africa would also remain within the Commonwealth as long as the country's sovereign rights – including the right to become a republic – were respected. This was a departure from his wartime assertions that South Africa had to break the British connection, and brought about a backlash from within Malan's own ranks.

58 Olga Solomon, who was only a few years younger than Le Roux, had been born in Johannesburg, and first exhibited paintings in Cape Town aged about 15 – this is probably where Le Roux met her. A year later, she moved to England with her mother and brother, where she studied painting, acting and ballet. Her first husband was killed in the Second World War. In 1946, she married Nicholas Davenport, an economist and journalist more than 20 years her senior (he died in 1979). She continued painting and acting, but also was the *salonnière* in her husband's house, where together they entertained influential and radical artists, economists, philosophers and politicians of the day. She died in 2008.

way back, we were immediately invited to dinner. John and I had a most amusing evening.

I have fallen for Elizabeth Rothenstein, and I can't imagine how John can see so little of her. But she loathes London and won't live there. They have been married for nearly 20 years, and the daughter, Lucy, is a sweet little thing who is crazy about riding. John has made me feel like a complete member of the family. I can't tell you how important and valuable his friendship is proving. He has taken the greatest pains to see that I meet people and that they should know I have his approval and confidence.

The Rothenstein house at Shillingford is charming and full of subtle colours and beautiful objects. It is clearly Elizabeth's whole existence, and she works very hard; although she is not beautiful, one is haunted by her lovely eyes and soft Kentucky drawl, which is so out of place in a country village. They are all extremely fond of animals, and apart from horses, they keep a black cat, a wire-haired terrier, and two huge Alsatians.

John's purpose in going to Stroud yesterday was to see the family lawyer about some aspect of his father's will. The country looks so exquisite at present that I loved every inch of the drive. His mother lives nearby, and after the legal conference, I drove them back to Lady Rothenstein's lovely house and had tea *en famille*. Lady Rothenstein must be nearly 80 but still shows signs of her remarkable beauty. She was perfectly sweet to me and though deafish, is full of vitality and can apparently be quite difficult, with the result that there has to be a not unkindly undertone of conspiracy in the family.

The great subject of discussion has been Sir Alfred Munnings's outbursts against modern art, particularly his rather drunken speech at the Royal Academy of Arts dinner on Thursday, which was broadcast.[59] As everyone was rather 'tight' and difficult, a certain amount of obscene language came over the air, and there was a strong reaction against such bad talk.

Yesterday morning Charles Gibbs-Smith[60] and I then went for a quick preliminary visit to the latest Royal Academy exhibition, which

---

59 Sir Alfred James Munnings, who was president of the Royal Academy of Arts from 1944 until 1949, was one of England's finest painters of horses. He was an outspoken critic of modernism, and in his valedictory speech in 1949, he dismissed modern art as 'damned nonsense' and claimed that the work of Cézanne, Matisse and Picasso had corrupted art. The BBC broadcast was heard by millions of listeners.
60 Charles Harvard Gibbs-Smith, who was Le Roux's age, was a British polymath

After the Dance

is, on the whole, quite atrocious. Then we had a quick lunch rather late, and I returned for the actual opening time at about 3 p.m.

At the entrance, I met John, who always has some glamorous young peeress in tow (a different one every time). We formed a kind of irreverent trio, with lots of people obviously dying to catch John's remarks. We had great fun, particularly as I mentioned that the most important work of art at the RA was Lady Sarah. Of course, the place was so crowded that one could hardly move, and the feeling in the air, what with this major battle between John and Munnings,[61] could scarcely be described.

I met Barry Craig[62] and his new wife at the opening. He is much the same. I had dinner with them that evening at their house in Maida Vale. I shall see them again before I leave. Barry's work has altered a bit but somehow without real progress being apparent.

Well, that takes me back to Thursday, the highlight of which was Brook's production of *Dark of the Moon*,[63] which I saw, having been lucky enough to secure a returned ticket. It is a most impressive production and unusual.

I am writing all this in John and Elizabeth's charming drawing room after a long and sunny walk with them and the dogs along the banks of the river. The countryside is exquisite, and many people claim it is the loveliest spring in living memory. It seems so green, with masses of blossom everywhere, and the houses and trees seem to float in the soft sunlight while the distances merge in a blue haze. The rooks are cawing more loudly than ever, and I was wakened this morning to the sounds of the blackbirds and thrushes with the almost bogus note of

---

and a historian of aeronautics and aviation. He earned an MA at Harvard in 1932, the same year he was appointed as an assistant keeper at the Victoria and Albert Museum; between 1947 and 1971 he was keeper of the museum's department of public relations.

61 Munnings's rabid antipathy to modernism was at the root of this long-lived 'battle'. In 1956 Munnings would paint a crude and clumsy satire on modernism, depicting several prominent connoisseurs of modern art, including Rothenstein, admiring an abstract sculpture in a gallery adorned with paintings by Picasso. Exhibited at the Royal Academy's summer exhibition, it caused outrage.

62 Frank Barrington Craig, also known as Barry Craig, was a British painter of portraits and landscapes. Born in England, he moved to South Africa and worked as professor of painting at the Michaelis School of Fine Art in Cape Town from 1926 to 1933, which is almost certainly where Le Roux met him.

63 *Dark of the Moon*, written by Howard Richardson and William Berney, was produced on Broadway in 1945. This London outing, at the Ambassadors Theatre, was a much-admired production by the distinguished director Peter Brook.

the cuckoo forming a kind of *obbligato*. One would be nowhere except in the English countryside.

Tomorrow I will move to Gwen's flat – the rest of the morning I shall spend at the Old Vic School with Glen Byam Shaw,[64] the director. I am lunching with Hugo Anson[65] and the director of the Royal College of Music (by the way, Marchant died a few weeks ago),[66] and I shall spend the first part of the afternoon with them. Then I go on to see the Tate Gallery, and I hope to have a seat in a show for the evening. (I feel awfully lonely when I go to shows by myself.) On Tuesday I go to Reading University for the morning, and at 3.30 I have an appointment back in London with Sir Kenneth Barnes of the RADA.[67] That evening I dine with Leif at the Embassy, and I am to meet some theatrical people at 11 p.m. with Gwen. The following day I spend with Robin Darwin, Head of the Royal College of Art,[68] and after lunch, I go to Stratford for the night to see *Midsummer Night's Dream*.

All my love
Le Roux

8 May 1949

Dearest heart

You have no right to make me miss you so much – it is unwarranted interference when I am supposed to have my mind on other matters.

This visit to London has meant a great deal to me, and I realise now how desperately I have needed a new stimulus. I am learning a great deal and finding a great deal of confirmation for many of my ideas.

---

64 Glencairn Alexander 'Glen' Byam Shaw, who was a few years older than Le Roux, was an English actor and theatre director. He married the actress Angela Baddeley in 1929, and in 1931 toured in South Africa with her, in a repertory of three plays, which is possibly when Le Roux met him. Between 1947 and 1951 Byam Shaw was the director of the Old Vic Theatre School.
65 Born in New Zealand in 1894, Hugo Anson moved to London in 1912 to study at the Royal College of Music. He became a well-known composer, particularly for the piano.
66 Sir Stanley Robert Marchant was principal of the Royal College of Music from 1936 until his death in 1949. Sir Reginald Sparshatt Thatcher, who had been appointed vice-principal in 1945, succeeded him.
67 Sir Kenneth Ralph Barnes, who was significantly older than Le Roux, was director of the Royal Academy of Dramatic Art in London from 1909 to 1955. He died in 1957.
68 Darwin, who was Le Roux's age, was born in London and studied at the Slade School of Fine Art, after which he exhibited at the Royal Academy of Arts and other main London galleries. He was the head of the Royal College of Art from 1948 to 1971. He died in 1974.

After the Dance

I have made some memorable (for me) discoveries. The mass of the people is much happier and healthier than they were, and they feel more secure. They don't fear the responsibilities of marriage and parenthood because they know that the state will look after them.[69] They work harder, but they have more interesting leisure. There is no doubt that 70% of the people are much better off than before the war. I have spoken to many people in buses, trains, restaurants – everywhere – and it has fascinated me to feel this new texture in the social and psychological fabric of the people.

I see very few smart-looking women, even in the most expensive and chic restaurants. The men, on the other hand, look extremely smart. I felt at once how much I had lowered my standards. I also realised how lazily I had learned to speak in South Africa.

A lot of the old-time reserve has gone, but enough remains to make life anonymous when one wants it. But, despite their impoverished circumstances and the shortages, people have, on the whole, a marked new tendency to say, 'Come and have a drink,' 'Can you take a meal with me?', 'I'd love you to come home for a bite and meet my wife,' etc., etc. That is certainly new. I have always known a great deal of hospitality here, but it has never been so forthcoming; contrary to what I was told, courtesy has by no means disappeared. Your bus conductors, taxi drivers, porters, shop assistants and office clerks are polite and helpful.

People don't talk about their war experiences, but sometimes one suddenly comes across drama and tragedy, poignantly, chatteringly. A taxi driver slid open his communicating window and said, 'Excuse me, guv'nor, but if you don't mind, I'd like to make a bit of a detour here – it only makes a difference of a few hundred yards.' Then he explained in a strained voice that he avoids passing the place where his only son was blown up while working in a bomb-disposal squad. That's all – no detail – no sob stuff.

London crowds have lost none of their fundamental good humour. The streets, incidentally, are much more crowded than they ever were. One hears quite a lot of laughter and leg-pulling. You hear much more discussion of news and events – things are not blindly accepted as inevitable. The little man-in-the-street and the man-in-the-backstreet feel that they matter.

---

69 The National Health Service had been set up by the Labour government in July 1948.

London's sex life has changed too, or rather the commercial aspects. For one, the chemists don't have those huge signs 'Birth Control Specialists' up any longer, although they still exist and show their wares. But there is a greater distinction about it. Prostitution must either have become more discreet or is declining – perhaps through amateur competition. Its ladies are scarce at night; I frequently walk home after a theatre or other event, and inevitably I pass through the favourite street-girl haunts. There, in the old days, particularly on a Friday or Saturday night, one had to push one's way along avenues of tarts in certain Soho and Mayfair streets. You now see only a few who look anxious rather than enterprising – and not too prosperous.

I managed to get two seats at long last (although I only wanted one) for *The Heiress*. Even string-pulling through Peggy Ashcroft[70] and Ralph Richardson[71] was of no avail in the time left – that was for last night. Peggy Ashcroft's performance is quite superb. It is the most challenging part and, in its success, the most significant achievement I have seen so far here.

I then called upon Hugh Agnew, the art dealer, who has invited me to participate in a small show of South African art he is organising – I am thinking of diverting my Italian works[72] here. Afterwards, I took Olga Davenport to lunch. I must say she is quite glamorous and very intelligent. We had a very pleasant lunch and indulged in a lot of intimate gossip and a good deal of laughter. In the afternoon, I attended to British Council matters and went to see Edith Evans's show in the evening.

This letter is to keep you going and tell you how much I miss and love and want you.

Always yours

Le Roux

---

70 Dame Margaret Ashcroft, who was about Le Roux's age, and known professionally as Peggy Ashcroft, was a notable English actress. She worked with many of Le Roux's connections, including Glen Byam Shaw and Gwen Ffrangcon-Davies, which is probably how Le Roux met her.
71 The English actor Ralph Richardson dominated, with John Gielgud and Laurence Olivier, the British stage for much of the 20th century. He also worked in films. In the 1940s, together with Olivier and John Burrell, Richardson was the co-director of the Old Vic company; he and Olivier led the company to Europe and Broadway in 1945 and 1946, before their success provoked resentment among the governing board of the Old Vic, leading to their dismissal in 1947.
72 These were the paintings Le Roux had made while he was in Italy with Eleanor.

After the Dance

20 May 1949

My dearest

I am having the most amusing time staying at a small mews house in Queen's Gate that Geoffrey Wylde[73] has lent me while he is in America. The mews house is purpose-built – not a conversion – so everything works, but my goodness, there is a lot of activity in the mews. The tinkering with cars seems to go on round the clock, and the endless revving of engines, fumes of petrol and so on, soon encourage me to explore this great city.

It has been useful to spend a couple of weeks in London seeing old friends, and I confess I have thrown the odd party, some of which were too great a success and were too noisy and went on too long. At any rate, I have received several reprimands from the three old ladies who live opposite.

Yesterday at 7 a.m., after a thoroughly enjoyable party that ended rather late, I was woken by two police officers standing on the roof of an adjacent house who began to bang on the upper window of my mews house. Would I allow the occupants of the vast block of flats behind me who were escaping from a gas leak to exit through my rear window, into my borrowed and temporary abode, and so into the mews itself? Indeed, I could see the residents of the flats, already lined up on the mews roofs, under the guidance of police officers and the fire brigade. At that time of the morning, they looked like people off a shipwreck, dressed in negligées and dressing-gowns, carrying their young and aged relatives, and so on. I was glad to help the police get them through my mews and into an assortment of what seemed like Black Marias, and ambulances were drawn up in the road outside.

The three old girls across the way had no idea of the emergency that had produced from my front door, at that hour of the morning, an unending stream of people in their pyjamas, nighties, etc., etc., clutching their young, their pets, their most precious belongings and so on. Obviously, they thought I had been having the party to end all parties, ending in broad daylight with the assistance of officers of the law. All I could do was throw up my hands in the most Italian manner and mouth how sorry I was.

Wish you were with me.

All my love

Le Roux

---

73 Born in South Africa, Wylde, who was a few years older than Le Roux, studied at the Michaelis School of Fine Art in 1925–26. He emigrated to the UK in the latter part of the 1930s.

3

Doubts

1949

16 June 1949

Dearest

First of all, let me explain about the 'party that got out of hand'. It happened while I was staying with my friends, Jill and Jean Rey, in Maastricht, Holland.

It was just that the womenfolk all got rather drunk and amorous, perhaps to show that they did not belong to the dull local types. Anyway, I was able to cope without difficulty with my particular little blonde cross. I had to see her home, but she was awfully insistent that she should make some coffee for me. But she was so tight that she literally could not stand without support when she got out of the taxi.

Here, I should like to tell a story of temptation nobly resisted, but it wasn't like that at all. There is only one way to hold a drunk and extremely amorous woman, and that is so that she can't embrace you and be difficult. I found her key, opened the front door, propelled her inside, put the key back in her bag – which, curiously enough, had a small .25 Schmeisser automatic in it – stood her up against the wall, closed the door and ran for the taxi. I didn't even wait for the thud when the floor came up to hit her. Very ungallant, I know, but the best thing.

There is nothing more to tell. I am not a bit promiscuous by nature so please don't worry about that sort of thing. I won't pretend that the spring does not worry me too at times, but that is usually only due to thinking too much about you.

All my love

Le Roux

After the Dance

23 June 1949

Darlingest

I had lunch with John two days ago, and he wanted to know how interested I would be in two art jobs over here, one of which is that of his second string. Humphrey Brooke has left, as he has gone insane.[74] Naturally, it is not just mine for the asking, and the salary is only £1,100 p.a., which means about £750 once taxes are paid. Anyway, I am taking no decisions, but if I do, they'll be taken very suddenly, I suppose. But don't discuss this with anyone.

Darling, I am so happy in London and feel so well here. I can't tell you how much I love it.

I love you but must end now.

All mine to you, dearest.

Your

Le Roux

In response to this letter, Philippa immediately sent Le Roux a telegram saying: 'Don't exchange one administrative job for another.' Le Roux cabled back that he had declined the job and would be back in six weeks.

The Hague
28 July 1949

Darling heart

It must be because I am so exhausted that I have a strange sense of foreboding about the next few days, excited as I am at the prospect of returning to you.

I love you. I love you more than I thought it possible to love anyone. Our marriage has really been marvellous, worth waiting for, worth experiencing, to know that such happiness is possible.

If anything should happen, always remember that, and forgive me for my own inadequacies.

I shall always love you.

All my love, my dearest one.

Always yours

Le Roux

---

74 Brooke, an art historian who was around Le Roux's age, was deputy director of the Tate. He suffered from bipolar disorder and was forced to leave the Tate as a result. He was the Secretary of the Royal Academy from 1952 to 1968.

Doubts

Philippa read this letter more than once, but when he cabled her that he was on his way back to South Africa, she forgot about it. She placed flowers in every vase she could find in their apartment, then drove to the airport to meet her husband. He had been away for four months.

Loaded with parcels and looking bigger than she remembered, Le Roux seemed to burst out of the aircraft as she watched from the upstairs lobby. He appeared almost like a stranger as he crossed the tarmac, and she wondered how she could have been so confident that she still knew him. Would he, upon seeing her again, find something lacking? He would be too kind to tell her, but gradually, she would come to know. She trembled as she fumbled for a cigarette, which she lit, and inhaled deeply before savagely treading it out. She took out a mirror to examine the face she would present to him and saw that her eyes looked large and anxious.

She put away the mirror, and as she did so, the doors opened, and Le Roux strode out. He glanced around the hall and then saw her.

She forgot everything as she ran towards him. His arms enfolded her, and she felt his familiar warmth. He kissed her, and she knew she was home again.

The next month, they were invited to drinks with some diplomats who had recently been in England and brought greetings from John Rothenstein.

Philippa was looking forward to the outing. She had an early bath with some of the perfumed oil Le Roux had brought her from his European trip, then sprayed herself with the matching scent. She slipped into one of her prettiest silk frocks; the pale background of gold with the long design of black corn stalks made her look taller than she was, and very slender. She put on gold earrings and slung a black bag over her shoulder.

She looked at her watch. It was early – only five o'clock. They had arranged that she would pick Le Roux up downstairs at 5.30, and they would drive out to the embassy in Waterkloof. She decided to go downstairs and wait for Le Roux in his office.

The painting studios were busy, and she heard Le Roux's voice in the distance. He laughed, and she smiled automatically. He had such a virile, full-bodied laugh; the sound made her happy.

In his office, Le Roux's secretary was putting the cover over her typewriter. She looked up and said, 'Good afternoon, Mrs Le Roux. Your

After the Dance

husband is expecting you, but he has been called to see a student's work. Would you like to wait in his office?'

Philippa thanked her and strolled in. There was a pretty bowl of roses on the desk, and she bent to smell them. His secretary must have brought them from her garden.

Her eyes strayed to the blotter where an open letter lay, upside down, the writing facing Philippa. The words stared up at her from the paper. 'With all my love, darling one, Jill.'

She picked up the letter and saw the address was that of the friends he'd stayed with while he'd been in Holland.

Suddenly, the letter was snatched out of her hands and Le Roux was towering over her. He smiled. 'A little early, aren't you? I thought we'd agreed to meet at 5.30?'

She looked at him, bewildered.

He laughed and said, 'Oh, this letter is nothing. I wasn't even going to reply to it.' Then he crumpled it and threw it in the dustbin, took up his hat and found the car keys. It all happened so quickly that Philippa wasn't sure it had happened at all.

⁂

Soon afterwards, Le Roux's large tin trunk arrived. It sat unopened in the penthouse for a week; then, passing the room one day, he called, 'Philippa, darling, could you unpack that trunk for me some time? It contains all my painting things. I'd be grateful if you would take a look at the brushes and clean them if they need it. Also, I bought myself a small easel which I shall need soon for some work I have in mind.'

That afternoon, Philippa unpacked the trunk. There were theatre programmes and some blank coloured postcards from various parts of England and Holland. She placed all these on the desk. His sketchbook she found next and lingered over, looking at the drawings and admiring the intricate detail that had gone into each design before he'd enlarged it and then drawn it on to the mural surface. She stacked his paint-brushes, upturned, in an old vase.

Ah! Here was his painting shirt, blotched and stained. He could decide later to keep it or discard it if he wished. Next, there were two pairs of grey slacks. One was stained beyond repair, and she put this with the old shirt. The other pair was in better shape.

Turning to put the second pair on the bed, she felt something in the pocket and took it out. It was a letter, postmarked in London, addressed to Le Roux in Holland.

Philippa sat back on her heels, looking at the envelope in her hand for a long time. Then she took the letter out. There were eight pages. She looked at the first page and the last: the letter started with 'Darling Le Roux' and ended with 'All my love, Naomi'.

She read the whole letter, trying to make sense of it. When she reached the phrase 'your slippers under my bed', she began shaking uncontrollably.

She put the letter back into the envelope, then, on trembling legs, she went into the bathroom and washed her face.

Sitting on the bed, still shaking, she thought back over their marriage. She thought of all the waiting – those long years – the agonies she had undergone to be with Le Roux. She felt very cold and put her arms around herself, hugging herself, rocking back and forth.

That evening, Le Roux let himself into the penthouse, full of news and laughter, but quickly became serious when he saw what she looked like. Putting a hand on her forehead, he said, 'Darling, you look so ill. Have you a fever? You look so strange. We were supposed to go to the Thompsons for dinner tonight, weren't we? Would you rather not go?'

He tried to take her in his arms, and she braced herself against them. It was the first time she'd ever done this, and he looked at her, shocked and anxious. 'What's the matter, my little snooks? Tell me. We've never kept anything from each other. You must tell me what's wrong.'

'We've never kept anything from each other?' she repeated and looked up at him. She took the letter from her pocket, where it had been weighing her down since earlier in the day, and handed it to him. 'I found this in your trousers in the tin trunk.'

'And you read it, of course.' He shook his head, then went over to the drinks tray and poured two. He handed Philippa a neat brandy. 'Here, you'd better drink that.'

She took the glass and sat down, but she could not drink. 'You had an affair with Naomi,' she said, dully. 'Do you love her?'

'Love her! Good God, no! I was just seeing something of her because her husband, Noel, is a madman.'

'I don't want to hear about him. You and Naomi – she writes that your slippers were under her bed.'

Le Roux burst out laughing. 'You're worried about that? Oh, it was just a game to make Noel jealous. Darling, please believe me.'

She edged away from him and got up. 'Why do you lie to me? You lied to me about Juanita, didn't you? You lied to me about this woman in Holland, Jill. You had an affair with her too. And now Naomi. Oh, Le Roux, I don't want to hear any more lies. I can't.' She wept silently.

'Here, drink your brandy,' Le Roux said, his voice warm and calm. He helped her with the glass, then led her to their bed and undressed her, helping her to put on her nightdress. He tucked her in, and shortly she heard him on the telephone cancelling their evening engagement.

An hour later, Koos – who had moved with them to their new home at the Pretoria Art Centre, and now occupied the servants' quarters at the back of the property – brought a tray with hot consommé, and she managed to swallow a little, but she felt ill and exhausted.

At last, she slept.

The following day, she remained in bed, and Le Roux sat with her all day, drawing in his sketchbook. He brought her their two Siamese cats, Ernest and Wilfred, whom they'd acquired when they moved back into Pretoria. He spoke to her as he drew, choosing his words carefully.

'Darling, this is all nonsense. I won't argue about it, but we must clear it up. When I had nothing to do, I visited Naomi, perhaps three or four times. She told me Noel was making her life miserable. As a joke, I suggested she write love letters to me and leave them where the servants could see them so they would report back to Noel, who she knew was paying them for information. I was annoyed with Noel and thought he needed a bit of teasing. When Noel realised we were toying with him, he was furious. He wrote to me stating he wouldn't rest until he'd destroyed me. The animosity with Noel goes back to my time in London in the '30s, I'm afraid.'

She listened, trying to accept what he was telling her.

'If you think I slept with her, darling, you simply do not realise my feelings towards women who've had children. She has five!' He stopped, took a deep breath, then said, 'You must believe me. I love nobody but you. I have never loved anybody the way I love you.'

4

Rothenstein's Offer

1949

In July 1949, a year after the Nationalist government came to power in South Africa, the minister of arts and science, J.H. Viljoen, announced plans to transfer the Pretoria Art Centre to the control of the University of Pretoria. Le Roux concluded that this meant the art centre would be run primarily as an Afrikaans institution, promoting Afrikaner culture.

Although letters to the paper and editorials expressed opposition, the Nationalist government was determined to stamp its authority on all aspects of South African life, including the arts.

When he realised the magnitude of the changes ahead, Le Roux resigned as director of the Pretoria Art Centre after six years.

News about his resignation reached John Rothenstein, who wrote to him immediately, suggesting for a second time that he should apply for the Tate post, as they had discussed when Le Roux was in London. 'If you arrive no later than March next year, the interview will take place immediately, and I can guarantee you the position, provided your qualifications are in order,' he assured Le Roux.

Philippa could see that Le Roux was overjoyed at the prospect of living and working in London. Even so, she voiced her doubts when they lunched with her parents the following Sunday.

Her father looked at her in astonishment. 'But what is the downside? It's such an honour for a South African to be selected, and it means that Le Roux will be in the centre of the art world. London! What more could you want?'

'It will be an administrative post, and it will take up time that Le Roux should spend painting,' Philippa said. 'Also, it's badly paid. Only

After the Dance

people with private incomes have held it in the past.' She put her arm on Le Roux's. 'I just feel it's wrong for you to stop painting.'

Le Roux remained silent but her father announced, 'I think you're mad!' Then he smiled warmly at Le Roux. 'You will, of course, accept?'

Le Roux nodded. 'As it happens, I have a bottle of champagne on ice. Shall we open it?'

Philippa and Le Roux boarded the *Stirling Castle* bound for England in mid-February 1950. The orchestra played, and they stood at the railing, throwing streamers to the people on the quay. They watched Table Mountain recede, with the city sprawling at its base, and Le Roux said, 'I can't wait to return to London. I'm determined to make a success of this opportunity.'

Philippa noticed the tension in her husband's face and slipped her arm through his. 'You will be a great success in London. Now, let's enjoy the trip.'

They shared a dining table with Gwen Ffrangcon-Davies, who was about to play the part of Queen Katherine in *Henry the Eighth* at Stratford, and over dinner one evening, she said, 'Perhaps Philippa will hear my lines? It would be such a help.' So Philippa spent a part of each afternoon tucked away in a corner on the top deck listening to Gwen creating an atmosphere of a bygone age in her lilting, heart-breaking voice.

As they dressed for dinner in their state-room one evening, Philippa confided to her husband, 'Le Roux, in the play, Queen Katherine says, "Haven't I always loved the king completely, second only to God? And obeyed him? Haven't I been so fond of him that he almost became my god, and I almost forgot to pray because I was focusing on making him happy? And am I rewarded thus?" She gave up everything for him, and divorce was her reward. Oh, Le Roux, I nearly cried.'

They arrived in London on a lovely, clear, cold day, and deposited their baggage in a boarding house at 18 Stanford Road in Kensington. While Philippa began flat-hunting, Le Roux went to the Tate Gallery.

Rothenstein was out at a meeting, so Le Roux's appointed personal assistant, Jane Ryder, a pretty young brunette in her late 20s, showed him to his office. It had huge windows with views across the River Thames: not the Thames of the verdant meadows of Oxfordshire, but the industrial river in the heart of Westminster; it was comforting nonetheless and susceptible to changes in the light.

'"Sweet Thames, run softly, till I end my song,"' Le Roux quoted from *The Waste Land*. When Jane looked blank, he explained, 'Eliot.'

'Elliot who?' she asked.

Le Roux smiled. 'I will get you the book.'

Rothenstein arrived a little later and invited Le Roux to join him for lunch in the restaurant in the basement. 'I'm so pleased you're here,' he told his new appointee over a meal of steak-and-kidney pie. 'The Tate is under-staffed, and we can't possibly fill all the exhibitions that are expected. You will be my deputy as the senior deputy keeper, and in charge of matters while I am away. When we have trustee meetings, I want you at my side, taking the minutes, so we have a record of what needs to be done. Norman Reid[75] will be the second deputy keeper. For the first year you will be on probation but that's a civil service formality.' He called for some water. 'Now, I want you to get a grip of the publications department. It's a major money-spinner for the Tate but also a large cost centre that poor old Brooke never managed to control. Do keep me informed.'

Le Roux nodded.

'Have a word with the Treasury. I've always found this chap helpful,' Rothenstein added, pushing a piece of paper across the table to Le Roux, on which the name 'Mr Perfect' was scrawled, along with a telephone number. 'Unfortunately, next week I will be away at the Venice Biennale. I'm sure you appreciate how boring it is to be constantly on the move as I am, but one must keep up with what is happening in Europe and America, don't you see.'

To many in the London art world, the appointment of a relatively unknown South African as deputy keeper of the Tate Gallery came as a surprise. Several factors influenced John Rothenstein's decision, foremost among them the Tate's chronic under-staffing since before the war, which made it unable to cope with the post-war demand for exhibitions. Additionally, Rothenstein struggled to dedicate enough time to the institution, as he was torn between finishing a glossy series of publications

---

75   Norman Reid was born in London in 1915. He won a scholarship to the Edinburgh College of Art, where he studied in the late 1930s. He joined the Tate Gallery in 1946 and became the right-hand man to Rothenstein.

on English painters and frequent invitations to travel abroad for artistic events. Furthermore, there was Le Roux's predecessor, Humphrey Brooke, whose dismissal had left many staff members feeling uncomfortable, and Rothenstein hoped that Le Roux, recognised as a charismatic personality with an artistic and academic background, would instil confidence in the staff.

But perhaps the most pressing reason for the sudden appointment was that Douglas Cooper, an art historian and wealthy art collector, was angling to be appointed to the position. Cooper was eminently qualified for the job, but Rothenstein suspected Cooper had ambitions to replace him as director, and that he would not countenance. In Le Roux, Rothenstein saw a very competent deputy who could pick up some of his tasks and who, as a South African and therefore not part of the British Establishment, would never be a threat to his position.

Le Roux called the Treasury as instructed, and a week later, Mr Perfect, who was responsible for systems at the Treasury, visited him. Le Roux explained that he'd been tasked by the director with setting up a proper filing and cataloguing system. 'So, how do you think we should begin?' he asked the other man.

'Well, we put in a jolly good system several years ago, so it would really mean improving on that, wouldn't you say?'

Le Roux was puzzled. As far as he could see, there was no system. Everything was simply dumped on the shelves of the storage area in the basement. He tried another tack. 'My priority is the Modern Foreign Catalogue, because we have a major Impressionist exhibition coming up. I'm afraid the system you introduced hasn't found its way to this section of our archive, so I will have to develop a system for that.'

'Excellent approach, Le Roux,' Mr Perfect said, standing and picking up his briefcase. 'I'll pop back next month to see how you're doing.'

After he left, Le Roux sat down heavily. No help there, then.

That night he and Philippa went out to dinner at the Six Bells in Chelsea. After their meal, as Philippa nursed a sherry, she asked Le Roux how the job was going.

'I'm worried about the Tate. It's in such a mess.'

'Meaning?'

'The filing is non-existent and nobody knows what's going on.'

'Surely you can fix that?'

'Not without making some sweeping changes that may not be popular.' He finished his drink. 'Come on. Let's go home. I have some work to do.'

Back from another trip, Rothenstein called Le Roux into his office. 'How is the filing proceeding in the publications department?'

'All done, John. I'd like to show you when you have time.'

'Not now. I'm off to Paris tomorrow. But do keep on top of it, that's a good chap.'

'John, I've been looking at the filing system generally at the Tate, and I think the whole place could do with an upgrade in terms of how we store information,' Le Roux said. It was something he'd wanted to raise since his arrival, and his fingers itched to impart some sort of order on the chaos he'd seen.

'I know what you mean. I have a devil of a job locating anything,' his boss agreed.

'Well, if you'd allow me, I will reorganise the filing system. It will be uncomfortable for a time, as we change systems, but I promise you that once it's done, you will know where everything is.'

'That would be a relief.'

Having been given the go-ahead, Le Roux wasted no time in implementing his new filing system.

As part of this reorganisation, he took over distributing the morning post. It was how his days generally started: opening the post, making a record of it, and handing it out to the appropriate people.

Norman Reid, the number two deputy keeper, approached Le Roux in the middle of the morning and said that he didn't understand why Le Roux was opening all the post.

'Because nobody knows what's going on here, Norman. There's no central system for processing and filing correspondence. The director has asked me to reorganise it.'

Reid looked unhappy but retreated without further comment.

A few days later, Rothenstein called Le Roux into his office again. 'I say, Le Roux, this new system of handling the mail isn't working. You're opening all my private correspondence.'

'John, all I'm trying to do is put in an orderly system so that, as an institution, we know what is coming in, who is dealing with it, and where it is filed in the future.'

'Elizabeth was most upset to hear that you opened a private letter of hers to me.'

'I do apologise. I didn't recognise her handwriting, but it won't happen again.'

Rothenstein continued to appear uncomfortable but wasn't sure how to confront his burly subordinate. Of course, it would be a godsend if he could organise everything, but wasn't this going a bit too far?

When Le Roux saw Rothenstein again several weeks later, his boss had just returned from a trip and looked relaxed and tanned.

'So, tell me, how are you getting on with the publications department?' the director asked.

'Well, I've seen the man from the Treasury on several occasions. He sees his role as a supervisor rather than a doer, so I've begun instituting the new filing system with the Modern Foreign Catalogue, and I've put John Hardy in charge of filing, and Miss Butcher will handle the cataloguing side.' These were two reliable staff members who knew the system.

'Oh, yes, good idea.' Rothenstein nodded his approval.

'By the way, John, when we discussed my position here, I said I would have to earn money from media work. That's okay, isn't it? Otherwise, it's very difficult to make ends meet on £1,100 a year.'

'Of course. I quite understand. But the Tate comes first as far as your time is concerned.'

Taking advantage of his boss's good mood, Le Roux added, 'John, do come to dinner at our new flat next week.'

Philippa had found a clean first-floor apartment in Rutland Gate, with floor-to-ceiling windows, a balcony and a neat kitchen. It fronted on to a quiet square, looking all the way up to Hyde Park. Rothenstein would be their first guest.

5

Delicate Subjects

1950

Philippa prepared a delicious fish pie, and the evening went smoothly. After the three of them had eaten and were sitting in the living room with snifters of brandy, Philippa remarked to her husband, 'We must dig out those letters of introduction we had from the diplomats in Pretoria, Le Roux.'

Seeing Rothenstein's questioning glance, Le Roux explained, 'Philippa is referring to the friends we had in the diplomatic corps in Pretoria. They gave us letters to the various ambassadors here and in Paris. Philippa was about to forward them to the embassies to say that we're here.' The letters of introduction would be a sign that the Le Rouxs were people to be included as guests at embassy parties. Le Roux added, 'We have done nothing about them yet.'

Rothenstein said nothing that evening, but the following morning, he called Le Roux into his office. 'My dear chap, I hardly like to mention this, but you know, when Philippa suggested presenting those letters of introduction, I did not like to point out to her that things over here are a little different from Pretoria. You, I am sure, will understand that, as a member of my staff, it would hardly be appropriate for you to have letters of introduction to important embassies rather than me. Philippa will understand these things when she has been here a little longer.'

When Le Roux relayed this conversation to Philippa, she responded, 'He clearly wants you to be subservient. Do be careful, Le Roux.'

'It's early days,' said Le Roux. 'Things will sort themselves out.'

Some weeks later, Le Roux and Philippa attended a dinner at the home of Sir Jasper Ridley, the chairman of the board of trustees of the Tate, in Marylebone.

As their host greeted them, another couple arrived, introduced as Mr and Mrs Humphrey Brooke. Brooke had held the position of deputy keeper at the Tate before Le Roux and, according to Rothenstein, had gone off his head. He was a large man, over six feet and slightly too heavy, and he did not look well, but he had a sympathetic air.

When they left the party, Philippa asked Le Roux if he'd had an opportunity to talk to Brooke. 'Well, he tried to bring up the Tate matter, but I excused myself,' he replied, shortly. 'I felt it was better left unsaid. After all, I am Rothenstein's appointee, and it's common knowledge that Rothenstein and Brooke are on bad terms.'

'He looked a nice man,' Philippa said. 'What I can't understand is that if Brooke is in such bad odour with Rothenstein, why did Sir Jasper invite him? Surely there must be two opinions about the Brooke case?'

April brought a flurry of social engagements, and it was with surprise that Philippa woke up one morning to find she was nearly 31. That night in bed, a little tipsy after a party, she whispered to Le Roux, 'If I don't have a child soon, I shall be unable to have one at all.'

Her husband pulled away from her and propped himself up on one elbow, looking down at her with a pained expression. 'How can we possibly have a child now, my sweet? We've just started our life here and certainly can't afford a child.'

One evening soon after, Philippa accompanied Le Roux to an exhibition at Agnew's, the gallery of Hugh Agnew, a prominent art dealer on Bond Street. Some of Le Roux's paintings were displayed alongside works by other South African artists. Philippa was disconcerted by the ease with which several women approached Le Roux, and when a beautiful blonde entered and wrapped her arms around his neck, exclaiming, 'Le Roux! How wonderful to see you again! When did you arrive? Oh, I've missed you!' she felt her face flush and her old suspicions resurface.

Seeing his wife's frozen expression, Le Roux quickly disentangled himself and put an arm around Philippa, saying to the blonde, 'I don't think you've met Philippa. This is Naomi Langley.' Le Roux turned back to Naomi. 'Are you still living in Hampstead?' he asked.

Le Roux's father, Johannes Smith, as head of the Cape Ossewabradwag, seated in the middle in a dark suit with two future prime ministers (BJ Vorster & PW Botha) at his feet.
(*Die Huisgenoot* magazine 7 July 1967)

Cartoon of Le Roux's father 'General Smith' driving the nationalist to Germany published in the *Sunday Express* 5 Jan 1941.

i

Le Roux aged 24 at the opening party for the SA House murals. (*Die Burger* Newspaper)

Le Roux's murals in the Old Mutual building in Cape Town.

Details of Le Roux's murals in the Old Mutual building. (Photo credit: Stewart Harris)

Le Roux and Eleanor Esmonde-White mixing the yolk of eggs with their pigments for their murals at South Africa House, 1936. (Photo credit: Smith Archive/Alamy Stock Photo)

 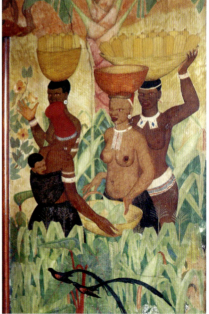

Details of Zulu murals in South Africa House, London. (Photo credit: Author's own)

Le Roux and my mother Philippa on their wedding day, 12 June 1947.

Philippa holding me at a time when the marriage was falling apart, December 1951.

Sir John Rothenstein.
(NPG collection)

Edgar Degas, *Little Dancer Aged Fourteen*,
1880–1, cast *c*.1922.

Controversial picture of Zsa Zsa Gabor
visiting the Tate.

Le Roux preparing egg tempera for the murals at South Africa House.
(National Portrait Gallery Collection)

Paintings by Le Roux. (Private collection; photo credit: Author's own)

Discreetly, Philippa moved away, looking at the pictures with unseeing eyes. She was relieved when Enslin du Plessis,[76] a South African journalist-turned-painter, suddenly appeared next to her.

'How are you, Philippa? It must be quite 18 months since I saw you and Le Roux in Pretoria.'

She turned to greet the bearded artist, who also had several paintings in the show. 'I saw one of yours when I came in.'

'I'm only over for a couple of weeks,' he said. Looking around, he added, 'It seems to be going well.' Then he caught sight of Le Roux and Naomi walking around the gallery and said, 'Ah, I see Le Roux is monopolising the lovely Naomi Langley. I must have a word with him. See you later.'

As Philippa and Le Roux walked home that evening, he was jubilant. His work had been well received, and there were already two little red stars on his pictures, indicating sales. 'By the way, darling, I've asked Naomi to have dinner with us one night next week,' he said, his tone bright. 'I said I would ask you which evening was convenient.' Perhaps feeling his wife's tension at his side, he continued, 'You'll like her when you get to know her. She's very sweet. Noel is divorcing her and being as nasty as he can. She's had to take part-time work in a local shop to make ends meet.'

'I don't want to have her to dine,' Philippa said, quietly.

'You're not still brooding about that letter?' Le Roux's voice was indignant.

'I don't want to know her or have her in my home.'

'I see,' said Le Roux. 'Well, I think you're being very silly.' He dropped her arm and speeded up his walking pace.

One evening a couple of months later, Philippa had news for Le Roux. She broke it over dinner.

'Are you sure? About the pregnancy?' Le Roux asked. His tone was dull and flat.

'Quite sure,' she said, smiling tightly. Following the Agnews' exhibition all those weeks before, Philippa had stopped using contraception.

Le Roux got up from the table and went to his study.

---

76 Born in South Africa in 1894, Enslin du Plessis settled in London in 1922, where he was a correspondent for South African newspapers, and began painting seriously about six years later. He returned to South Africa intermittently and from 1938 he exhibited with the New Group. He would retire from journalism in 1956 to focus on painting full-time.

For the following week, he ignored Philippa during the day, but at night, he made love to her with increased intensity.

Philippa responded with all the love she had for him, and while she caressed him and told him how much she loved him, she prayed that he would accept the child and her.

One day, late in July, Philippa announced, 'Diana Malherbe is in London. You remember her; she was on the *Rand Daily Mail* with me? She now has a job with *Life* magazine in Paris. I've asked her to dinner tomorrow night.'

Diana arrived punctually at 7.30 p.m., before Le Roux returned from work. She was tall and dark, a willowy woman several years older than Philippa. As she had been away from South Africa for some time, she exuded the sophisticated air of a European.

Philippa was delighted to have a moment alone with another woman she could trust, and confided that she was pregnant.

'How lovely for you! I'm sure Le Roux is delighted.'

Philippa said nothing.

Diana went on, 'I have a great friend who is a gynaecologist, Walter Spicer. I'll introduce you to him. He'll look after you, and you'll like his wife, Leila.'

The sound of a key turning in the door announced Le Roux's arrival as he entered, apologising profusely. 'Sorry to be so late. I hope I haven't missed the gossip,' he said while unbuttoning his coat.

'Philippa was telling me her exciting news.' Diana sipped her wine. 'If you've never been to Paris, Philippa, why not come over while I'm there? After all, when the baby arrives, you won't be able to travel. Don't you agree, Le Roux?'

He nodded, and Diana continued, 'I could find you very reasonable accommodation near where I live, and I would give you directions to the various places of interest. I work during the day, but we can meet each evening for dinner.'

'Oh, how wonderful,' Philippa said, turning to Le Roux for approval while attempting to mask the tension between them.

'I think it's a lovely idea!' Le Roux said with enthusiasm. 'I've always meant to take Philippa myself, but we've been here only a few months, and there's been so much to arrange, apart from moving into this place and getting settled.'

Within a couple of days, and disregarding Philippa's numerous reasons why it wasn't a good idea, Le Roux had sent her off to Paris. 'You know you want to go!' he told her as he saw her off at the airport. 'I'll join you as soon as I can. I know there's some work to be done in Paris, and I'll see if John will let me go over instead of going himself.'

A week later, Le Roux arrived in Paris. 'Darling!' He greeted Philippa warmly when she met him in front of where she was staying. 'Look at you!' He held her at arm's length and ran his eyes down the length of her body. 'You've grown sleeker, and there's a finished roundness in your face.'

He put his arm around her and kissed her passionately. 'It seems such a long time since we've been alone.'

She led him up the six flights of stairs to their room. 'The higher the floor, the cheaper it is,' she announced, as she opened the door. 'But look: a bath!'

'And a double bed!' Le Roux threw his things down. 'How I've longed for you, my love.'

He undressed her in the dim little room and tore off his own clothes, joining her on the hard bed with its thick cotton sheets. Her joy at having him with her – at him wanting her so much – was such that she wanted to be absorbed into his being.

'I love you,' she whispered, as she melted into his arms, losing herself in the moment.

It was some time before she realised that he wasn't responding. Holding his head close to hers, she whispered, 'What is it, Le Roux? I want you so much.'

He lay beside her for a few moments, limp, his body warm and damp, his head turned away from her. Then, suddenly, he got up and went into the bathroom, leaning over to turn on the bath taps.

She lay, eyes wide, watching him gravely. 'Do you not love me?' All her fears came flooding back.

'It's not that. I just can't do it.' His voice was hoarse, and he stood with his back to her. 'I can't make love to you!'

'What ... what have I done?' she asked. He must love her, surely? She couldn't bear it if he didn't.

'You've changed.'

'I don't understand.'

'Your body has changed.' He could hardly bear to speak the words.

'Of course it has! I'm pregnant.'

'I just can't do it,' he said, angrily, and slammed the door shut.

After the Dance

She lay in the bed, feeling utterly weary. The shock of his sudden withdrawal had left her numb. She wished she could be alone quietly to absorb this new sense of hurt. But the bathroom door opened and Le Roux came out, a towel draped around him, a stiff smile on his face.

'I've run a bath for you, and then I think we should go and discover some marvellous little restaurant and have a good bottle of wine. I've had a trying week with John, and I'm tired.' He sat on the bed and brushed the hair back from her face. 'Come on, darling. I want you to show me what you've been up to over here.'

She looked up at him. His face was pale and his eyes remote.

The following evening, Le Roux organised a dinner to thank Diana. He invited a well-known artist friend, Terence Nomen,[77] and his young French wife, Coco.

Terence was a tall, good-looking man, with close ram-like brown curls above his temples and a touch of grey lending distinction. He usually wore the rapt expression of a small boy absorbed in something. His fine voice, dark, glowing eyes and strong cleft chin were things that made people notice him, particularly women.

Coco was a striking redhead of about 30, a model by profession and a lively addition.

Diana took them to a smart new restaurant, having rung ahead to explain that she would be bringing some very important people to dinner, and to make sure they would have the best attention – and they were indeed welcomed with open arms by the owner.

Looking through the menu, Philippa was uneasy because the prices were extremely high. As Le Roux planned to pay for the meal, it looked certain to consume their entire yearly allocation of French francs.

Coco was engaged in an animated conversation with a waitress who kept looking at Le Roux, and then went to speak to the restaurateur, who came over to the table to suggest to Le Roux that the chef choose the menu for the table.

The meal served with accompanying wines was memorable. It ended with coffee and brandy from the 19th century, and the owner made a tremendous fuss of Le Roux. Finally, nearing midnight, he called for the

---

77 Terence Nomen is a pseudonym used by Le Roux in *The Contemporary Scene no. 412*, broadcast on the SABC on 9 June 1958.

bill and was told that the meal was on the house – a present from the restaurant owner.

'What? No, I can't accept such a generous gift,' said Le Roux, flushed and happy from all the good food and wine.

'*Non, non*, I insist,' the restaurateur said, then shyly held out a menu and a pen. 'If I may, monsieur, it would be a great honour for us if you would sign our menu. It is not often that a film-maker of your fame and accomplishment visits a Paris restaurant.'

Coco leaned over to Le Roux and whispered, 'Oh dear, this is my fault. The waitress asked me whether Le Roux was "the famous man" and I said yes. She obviously imagined you were Orson Welles.'

The American *Citizen Kane* director and star – who was only a few years younger than Le Roux, and to whom Le Roux did bear a striking resemblance – had, coincidentally, been spending time in Europe, starring in *Black Magic*, *The Third Man*, *Prince of Foxes* and *The Black Rose*.

'Oh, my good man, there's been an awful mistake,' Le Roux laughed, embarrassedly. 'I'm not Orson Welles. I'm a painter.'

The restaurateur laughed too, and tapped the side of his nose. '*Ah, oui, monsieur*, a painter.' He nodded knowingly and winked. 'I understand. But still, an autograph...?' Once again, he held out the menu and pen.

Philippa, who was exhausted, whispered to Le Roux, 'Oh, please just sign it! I want to go to bed!'

'What will you be using it for?' Le Roux asked the restaurateur.

'*Un souvenir*,' he assured his special guest, with the broad smile of someone who knows he's finally got his way.

Sighing, Le Roux scrawled an illegible signature on the menu with a great flourish.

It was a sombre taxi ride back to the hotel. Le Roux said he felt more of a fool than a forger, and wondered what the trustees of the Tate might say about the incident if it ever got out. Diana assured him that the publicity the restaurateur would squeeze out of the supposed visit of Orson Welles would be worth many times the price of the feast.

Several months later, Le Roux was very surprised to read Terence's short obituary in *The Times*. No sooner had he absorbed the news than Jane Ryder's fresh voice informed him that Mrs Nomen was waiting for him downstairs, and should she show her to his office? Le Roux remembered the striking French redhead who had caused the misunderstanding about Orson Welles, and asked Jane to show her in.

To his surprise, a woman of about 40, with candid grey eyes and warm brown hair, came into his office, her hand held out. 'Hello, Mr Le Roux, I'm Betty Nomen. My husband always spoke fondly of you.' Her black suit was well cut and obviously expensive, as were all her accessories. 'I'm here to trace the whereabouts of my late husband's pictures that were submitted to the selection committee.'

'Oh, Mrs Nomen, how nice to finally meet you,' Le Roux blustered, trying to cover his confusion. 'We have 25 of your late husband's pictures, which we can release to you whenever you are ready.'

'That's why I came. I can't store them, as I'm in the process of giving up our studio cottage in Hampstead.'

Le Roux was pleased to help and said the Tate would store the items until it was convenient for her to collect them.

A couple of days later, Jane called to say, 'Mrs Nomen is at the reception desk again, and very much wants to see you.'

'She doesn't have an appointment,' said Le Roux, with a note of irritation, 'but, of course, show her up.'

To his astonishment, Jane came into the office with a wicked smile and introduced a familiar glamorous 30-year-old redhead in a smart dark frock.

She held out her hand. 'You remember me, Monsieur Orson Welles? We had dinner in Paris.'

'Yes, yes, of course I do, Coco. How are you?' Le Roux said. His mind was spinning.

'I am in shock,' Coco said sadly. 'Terence was a great talent – so handsome and so much fun, wasn't he? It's terrible that he died so young. We met ten years ago in Cannes and married soon afterwards, but poor Terence had no money, so I continued my work as a fashion model.' Coco smiled as she reminisced. 'He was so passionate and moody. Our home in Paris would descend into chaos from the moment he returned from a trip, eager to express his new ideas and sketches, wanting me to account for every moment he had been away, and ultimately leaving the house in the biggest conceivable mess. I'm glad we had no children; Terence would have been a shocking father.'

Coco, too, wanted to know about Terence's pictures, and Le Roux cautiously undertook to make enquiries.

As she made to leave the office, Coco turned back and said, 'A few days ago, I ran into the owner of the restaurant in Paris where we ate together that night. The little man grabbed my arm and said that the most terrible thing had happened. The autographed menu had been stolen, and he had notified the police.'

'Oh, good God,' uttered Le Roux. 'What happened?'

'The police believed the matter did not warrant their intervention and advised our friend to write to the actor to request another autograph. Consequently, he wrote to Orson Welles, recalling the meal and explaining the circumstances, while inquiring if he could obtain another autograph. Orson Welles' secretary responded in delightful terms and included a large photograph featuring, above Orson's signature, the inscription, "To commemorate a marvellous dinner!"'

A week later, the telephone rang, and a bright voice said, 'This is Carol Nomen.'

'Ah, yes,' said Le Roux, resigned to yet more confusion. 'You must be the widow of Terence Nomen?'

'Oh, no,' came the reply, 'I'm the daughter. But I am here with his widow, Jacqueline, my stepmother. I've come over from Saint-Tropez with her to sort out my father's affairs.'

Le Roux invited Carol to visit his office, and she turned out to be an enchanting 25-year-old woman dressed in a low-cut Dior suit, with lovely dark hair cascading over her shoulders. 'You see, Mr Le Roux, my mother died shortly after I was born, and I was partly raised by my father's relatives in Ireland and partly in Saint-Tropez, where Jacqui and I attended the *lycée*. I adored Daddy, but ever since my mother died, he has always been pursued by women, and he is much too kind-hearted to shake them off.' Then, leaning forward so Le Roux could admire her full form, she confided, 'To protect him, I married him off to Jacqui.'

'Did your father make a will?'

'Of course,' she said. 'Daddy was a man of considerable means, you know. I'm seeing his lawyers tomorrow. Jacqui is a successful photographer with a career of her own, but I know Daddy will have left her well provided for.'

'Ahh, yes, Carol, on that point, I have something to tell you,' Le Roux said, and proceeded, as gently as he could, to break the news about the several other Mrs Nomens.

When he'd finished, Carol sat quietly for some moments, thinking. Then she gave Le Roux a bright smile. 'Daddy was such a kind and generous man. I am sure he made adequate arrangements,' she said.

Le Roux certainly hoped so.

6

Duties at the Tate

1950

It was one of Le Roux's duties at the Tate to inspect and certify sculptures imported in preparation for the Festival of Britain. This spectacular cultural event, to be held in Battersea Park in mid-1951, was intended as a 'tonic for the nation', to raise the spirits of a country still in the grip of post-war austerity and rationing. The Arts Council was importing many massive sculptures for the open-air section of the Festival.

Even though the certification was little more than a formality, it still had to be done. Le Roux made several trips to a large stonemason's yard on the south side of the Thames, where the customs and excise inspectors broke the seals of the crates, and Le Roux had to fill in and sign forms to certify that the works were indeed original works of art, not commercially produced, and made of the material stated. The forms also required Le Roux to say whether the sculptures were 'in the round' or 'in relief'.

The first time some sculptures were unpacked, about 30 men on lunch break watched the proceedings with interest. By any standards, many of the works imported to England for the exhibition were controversial. As Le Roux signed the forms, there were grunts and groans from the men and the odd ribald comment. Jim, the foreman, was the only one who formally voiced his doubts about the works of art. 'Guvnor, you've been done. That is no more a sculpture of a woman than it is of an elephant's behind.' To guffaws of laughter, he added, 'Not even my missus looks like that, an' she's a big un.'

Then the customs inspector unpacked a mobile by Alexander Calder[78] that had been packed flat. Le Roux, who had seen this particular mobile exhibited in Paris some months before, looked briefly at the assembly diagram and signed the paper.

The customs inspector had, to this point, maintained an objective outlook, although he clearly shared the workers' scepticism. But on this particular sculpture, he begged to differ. Clearing his throat, he said quietly to Le Roux, 'I think you made a mistake, sir. You have called it sculpture in the round.' He pointed at the collection of rods and pieces of metal that looked like flattened ploughshares.

'I see your point, inspector,' said Le Roux in a conciliatory tone. 'When a Calder mobile is dismantled, it does look like a deconstructed toy. But when it is mounted, the sculpture occupies a space almost like some kind of moving plant, making it a sculpture in the round, to my way of thinking.'

The customs inspector nodded but still couldn't see how a collection of flat pieces of metal could ever become a sculpture in the round.

The workers were under the misapprehension that there was a dispute about whether the Calder could be considered a work of art. 'It's a child's toy, that's what it is,' said the foreman, who was beginning to feel he had a good grasp of the subject. 'I got kids, and this is the kind of stuff they like.'

A fierce argument broke out among the men, and Le Roux found himself involved in giving an impromptu lunchtime lecture on modern art. As he looked around at the blank faces, he ended by saying, 'If you visit Battersea Park to see the exhibition in the spring of next year, and I hope many of you will, this "toy" will be suspended from the high branch of a tree, spinning gently, reflecting the light, and conveying different shapes as it spins.'[79]

'The Agnews telephoned and asked us to lunch on the 15th,' Philippa told Le Roux one evening. Fortunately, she'd had no morning sickness,

---

78 An American sculptor, Calder was known for his innovative mobiles (kinetic sculptures powered by motors or air currents), his static self-supportive abstract 'stabiles' and his monumental public sculptures.
79 From a transcript of a recording for the SABC, no. 63 in the series *London Review* by Le Roux Smith Le Roux, 20 June 1951.

and was keeping herself busy with invitations to luncheons, dinners and country weekends.

'Did you accept?'

'Yes. And the Bertrands suggested we might care to join them in the country the following weekend. I have to let them know. And there was a telephone call from a Mrs ... I wrote it down because she was so insistent.' She got up and went to the table next to the phone. 'Ah, here it is. Mrs Bilton. She said she and her husband had met you when you were here last year. She's given her number and wants you to ring her. Something about the valuation of a picture she wants to sell.'

'Why didn't she ring my office?'

'I don't know. Do you want her number?'

Le Roux put down the book he'd been reading. 'I remember her. I sat next to him on the plane from Holland a while back. They lent me a car when I was in London. Fabulous apartment in Mayfair. I wrote to you that I went there for a drink.'

'Do you want the number or not?' Philippa's uncharacteristically impatient response reflected the atmosphere between her and her husband. Things in the bedroom had not improved since they returned from Paris.

'Not really,' he said, returning to his book.

A few days later, a lengthy letter arrived from Diana detailing her working trip to New York for *Life* magazine, along with the atmosphere in New York and Washington amid all the discussions regarding a potential war in Korea. She included a copy of the 18 September 1950 issue of the magazine featuring a 15-page article titled 'South Africa and its Problem'. The article highlighted that the Nationalists, who attained power in 1948, had supported Nazi Germany during the war. It further described the injustices that the Nationalist government had imposed on 'non-European' South Africans. The Nationalists justified their policy as the best means 'to preserve racial integrity'.

Philippa read the article to Le Roux as he ate supper.

'It casts us all as Nationalist supporters. I don't support them. You don't. There are plenty who don't,' Le Roux said, irritated.

'But not enough,' Philippa responded.

'Articles like that make it difficult being a South African abroad.' There was a pause and then, out of the blue, Le Roux asked, 'Have you still got Mrs Bilton's telephone number?'

Philippa took a moment to place the name, then she said, 'No, I threw it away because you said you didn't want it.'

'I feel perhaps I should get in touch with her, as they were very nice to me,' Le Roux said. 'I'll drop her a line. I remember the address of their apartment.'

Le Roux retired to his study, and Philippa went to bed. She never saw him these days. He was always working. And when he went out, he left her at home.

⁂

'Is that usual?' Philippa asked Walter Spicer at her next appointment, as he finished his examination. She was referring to the fact that her husband had not even tried to make love to her since their return from Paris.

Washing his hands and speaking over his shoulder, the doctor said, 'Sometimes a man is sensitive about these matters, but when he sees the child, and the mother has returned to normal, it will be forgotten.'

'He didn't want the child, and I did force matters.' Philippa was relieved to be able to admit this to someone in confidence. 'You see, I think he feels I acted deceitfully – and I did. I knew he would never agree, so I took a chance that he wouldn't mind. But he does.'

'My dear Philippa, please go home and try not to be so anxious. You're in excellent health. You will have a beautiful baby, and all will be well; I'm certain of that.'

But one evening not long after, Le Roux was late for dinner without letting Philippa know. She sat despondently at the kitchen table, waiting for him. At last, past 9 p.m., she heard the key turn in the latch.

She rushed to the front door. 'Where have you been?' she cried, throwing her arms around him. 'I was so worried. I've kept dinner for you.'

'Don't worry about food, snooks,' he answered as he took off his coat. 'I'm sorry I never called. It all happened rather suddenly. I got through to Mrs Bilton late this afternoon, and she asked me to call round and have a drink. I was late getting there and thought it would only take an hour, but she wanted my opinion on a couple of paintings and then she opened a bottle of champagne, and I never realised how late it was.'

She noticed his eyes were shining, and he looked excited.

'I had forgotten how young she is. She's been very ill and still is. She was in bed and had a nurse in attendance. I couldn't very well leave her immediately. She's going abroad next week, which is why I went today. She wants to meet you, and will contact us when she returns.'

'And her husband?' Philippa asked.

'Oh, I gather they are separated,' Le Roux said, and Philippa noticed that he avoided her eyes. 'I don't know the full details. So, what has your day been like?'

There was a heavy snowfall over Christmas in 1950. Philippa loved the white carpet and the crunching sound people's footsteps made as they walked along. She went out to do her shopping, feeling well and happy.

One Saturday evening, she and Le Roux caught a bus to Piccadilly Circus. Looking out of the window, she could see the great white plumes of people's breath in the chill air as they tramped along the pavement. It was quite dark at four o'clock, as it was almost the shortest and darkest day of the year – not a day to be outdoors much, thought Philippa, as she watched Le Roux staring at the showrooms of the most expensive cars.

'Do you think Father Christmas will bring you one of those?' she teased.

He lifted his head as if to say 'perhaps'.

At Piccadilly Circus, Le Roux was anxious to buy a late edition of the evening papers that still contained news. 'Before their pages are smothered with classified results of the afternoon's football.'

She watched the traffic circulate around the island.

Le Roux gripped her arm. 'Trust me,' he shouted as he led her across to the statue of Eros. They got there safely, attracting no more than a couple of hoots and a reproachful glance from a tall policeman in his smart winter coat.

Le Roux put his arm around her. 'No one really knows Piccadilly Circus unless they've stood here on that central island, beneath Eros, with its ceaseless merry-go-round of vehicles.'

She felt dizzy, not only from the gyrating traffic but from the blaze of those enormous electric signs whose energetic and unbroken repertoire always lends a festive air to Piccadilly Circus. The only thing that slowed the traffic temporarily was the warning sound as a police car flashed through the Circus, twisting and turning at speed, often on the wrong side of the road, off on some urgent errand.

Looking up at the enormous Christmas tree in Leicester Square, she whispered, 'Oh, it's so so magical, Le Roux.'

Le Roux took her arm. 'Come along; we can't have you catching a cold just before the birth of our child. *King Solomon's Mines* is playing at the pictures. It'll keep us warm before we go to dinner.'

But it was a subdued festive season for the Le Rouxs. They listened to the King's speech on Christmas Day, which was depressing, and then took a walk in Hyde Park. On New Year's Eve, they enjoyed a quiet evening listening to Edith Evans in *Queen Elizabeth*; by 11 p.m., they were in bed.

When Philippa woke one night in late January and found that she was wet, at first she didn't understand. But then, when the pain began, she realised the baby was coming. She looked at her watch. It was two o'clock.

She woke Le Roux. 'Darling, I think this is it!'

They phoned Walter Spicer and then took a taxi to a private clinic in Hampstead. Once Philippa was settled, Le Roux left her to it.

That evening, Walter called Le Roux to say he had a beautiful son. But it had been a tiring labour and, frankly, touch and go at the end. 'I had to do an episiotomy because the cord was around the baby's neck, and we had to get him out,' he explained. 'Anyway, both mother and child are now doing well.'

Philippa's room was a bower of flowers, with out-of-season lilacs, daffodils, hyacinths, tulips and tuberoses. And when Walter did his rounds, she told him, 'I'm so relieved. Le Roux is as proud a father as I could have hoped. He wants to name the baby after me.'

Le Roux visited her most days and was surprised by the number of other visitors.

On one occasion, he waited for visiting hours to be over, and lingered while the nurse ushered the others out of Philippa's room. Then, sitting down next to her bed and taking her hand, he said, 'Darling, there is something I want to tell you, and I don't want you to be hurt, but you mustn't tell people all the details of the birth. I am afraid it bores them. I noticed Kitty's eyes rolling when you explained some of your reactions.'

Philippa looked at her husband. Was this how *he* felt, or had she genuinely bored her guests with her chatter?

A week later, Philippa took her baby home. Feeling tired and weak, she put Philippe in his cot, then undressed and got into bed, leaving the new-born to the night nurse Le Roux had employed.

The following day, she had difficulty getting up. The nurse checked her temperature and quickly went to get Le Roux. 'You need to call the doctor immediately. Your wife has a fever.'

'She has a slight case of pneumonia,' Walter told Le Roux. 'Fortunately, you have an excellent midwife who can care for the child, along with the night nurse, and I will send a Swiss doctor, a friend who will take care of her.'

Le Roux moved out, saying he would lodge temporarily with a friend.

After the Dance

For the next three weeks, the apartment in Rutland Gate was converted into a makeshift hospital room and nursery. Philippa remained delirious for the first week, unable to feed her baby properly and constantly calling out for Le Roux. The hungry child cried at all hours.

Finally, one evening, she opened her eyes and saw a nurse sitting placidly, knitting, in the corner of the bedroom. A small lamp on a table softly lit the room.

The nurse got up and crossed over to her. 'Feeling a little better, are you? Would you like hot soup or a cracker with a little milk?'

'Soup, please.'

'It would be good if you could feed the baby, dear. The poor little mite is so hungry. I'll fetch him now.'

As Philippa regained her strength and was able to feed Philippe, some normality returned to the apartment, and Le Roux came home.

One evening, Le Roux arrived home in great excitement. 'Darling, I have tickets for the Henry Purcell[80] concert to be held in the Victoria and Albert Museum, in a large exhibition hall, specially re-adapted for sound, the same hall where the famous Raphael Cartoons[81] are on view!'

'How lovely! I would love to go.'

'Constant Lambert,[82] with the Philharmonia Orchestra and the Covent Garden Choir, will produce an unforgettable recital, particularly as Arnold Goldsbrough[83] is playing the harpsichord.'

'We could have dinner in that little bistro in South Ken and walk over. Shall I book?'

'Well, there is a complication. I also have tickets on the same day to the first night at Sadler's Wells of the ballet *Harlequin in April* with

---

80 Purcell was the outstanding 17th-century English composer of Baroque music.
81 The Raphael Cartoons are seven large cartoons for tapestries, surviving from a set of ten designed by the High Renaissance painter Raphael in 1515–16 for the Sistine Chapel. Since 1865 the cartoons have been on loan to the Victoria and Albert Museum.
82 Leonard Constant Lambert, who was a few years older than Le Roux, was a British composer, conductor and author, and the first music director of the Sadler's Wells Ballet (later called the Royal Ballet); married, he had an on-off affair with the great ballerina Margot Fonteyn. Lambert would die later that year, on 21 August 1951, two days short of his 46th birthday, of pneumonia and undiagnosed diabetes complicated by acute alcoholism.
83 Arnold Wainwright Goldsbrough was an organist, harpsichordist and conductor. A musical prodigy, he became a church organist at the age of 12 in 1904.

choreography by John Cranko,[84] specially commissioned by the Arts Council, so there will be a lot of South African talent on show.'

'What will you do?' Philippa asked, with a sinking feeling. She anticipated that her husband's plans would not include her.

'Well, it's not much of a choice for me, particularly as I have to think of a subject for my broadcast to South Africa this week. It has to be *Harlequin*. I also need to see the production because John Piper,[85] one of the Tate trustees, is doing the sets and costumes.'

'Oh, I'm happy to come with you to *Harlequin*, although I would be sad to miss the Purcell.'

'No, darling, let's do both. You go to the Purcell. Take someone. I shall improve my stock at the embassy by asking one of the senior people.'

So she invited Leila Spicer to the Purcell and had a thoroughly enjoyable evening. She didn't consider whom Le Roux had asked until he woke her in the dark hours of the next morning, getting into bed at 4 a.m. and bringing a strong whiff of a woman's scent.

She lay awake for a while, thinking about Le Roux and their life together, and then got up and made herself a cup of tea.

At dinner the following evening, Le Roux was enthusiastic about the ballet. 'Darling, I wish you could have joined me. It was wonderful. *Harlequin in April* is a ballet about a mad king, set in a timeless Commedia dell'Arte world filled with characters like Harlequin and Pierrot. The theme of the ballet is inspired by the first line of *The Waste Land*: "April is the cruellest month". Like the flowers of April, man rises and grows in stature and beauty. Soon, he believes he can overcome nature, dominate the very origins from which he came, and harness everything to his own will – or so he thinks. Yet, he encounters forces greater than himself: the internal weaknesses and ultimate subjugation to the rigid conventions that always seem to govern human life. Cheated of his prize, he dies like the April flowers and returns to the earth.'

'Oh, Le Roux, you describe it so wonderfully,' she responded. 'I wish I had been there.'

---

84 John Cyril Cranko received ballet training at the University of Cape Town Ballet School, and choreographed his first ballet for the Cape Town Ballet Club in 1945 when he was only 18. The following year he moved to London, studying with the Sadler's Wells Ballet School (later the Royal Ballet School), and danced his first role with the Sadler's Wells Ballet in 1947 at the age of 20. At 23, he was appointed resident choreographer for Sadler's Wells Theatre Ballet's 1950–51 season.

85 John Egerton Christmas Piper, a painter, printmaker and designer of stained-glass windows and opera and theatre sets, served as a trustee from 1946 to 1954.

IV

The Great Tate Affair

1

Rumbles About Rothenstein

1951

Le Roux's time at the Tate was split between editing the new Modern Foreign Paintings catalogue and turning the publications department from a loss-making into a profitable operation. The first several months had gone well, and Rothenstein spoke warmly of his appointee to the trustees and said he was able to build excellent relations with the staff.

One day, Paul Hulton, an assistant keeper responsible for the drawings at the Tate, suggested to Le Roux that they have lunch together. He didn't appear eager to meet at the Tate, so they walked around the corner to the Morpeth Arms, where the tunnels beneath once served as the final path for the unfortunate souls leaving Millbank prison to be deported to Australia. They found a table upstairs, overlooking the Thames.

'I thought it would be good to have a chat, one colonial to another.' Hulton was from Auckland, and although he'd been in the UK for many years, he still talked with a strong New Zealand accent. After they had ordered, Hulton continued, 'Have you heard anything about your predecessor in the publications department?'

'Not really. Some vague mumblings that Brooke wasn't treated well, but as John brought me over, I haven't liked to inquire too deeply. I met him a few months ago at Sir Jasper's house, actually, but I didn't engage with him.'

'Sir Jasper had him over? Well, that shows what he thought of the situation. Sir Jasper is a decent man. As long as he is the chairman, sense will prevail.'

'What do you mean?'

'The Tate under Rothenstein can be a thoroughly unpleasant place to work.'

'Why?'

'It's badly run by one man with scant reference to anybody, including the trustees. Do you know what *The Burlington* magazine wrote in an editorial when the Tate Gallery turned 50 in 1947? "The Tate Gallery has stumbled into its fiftieth year."'

Le Roux raised his eyebrows in surprise, and Hulton continued. 'Humphrey and his deputy, the lovely Honor Frost[86] – incidentally, a favourite of Rothenstein – fell out because although she nominally reported to Humphrey, she was on a project that Rothenstein devised for Humphrey's department. I'm not saying Rothenstein was wrong – the publications department certainly needed help – but Honor was a divisive character. Then, in May '48, there was a blow-up between Humphrey and Honor because he reported that she had formed an external private company, with no connection to the Tate and no authorisation, to take on some of the department's printing work. Rothenstein did nothing.

'The row simmered for most of the year, and then Honor accused Humphrey of trying to rape her, and Rothenstein took her side and got the Treasury to insist that Humphrey go off to the hospital to calm down. After that, try as he may, Humphrey could never shake off the tag that he was unstable. With the Treasury's help, Rothenstein managed to move him out of the Tate. Rothenstein tried to hold on to Honor, but Sir Jasper insisted that she go.'

Le Roux, who had been listening in fascination, asked, 'Are you saying that John and Honor had some sort of relationship?'

'No,' said Hulton, 'it was just that he could see no wrong in her, while the rest of us saw her for what she was.'

'And how does this affect me?'

'Consider it a friendly warning. Rothenstein is insecure and incompetent, and certainly doesn't like any lights to outshine his own. We must all be utterly subservient. As you've adopted a high profile on radio and television, I just thought you'd better be aware.'

---

86 Orphaned at an early age, Honor Frost became the ward of Wilfred Evill, a London solicitor and art collector. She studied art, and became the director of publications at the Tate. She later worked as a scuba diver on the underwater excavation of shipwrecks. The substantial art collection she inherited from Evill was auctioned after her death in 2010 to endow the Honor Frost Foundation, which supplies funds for underwater archaeology in the Mediterranean.

'Well, thank you very much.' Le Roux looked across at the sincere young man. 'And you? What about you?'

'I'm sure Rothenstein will move me on at some point. I'm a friend of Humphrey's, and I objected publicly to how he was handled.'

Rothenstein had just finished the first volume of his *Catalogue of Modern English Painters*, and returned to working full-time at the Tate. What had surprised him and made him uneasy was that Le Roux had taken over many of the functions of running the gallery.

A month later, when Rothenstein fired Hulton, Le Roux informed Philippa about it and what Hulton had said so recently during their lunch.

'So, what are you going to do?'

'Well, I feel I should say something.'

'Oh, Le Roux, don't get involved while you are still on probation,' Philippa pleaded.

Le Roux's probation expired in mid-1951, at which stage he was to be appointed permanently to the post of deputy keeper. When his appointment came up for confirmation before the Civil Service Commission,[87] he attended the hearing, and shortly thereafter, Rothenstein summoned him to his office.

'I've had the results of your interview with the Civil Service commissioners regarding your probation,' he said, steadfastly looking down at the paper in front of him to avoid Le Roux's eyes. 'The commissioners feel that they are not ready to confirm your appointment. They complained that you appear too flamboyant and are too interested in your media work and things outside the Tate. So they've extended your probation for another year.'

There was an uncomfortable silence as Le Roux shifted in his chair. 'Well, John, that is fine if you say it is. After all, I work for you, don't I?'

'Yes, yes, of course.'

A few days later, Rothenstein received an irate call from Philip James, art director of the Arts Council, about comments Le Roux had made on the BBC about an Arts Council exhibition of British painting.

---

87 The Civil Service Commission, which was (and is) independent of the government and the civil service, regulates recruitment to the UK's civil service, providing assurance that appointments are on merit after fair and open competition.

'There is a matter I must raise with you that reinforces the commissioners' concerns,' Rothenstein said to Le Roux after he answered the summons to his office. 'The trustees and I were displeased with your criticism on BBC Radio's Third Programme, published in *The Listener*[88] last week, regarding the two anthologies of British painting, and Philip James is quite upset. This was a show organised by the Arts Council, and having a senior member of my staff criticise it while we receive funding from the Arts Council for our exhibitions is unhelpful.'

'All I said was that it was a timid and unimaginative representation. Do you and the trustees disagree with that?'

'That's not the point. I support you, of course I do, Le Roux, but your media work – as my deputy – makes my life difficult.'

'My outside media work is a question of money, John. As we agreed when I joined, I do undertake outside media work to supplement my meagre salary at the Tate. I'm happy to explain this to the trustees.'

'That will not be necessary.' Rothenstein put a file in his desk drawer and locked it, indicating that the meeting was over.

When Le Roux arrived home that evening, he told Philippa about the postponement of his confirmation and John's reprimand over the Third Programme.

'I've never trusted John,' she said. 'He's being underhand. You need to explain your outside work to the trustees.'

Le Roux was unwilling to rock the boat. 'I'm just beginning to understand how John likes to work. I'm sure it will be all right,' he said.

John Rothenstein was knighted in the 1952 New Year's Honours. Then, at the beginning of February 1952, George VI died, and Le Roux made his weekly broadcast to South Africa.

> Each person learned in their own way of the passing of that good and beloved man, King George VI. I was being driven through the streets when I noticed the crowds jostling to buy special editions of the papers at the street corners. As the traffic lights held us up, someone

---

88 The BBC Third Programme was a national radio station broadcasting cultural and intellectual material from 1946 to 1967, when it was replaced by BBC Radio 3. *The Listener* was a weekly magazine established by the BBC for reproducing broadcast talks, commenting on the intellectual broadcasts of the week, and previewing major literary and musical shows and books.

leaned towards me from the adjoining car in the close traffic and asked anxiously, 'Has war been declared?'

Then, through a gap in the throng, we saw the first stark poster of four words: 'The King is dead.' Soon flags everywhere were being hurriedly hauled to half-mast, and a great hush began to fall over the city, so that miles away, one could hear the tolling of Great Tom, the historic 17-ton bell of St Paul's Cathedral, which is only sounded on these occasions.

That the change of atmosphere which affected all London sprang from deep and sincere emotion, one could see from the expression of every passer-by. For the sorrow of the people here is tinged with guilt – a feeling that they had allowed this duty-conscious, unassuming and uncomplaining king, much as they loved him, to work himself to death.

This thought was to be echoed on many levels during the following days. Physical changes overtook the great city. Bright notes began to vanish from the streets as shop windows throughout London underwent a transformation. Gay colours and frivolous displays made way for simple arrangements of black and grey and purple and perhaps a few touches of white. The brilliant electric signs and advertisements were not switched on when dusk fell, nor, on that first evening of mourning, were the cinemas or theatres open, so that the West End by nine o'clock had assumed a dim and deserted air.[89]

During this gloomy time, Le Roux was absent more than ever. Philippa wondered where he was and what he was doing. Because of her loneliness and inner turmoil, she spent the greater part of her waking hours with her little boy, Philippe. The trees were bare, and the weather was bleak and cold, but she liked it, and took Philippe out of the flat whenever she could.

A few days later, she was putting the baby to bed when the bell rang. It was Le Roux's friend, Peter, from BBC Television, who had come to the flat to discuss a new script for Le Roux's Monday broadcast.

While the men were talking, Philippa gave them a drink. 'I'm so looking forward to the show,' she said. 'We don't have a TV set so it would be fun to see it live.'

'Of course,' responded Peter at once. 'I will arrange a ticket.'

---

89 Part of the transcript of the broadcast *The Contemporary Scene* on 13 February 1952 for the SABC.

After Peter left, Le Roux turned on Philippa. 'Why were you fishing for an invitation? I've told you that wives aren't allowed.'

'I was only making conversation. I'm sorry. I won't go,' she hesitated. 'But I don't understand why, if wives aren't allowed, Peter offered me a ticket?'

Le Roux stared at her, his expression unreadable. 'I don't want you at the studio while I'm working.'

'Okay, okay. I understand.'

'And I don't want you asking me the whole time who I had lunch with and what I've done during the day,' he added, his tone biting. 'Between you and Rothenstein, I have no privacy.'

'But —'

'And please don't accept invitations from the girls at the Tate to come in for tea either. I don't want you there.'

Philippa looked at the floor and shook her head. 'Le Roux, I don't know what's going on. You are never here. You cut me out of your life. You only tell me the truth when it suits you.'

'Oh, forget it, Philippa. I don't have time for a row.' He marched out of the flat, slamming the door behind him.

Philippa retired to bed, very upset, and lay thinking about what had happened. It was clear Le Roux didn't want her anywhere near his work life. What with his lies and omissions, she didn't know where she was. He always told her he loved her but she was so lonely and so unhappy. How had it come to this?

2

Misgivings at the Gallery

1952

By the spring of 1952, the Le Rouxs had been living in London for two years.

'This flat is too small. You will have to find something larger,' Le Roux told Philippa one day. 'The child cannot continue to sleep in the living room indefinitely. Also, I need a study.' He didn't look at her as he talked, but she knew he was fed up.

He was right about Philippe, though: the child was thriving, and growing larger and rosier, until he became too heavy to carry. Just as she had given up hope that he would ever stand on his own two feet, he had risen one day in his playpen and, holding on to the rails, shakily taken his first steps. He had soon tired of his pen and demanded to walk everywhere.

She scanned the newspapers for apartments, and was fortunate to find one on Elizabeth Street. It had three floors that needed repair; the lease ran for nine years, and the owner didn't want any key money[90] if the tenants would put the place in order. Within a month, the family had moved in.

One evening, returning early from work, Le Roux said, 'Let's eat and then walk in the park. I want to tell you something.'

Philippa hurriedly prepared supper, and while Le Roux ate, she changed Philippe and put him in the pram. Between them, they carried the pram downstairs. It was twilight, and they didn't speak as they walked. Philippa

---

90 Key money is the same as paying a premium on a lease: the premium is derived from the difference between the rent for the next (in this case) nine years, and market rent, and capitalising that.

didn't want to disturb Le Roux's train of thought: it had been a long time since he had discussed anything important with her.

Finally, when they were across the main road and strolling along a path in Hyde Park, he said, 'You remember that chap we met, Humphrey Brooke?'

'The one who held the position before you at the gallery?'

He nodded. 'Well, I had lunch with him today, and his version of what occurred is different from the official line, and somewhat disturbing.'

'In what way?'

'He claimed that he had brought to Rothenstein's attention the unpalatable fact that printing the Tate Christmas cards had cost £7,000, which was a ridiculous amount of money, even though they recouped the costs through sales. Apparently, Rothenstein had hired a woman named Honor Frost, who was responsible for this special project and had established a company independent of the Tate to undertake the work. By chance, Brooke discovered that the cost billed by Frost's company to the Tate was significantly higher than budgeted and eliminated any profit from the cards. Brooke immediately reported this to Rothenstein, stating that Frost had not been authorised to set up a company outside the Tate's corporate structure for the work. Nothing happened, and when Brooke raised the matter again, Rothenstein exploded and informed Miss Frost of Brooke's complaint.'

'And then?'

'Brooke said that one day, when he was leaving the Tate for a luncheon, he hailed a cab in front of the building. As he was getting in, he heard his name being called. Honor Frost asked if she could share the taxi, as she was late for an appointment.' Le Roux suddenly laughed. 'You know, the rest of the story is so unbelievable that I can hardly put it into words.'

'You can't stop now. Go on, please.'

'Suddenly, as the taxi pulled out on to the Embankment, Frost started tearing her clothes and hitting him, screaming. The taxi stopped, and she jumped out, shouting that he had tried to rape her. She rushed back to Rothenstein in disarray and accused Brooke of the attack. Brooke was completely bewildered.'

Philippa stopped. 'Why didn't he deny it?'

'Well, Brooke said the whole thing was so beyond his experience that when Rothenstein called him into his office for an explanation, he didn't take his questioning seriously. But Rothenstein referred Brooke to the Treasury, who sent him to a psychiatrist to be "assessed". By this time, Brooke says he didn't want to be associated with the whole sordid mess, and he took leave to think matters over. He told his wife and she persuaded him to resign.'

'What a horrid story. Why did he tell you all this?'

'He said he wanted to warn me. He said I should be aware that Rothenstein wasn't what he seemed, and that I had better protect myself.'

'What will you do?'

'Nothing, at present, but I think I need to take a closer look at the archives.'

Impulsively, Philippa put a hand on his arm. 'Oh, darling, do be careful. Rothenstein may be awful, but he's not your enemy. Don't do anything that might annoy him. After all, the past is none of your business.'

'Maybe, but if Rothenstein is the type of man Humphrey suggests, then the sooner I know the lie of the land, the better.' With a forced laugh, he added, 'I certainly do not want to be unprepared if "the great man" wishes to get rid of me.'

⁂

One evening in June 1952, Le Roux arrived home after dinner. He didn't say where he had been, and Philippa didn't ask.

He made himself comfortable on the sofa and opened the newspaper. 'By the way, I shall be in Paris on business next week,' he told his wife. 'Rothenstein wants me to see some pictures there with the possibility of buying them. I'm taking Jane Ryder with me, as she speaks French fluently, and mine, as you know, is not good.'

'When do you leave?' Philippa asked as she walked into the kitchen, an unwelcome but vivid picture of the pretty young Miss Ryder with her pert physique forming in her mind.

'Let me see ... the board meeting is next Tuesday, so probably Wednesday.'

'Very well. I must remember to fetch your suit from the cleaners.'

After the board meeting, Le Roux returned home from work in a strange mood. Pouring himself a strong brandy, he told Philippa about what had transpired.

The director proposed that the Tate purchase a Degas bronze statue, *The Little Dancer*, for over £9,000 from a dealer in Bond Street. Le Roux pointed out to the trustees that the same dealer had offered the Tate the same bronze statue as part of a complete set of 73 Degas bronzes, valued at £4,500 to £5,000 the year before.

Rothenstein, supported by Norman Reid, his loyal second deputy keeper, strenuously refuted this, saying that the complete set of bronzes previously offered to the Tate did not include *The Little Dancer*.

'I'm certain they're wrong – it's highly unlikely that the set would have excluded *The Little Dancer* – but I can't prove it. And if *The Little Dancer was* part of the set, it would have had a much lower value than what they're asking us to pay.'

'Does it matter, Le Roux, if the trustees are happy?'

Le Roux clicked his tongue impatiently and gave his wife an annoyed look. 'Of course it matters. Pricing art is a very important part of the Tate's business. And that's not all. After the meeting, the director told me that Norman would take the board minutes in future.'

'Why?'

'Because I had questioned his decision, I suppose. He's trying to show me he is in charge.'

On Wednesday evening, Le Roux sat on the pavement of his favourite Champs Elysées café, Fouquet's, the famous brasserie with red awnings where people from the arts had met for decades. He didn't mind that Jane Ryder was late, as the evening was so perfect. He hoped she was making the best of herself as he sipped a glass of Pernod, enjoying the last rays of the sun and watching the endless pageant of people walking up and down one of the great pedestrian highways of the world.

His musing was disturbed by the young and beautiful Jane standing before him. 'You look ravishing,' said Le Roux in his guttural tones, and Jane blushed. He ordered champagne to celebrate the successful meetings they had had with several galleries that day.

They were toasting each other when Tony Kloman stopped by their table. Kloman ran the Institute of Contemporary Arts, a recently founded London space where artists, writers and scientists could debate ideas outside the traditional confines of the Royal Academy. He was there with his wife, Theo, and the four of them talked about this and that until Kloman asked how Le Roux was finding the Tate.

Le Roux, who was on his second glass of champagne and feeling expansive, said, 'I love it, but working under Johnny is a nightmare. He can't organise anything, and he won't delegate.'

'Oh, I am sure it has its ups and downs,' Kloman said.

Le Roux opened his mouth to expand but Theo interrupted, saying they would be late for dinner, and whisked her husband away.

After a couple more drinks, Le Roux and Jane headed to dinner at a nearby restaurant. But Jane's high heel caught in a hole in the cobbled street, and she fell, twisting her ankle. What had begun as a promising evening ended up as a visit to Saint Louis hospital.

The following day, with Jane under doctor's orders to keep the weight off her foot for at least a month, Le Roux hired a car and driver to get around Paris. It was a nuisance, but Le Roux felt the Tate could jolly well pay.

Le Roux's good humour was spoiled when he returned to the gallery, only to have a junior accountant in the publications department, Mr Hockaday-Dawson, write to him saying he should obtain approval for his Paris expenses.

'He said I needed authority from the trustees. Bloody cheek!' he told Philippa that evening, as they ate dinner together.

'But it's your department, isn't it?'

'Yes. I gave him an official written warning.' Le Roux drained his glass of wine and poured himself another. 'This is Rothenstein's doing. Ever since I questioned his valuation of the Degas *Dancer*, he's had a frosty attitude towards me.'

Le Roux was in Paris again on Wednesday 16 July 1952, the day before the next board meeting. He phoned to speak to Rothenstein but the director was unavailable, so he left a message with his secretary to suggest that, as the Bond Street gallery was now charging a further ten per cent for the Degas *Dancer* – something he had discovered while he was away – the board should be informed.

The next day he arrived late at work at the Tate, and, at the board meeting, more out of habit than pique, took the minutes. Rothenstein did not say anything at the meeting. But afterwards he was furious.

'I told you not to take the minutes.'

'I am sorry. I forgot.'

'You phone from Paris demanding the price of the Degas be added to the board agenda. It's not your concern. And what do you think you are doing going to Giverny to see the early Monets? That's my job.'

'John, I was in Paris and Sutherland questioned the purchase at the June board meeting. I thought —'

'You are constantly exceeding your authority, Le Roux.'

Le Roux apologised. But Rothenstein wasn't satisfied and called Le Roux into his office a couple of days later. 'I must say, you seem to create a secret around everything you touch. Everything is under your control.

And I must tell you, I don't feel comfortable about it,' the director said, coldly. 'If I may be frank, I think it's time you looked for another job. There are plenty of suitable positions around. I understand they're looking for a new curator of the Imperial Institute.'[91] He handed Le Roux the advertisement for the job.

'Well, John, I will certainly consider your suggestion and come back to you.'

'Do, do. I only want to help.'

When he arrived home late that night, he seemed so upset that Philippa asked him if anything was the matter.

'Rothenstein called me in to his office and said I should look around for something else, "more suited to my great ability", is how he put it. He's beginning the same underhand process to get rid of me that he did with Humphrey Brooke.'

'What did you do?' Philippa asked, worried.

'I told him I'm happy in my job, of course. Then he said that the curatorship of the Imperial Institute was becoming free, and if I were tempted to apply, he would see that I was appointed. Can you beat it?'

'Oh, Le Roux, wouldn't that be much better? You would be your own master, and I'm sure the salary is much larger.'

'Of course it wouldn't be better! Even if the salary were double, the Imperial Institute doesn't interest me at all, nor does the directorship of the Salisbury Art Gallery, which he heard I'm also to be offered.'

'Well, I think you're making a mistake fighting with Rothenstein,' Philippa said. 'The powers that be will never support a colonial to replace one of their own. But I do understand why you wish to remain in London, and if you insist on fighting, you should write Rothenstein a note. After all, if this were to get nasty, it would be best to have a record.'

The next day Le Roux left a note with Rothenstein's secretary that read, 'While I do not want to appear ungrateful for your drawing my attention to the possibilities of posts outside the Tate, I must explain that I am completely happy about the scope and duties of my job under you. Indeed, if you foresee the possibility of my abilities becoming frustrated at the gallery, the remedy is in your hands, as I am in the full sense your own deputy.'

---

91 The institute buildings were used for a number of events, and included exhibition galleries that were used to promote trade and research.

3

Domestic Dissent

1952

Late one night, Philippa woke up and lay in the darkness, aware that Le Roux was also awake. She moved towards him and, touching him, whispered, 'Darling, I am also awake. I love you.'

He turned to her and enveloped her in his arms, drawing her to him as he buried his face in her hair. 'I love you too. It has been so long.'

'Oh, Le Roux, I've longed for you!'

She felt him stiffen as his hands ran over her body, and he kissed her wildly. The familiar taste of his mouth on hers was almost unbearable, and she responded urgently to his questing tongue, rediscovering the unbearable ecstasy of waiting until he guided her through the difficult ascent. She waited for the final moment when his entire body would communicate itself to hers. Then she felt him go limp and heavy.

Refusing to believe what was happening, she cried, 'Now, darling, now!' and was carried away on a long journey – by herself.

Afterwards, she lay beside him, weeping softly, caressing him. 'What happened? Was it not good for you?'

At last, she couldn't bear his silence, so she rose, put on her gown, and turned on the light. He was lying face down among the pillows, so she walked round the bed and sat next to him, stroking his hair until he turned and looked up at her.

'Tell me,' she said, 'was I no good? Did I do something that put you off?' She tried to laugh. 'It's been so long. I've probably forgotten how to make love.' His face was set, and she could see he was angry. Uncertainly, she stood up. 'Shall I make some tea? Or would you like a drink?'

He got up and found his gown. 'I've got some work I must do.'

She followed him into the living room, and when he had poured himself a brandy, she sat down on the arm of the wingback chair. 'I must know. We can't go on like this. What is it?'

He shrugged. 'I don't want to talk about it.'

'But we must talk. We have to talk. Tell me, please!'

'I can't make love to you.'

'But why? There must be some reason!'

He got up and set his brandy down on the coffee table, then began pacing. 'It's like making love to a different woman. I don't want to discuss it.'

'But I saw Walter. He said I was all right.'

Le Roux didn't respond.

'You must tell me what it is. I will do anything but I have to know what's wrong,' Philippa said, the desperation making her voice hoarse.

'I can feel your device.'

She laughed with relief. 'Is that all?' She threw her arms around him and kissed him. 'Oh, darling, you had me so worried. Come to bed. I'll make an appointment to see Walter at once. I'm sure he can fit me with some other form of birth control.'

He gave her a tight smile and a quick kiss and said, 'Run along to bed. I'll come as soon as I've calmed down.'

The next day she phoned Walter Spicer, and asked him to refer her to a female gynaecologist.

That afternoon, she was in Dr Gaunt's office, and explained the issue. 'I am most concerned, because before I had my baby, my husband and I never had any problems with our sex life. I feel it is all my fault,' she said, miserably. 'He warned me that he didn't like women who'd had children, that it spoiled them, and I didn't understand what he meant.'

After the examination, Dr Gaunt said, 'I can find nothing wrong with you.'

'But ... but my husband —' Philippa said, helplessly. 'What can I do?'

'I don't think there is anything you can do,' the doctor said gently. 'There's nothing wrong with you, and if he complains that he cannot sleep with you, then, Mrs Le Roux, I'm afraid he does not want to sleep with you.'

A few days later, Le Roux's mood had improved. He came home earlier than usual and called to Philippa from the front door. 'Come down here quickly. I have a surprise!'

Picking up Philippe, she ran down the stairs, and Le Roux led her on to the pavement.

'Look,' he said proudly, pointing to a large, elegant car parked at the front door. 'Isn't it perfect? It belongs to Lois Bilton. She's asked me to take care of it while she's away. It's a Daimler.' He opened the front passenger door. 'Hop in. I'll take you for a spin.'

After settling Philippa and the little boy in the front passenger seat, he took his place and turned on the ignition, then pulled out into the road. 'We can use it for a few months. Lois is going to the south of France and intends to sell it when she gets back. I helped her sell a painting, and I believe this is her way of repaying me. I jumped at the chance. After all, summer holidays are approaching, and I thought it was ideal for our weekends. We can take Philippe and escape the city!'

Philippa's suspicions made it impossible for her to admire the car as much as her husband did. 'I think it odd that Mrs Bilton lends us an expensive car like this out of the blue,' she said, and earned herself a scowl from Le Roux.

When Gwen Ffrangcon-Davies heard about the car, she offered her cottage in Essex for the family's use for the summer. 'You would be doing me a kindness to go down and air out the place. I'll be tied up for months in Stratford. Please use it,' she told Le Roux.

For their summer holidays, Philippa packed suitcases and took food in boxes so they wouldn't have to shop when they arrived. It was cosy in the car, with Philippe sleeping peacefully on the back seat, and she loved the long drive down to the cottage. She had so little time with her husband these days that any snatched moments were a joy. But even the car ride was tinged with doubt: what was Lois Bilton to Le Roux that she should lend him such a car?

The cottage was quaint, with a sloping roof and beamed ceilings, an attic to explore and two lovely bedrooms. Once she had unpacked, and was washing and changing Philippe before she gave him his dinner, she marvelled at how happy she was, here alone with Le Roux and their son.

When she had laid the child down to sleep, she went downstairs. She looked out of the kitchen window at the field beyond, dotted with buttercups and daisies. There was Le Roux armed with a large pillowcase, picking mushrooms. She ran out to join him, laughing happily.

'I can help you, but I have no idea which is poisonous.'

'Look for these,' he said, and fished out of the pillowcase a mushroom, fleshy and thick, with a pale hood and dark brown underside. 'They have a wonderful flavour. I remember them from my student days, and I'll show you how to cook them. I could eat a plate by myself.'

When the pillowcase was full, they went inside, and Le Roux chopped an onion and browned it in butter, then added the sliced mushrooms and let them soften. 'I wonder if Gwen has a drop of sherry?' he said.

Philippa opened several dark cupboards in the dining room and found half a bottle of Fino. Le Roux poured a little of the golden liquid into the pot and, when he had swirled it around, piled the delectable mess on to two plates and carried them to the table.

They each took a mouthful and looked at each other, delighted. 'Delicious!'

After they had eaten, Le Roux settled down to some paperwork he had brought with him.

'Must you work this evening?' Philippa asked, keeping her tone bright and light.

He looked up. 'I wanted to tell you but haven't had much time to think about it. I've been asked to appear on a new television programme on the major art exhibitions in London.'

'Why, that's wonderful, darling. I'm sure you'll do it very well.'

'I need to come up with something interesting, and since the first one is in less than a month, I thought I'd work on it here. The producer will see how the pilot performs, and if it's successful, they'll create a series.' He paused, looking thoughtful. 'I'm not sure how Rothenstein will react.'

'Haven't you spoken to him yet?'

'I want to first get it clear in my own mind during our stay here. Of course, if he's against the idea, I'll have to drop it.'

'But how could he be? It's such wonderful publicity for art generally.'

'Well, we'll see.' He turned back to his papers.

She walked over to him and gave him a kiss. 'I'll leave you, then, and go up to bed.'

'Goodnight.'

As she undressed in the dim light, she reflected how little she knew of Le Roux's life these days. She put on her nightdress and crawled into bed. Everything would be okay; she must just give him time – these were her last thoughts as she fell asleep.

4

Scandals and Complaints

1952

On Le Roux's return to the office, the new chairman, Lord Jowitt,[92] asked to see him. 'It has come to my attention that you threatened to dismiss Mr Hockaday-Dawson when he refused to reimburse some of your French travel expenses,' he said, getting right to the point. Tapping a piece of paper on the desk, he went on, 'I have a copy of your letter of 30 June.'

'I thought he was impertinent, Chairman,' Le Roux said. He kept his voice even but was furious inside: this was undoubtedly Rothenstein's work.

'I am afraid this is not how the board saw it.'

'The board?' Le Roux was now indignant. 'How is this a matter for the board?'

'You cannot threaten a junior member of staff with the sack if he questions your expenses.'

'But I'm responsible for the finances of the publications department. Hockaday-Dawson works for me.'

Lord Jowitt cleared his throat uncomfortably. 'Nonetheless, it is not how a senior manager should behave.'

Realising that this was not an argument he could win, Le Roux apologised. 'I am sorry, Chairman. It will not happen again,' he said, stiffly.

---

[92] William Allen Jowitt, 1st Earl Jowitt, was a British Liberal Party, National Labour and then Labour Party politician and lawyer who served as Lord Chancellor under Prime Minister Clement Attlee from 1945 to 1951. He was chairman of the Tate trustees until 1953, and died four years later, in 1957, aged 72.

After the Dance

When he got home that evening, he was fuming. Philippa was careful not to ask any questions. Finally, when she had cleared away the dinner dishes, he spoke. 'Can you believe it? I learned today that Rothenstein tried to discredit me.'

'Discredit you? In what way?'

'Rothenstein brought up the question of my expenses on my last Paris trip with the board.'

Philippa was just as indignant as Le Roux. 'If you'd spent too much, Rothenstein only had to tell you personally, and you would have put it right!'

'Exactly.'

'Are you going to speak to Rothenstein?'

'He's away on one of his many trips.'

'So, what did you say to the chairman?'

'I pointed out that it cannot be that a junior accountant has the say-so on what I, as head of the department, can spend.' Le Roux got up and gazed out of the window. 'It's Rothenstein up to his tricks. He feels threatened by my media work and wants to get rid of me. I'm sure of it.'

⁂

By raising the question of his expenses with the board while he was away, Le Roux felt Rothenstein had fired the first shot. Much against Philippa's advice, he chose this moment to send the chairman a written brief on the director's dealings with the Marlborough Fine Art Gallery on Bond Street regarding the purchase of the Degas bronze. In it, he displayed the most important characteristic of the whistleblower: the ability to collect and analyse information so that his accusation could be delivered with care to extract the most impact.

> Lord Jowitt, the facts are these. When *The Little Dancer* was first offered, the price quoted was eight million francs (£8,000). I pointed out to the director in the presence of Norman Reid that this price was excessive for a Degas sculpture. The director said that the trustees were determined to acquire this work.
>
> At the board meeting of 19 June, the Degas bronze was discussed as a possible purchase. I said that this price was twice that charged by the same dealer a year earlier for the full set of 73 Degas bronzes. The director, supported by Norman Reid, refuted this, saying that the full set of 73 Degas bronzes offered to us previously did not include *The*

Little Dancer. If you compare the two letters[93] you will see this is not true.

When the final account came from Marlborough Fine Art Company towards the end of June, the price had increased by 10% to £9,076. I said to the director that the account should not be paid until the board had sanctioned the increased price.

On 8 July, while I was abroad, the director approved the payment. I did not know it had been authorised and rang from Paris on 16 July to say that the purchase price should be placed on the board agenda for 17 July. According to the minutes of that board meeting, the director merely reported that the transaction had been concluded, without mentioning the price.

Subsequently, I broached the subject several times with the director, who said it was something he would take up with yourself.

On 27 August, before going on holiday, I wrote to the director asking that the price increase be put on the agenda for the board meeting of 4 September. At the meeting of 4 September, trustees Graham Sutherland, Henry Moore[94] and John Piper expressed alarm about the amount paid, as it seemed to be much higher than that for any other Degas bronze. They suggested the director enquire of the American art dealer Curt Valentin[95] whether the price was, as some of the trustees surmised, 'very excessive'. Curt Valentin responded on 25 September that he had been amazed to read of the high price paid in the London *Times*. Valentin had sold one of the six Degas bronzes to the Virginia Museum of Fine Art for $4,300 in 1945.

On the evening of 7 October, Rothenstein got wind that Le Roux was briefing the chairman privately about the price of *The Little Dancer* and called his subordinate to his office. The director did not mince his words. 'I want to discuss a matter of great importance to you, which I

---

93 The letter of 27 June 1951 to John Rothenstein at the Tate Gallery from David Somerset of the Marlborough Gallery on Bond Street lists 'bronze pl. No. XX (The Little Dancer) at £4,000-£5,000'; the letter of 17 June 1952 lists 'bronze pl. No. XX (The Little Dancer) at 8 million francs (£8,000).
94 The artist Graham Sutherland had served as a Tate trustee since 1948; the sculptor Henry Moore served as a trustee from 1941 to 1956.
95 Curt Valentin was a German-Jewish art dealer. In 1937 he emigrated to America, and opened a modern art gallery, the Bucholz (later renamed the Curt Valentin Gallery), in New York City. His gallery handled works by many notable artists, including Alexander Calder and Henry Moore. Valentin died, aged 52, in 1954, in Italy.

can do in one of several ways. First, you must listen to what I have to say without interruption or challenge, because these matters are beyond dispute. Second, I will have Norman Reid join us as a witness, making my charges against you more formal.'

Le Roux hunched forward in his seat, looking across the desk at the director with evident annoyance. 'Norman has left the building for the day, and, John, I must remind you, he has made it clear several times that he does not want to be involved in our discussions about my role.'

'Do not interrupt me, Le Roux!' Rothenstein slammed his pen down on a pile of papers. Then he took a deep breath, and, in a more even tone, said, 'Third, I can put my comments in writing.'

'Well, John, I think putting them in writing would be a good idea,' Le Roux said.

'I must warn you that besides taking up my precious time, you will regret my written statement because I have considerable skill in compiling written criticisms, and this will have serious consequences for you. It will go on your personal record at the Treasury and become a permanent black mark against you.'

'John, you do what you think best.'

'Very well, Le Roux.' But the director was not yet done with his deputy keeper, and needed to have his say. 'This is a delicate matter, but I would be derelict in my duties if I did not mention that your attitude to your work and your colleagues has not been entirely normal in recent months. Several colleagues have brought to my attention that you spend hours in the archives and create an iron curtain around your work that prevents any of us from knowing what you're doing.' Rothenstein looked down at his notes: 'You must stop all the secrecy. You must make a new beginning, because you are entirely in my hands, and I can and will change each and every one of your duties without question.'

Le Roux, seething with rage, said nothing. What the foolish gossips who surrounded him at work saw as 'secrecy' – what Rothenstein described, ridiculously, as an 'iron curtain' – was simply a modern way of organising and filing information. As he was the only person in senior management interested in the files, he was branded secretive.

'Well, what do you say, man?' The high colour in Rothenstein's cheeks showed his anger.

Le Roux remained silent, staring across the desk at the man who had given him this opportunity at the Tate but who had turned out to be incompetent and malicious.

'Typical,' Rothenstein spat out, and then seemed to read Le Roux's mind. 'I have raised these matters as a friend, and you say nothing. It's clear that you have psychological problems.'

That, Le Roux could not allow to pass. 'John, I will not be sent to a hospital for psychological assessment, like Humphrey Brooke, simply because you want to get rid of me.'

At the board meeting the next day, Le Roux asked to make a personal statement in which he defended his expenses in Paris and his response to Hockaday-Dawson. He denounced the director's handling of the matter as 'tyrannical and underhand' and typical of how he dealt with staff. He then recounted the previous day's meeting, also mentioning the director's suggestion that Le Roux take 'his immense talents' to some other artistic institution.

'I want to end by saying this,' Le Roux said. 'People have long since ceased to believe that a procession of men come here with excellent reputations and then mysteriously turn into monsters of inefficiency, or disloyalty, or whatever they are supposed to be, and then, in spite of the slurs cast upon them, can continue their careers elsewhere with distinction. I, of course, refer to Messrs Brooke, Hulton and perhaps myself.'

Rothenstein and Le Roux were asked to leave the meeting, and in their absence the trustees discussed the issues. They agreed that Lord Jowitt should conduct a review of the Tate's management and report back at the next board meeting on 20 November.

The following month, as Lord Jowitt prepared his report to the board on the Tate's management problems, his attention was diverted by two complaints about the director. The first concerned an article in *The Illustrated*[96] about the actress Zsa Zsa Gabor's visit to the gallery to promote *Moulin Rouge*, a John Huston film about Henri de Toulouse-Lautrec. The magazine printed a picture of Gabor posing provocatively with her leg draped over a nude male statue.

Lord Jowitt's mailbox overflowed with objections, including one from the wife of the chancellor of the exchequer, Rab Butler, whose family had given generously to the Tate.

---

96 *The Illustrated* was a weekly magazine carrying news and photos of fashion trends, celebrity gossip and aspirational lifestyles.

After the Dance

Jowitt, incandescent, summoned Rothenstein. 'I am ashamed to be the chairman of this great institution with vulgar pictures like this appearing in the press,' he told him.[97]

No sooner had this incident blown over than a second one arose. Rothenstein was once again absent from the gallery, and Le Roux was persuaded to supervise the filming of *The Fake*, a British crime movie whose plot involved an American detective trying to solve the theft of a priceless painting from the Tate. A contract drawn up two years earlier by Rothenstein permitted the film to be shot using public rooms at the gallery.

Following the Gabor scandal, Le Roux was hesitant to expose the Tate to further potential embarrassment, so he reviewed the contract to determine if there was any exit clause that could release the gallery from its commitment. To his astonishment, he found that Rothenstein had received a fee of £200 for 'helping with the script'.

Le Roux, now at war with the director, sent the chairman the contract signed by Rothenstein. The contract had been approved at the board meeting of 17 January 1950, but it did not mention the fee.

In response, in a letter in early November 1952, Rothenstein informed the chairman that the minute of 17 January 1950 was merely incomplete in that it did not mention that he was to receive a modest remuneration. Norman Reid, who had taken the minutes, confirmed to the chairman that the director had mentioned the fee and apologised for the omission in the minutes.

Chairman Jowitt responded: 'It may well be so – I have no independent recollection, apart from the minute,' and sent the director to explain the matter to the Treasury.

Sir Thomas Barnes, the Treasury solicitor, expressed disapproval of the arrangement whereby the director of a public gallery could profit for himself by a film shot in the gallery. Rothenstein decided to concede gracefully. 'Yes, I see the point,' he said, and agreed to pay the money into the trustees' account to contribute to the purchase of works of art.

These matters delayed Lord Jowitt's review of the documents regarding *The Little Dancer* until the second week of November, by which time questions had arisen in Parliament. He concluded that Le Roux was

---

97 Rothenstein, who described the complaint as a 'non-event conjured up by Le Roux', later wrote, 'Perhaps the photograph was strong meat for some people in 1952; Miss Gabor had slightly lifted her skirt so that a knee was almost entirely visible.' Today the Gabor 'incident' may appear a storm in a teacup but it must be borne in mind that the 1950s were a period of extreme respectability and conformity.

correct about the overpayment for the Degas bronze but added that the deal had already been made and that renegotiating the price would be costly and embarrassing. After all, the board of trustees had agreed to the payment. However, he felt the director had been negligent in not circulating the letter from the Marlborough Gallery dated 27 June 1951, in which the Tate was offered 73 Degas bronzes, including *The Little Dancer*, for between £4,000 and £5,000.

When the board of trustees next met, on 20 November, Lord Jowitt's formal report was presented. 'Le Roux has done excellent work restoring the publications department from a sickly infant to a thriving child,' he had written. 'There are not the slightest grounds to impeach his integrity. Rothenstein has been the director for many years and has done the most valuable work. We have here a clash of personalities for which neither of the two is wholly to blame. Le Roux is enthusiastic and ambitious and would like to extend his sphere of activities. Rothenstein is, I think, inclined to keep too many things in his own hands.'

Given their clash over the Gabor incident, Rothenstein anticipated that Jowitt's report would be hostile. So he did what he had found successful in the Humphrey Brooke saga and called in the Treasury. He knew this ploy generally favoured the senior man, as the Treasury was determined to support the status quo.

For his part, Lord Jowitt was not against the Treasury's involvement, particularly as it exonerated him from making the unpleasant decision of sacking the director.

Sir Edward Ritson, deputy chairman of the board of the Inland Revenue, and his colleague Sir Edward Playfair were the Treasury officials detailed to sort out the management affairs at the Tate.

As Ritson wrote in a note to Playfair: 'I hope the artists [on the Board of Trustees of the Tate] will appreciate my contempt for detail and my admiration for Significant Form.'[98]

Le Roux understood that things were about to escalate when, within a week, Humphrey Brooke phoned him and invited him to the Royal Academy, where he was now the secretary.

Brooke greeted him on the stairs. 'Welcome, Le Roux, although I fear it is not in happy circumstances.'

When they had sat down in his office and Brooke had called for tea for the two of them, the secretary began. 'I was at a party given by Mrs

---

[98] Note from Edward Ritson to Edward Playfair in the National Archive dated 9 December 1952.

Maud Russell[99] the other night, and Sir Philip Hendy[100] took me aside, saying, "Johnny has got himself into serious trouble this time." Hendy went on to say that at the most recent board meeting, he had found himself in a minority of one in wishing to see the director retain his post.'

Le Roux, who had been at that board meeting, sipped his tea and listened.

'Hendy said he was organising a "Save Johnny" campaign and needed my assistance and – you're not going to believe this – he wanted me to write a letter clearing Rothenstein of any blame in my dismissal.'

'What an absurd suggestion!' Le Roux was taken aback at how poorly informed Hendy seemed to be: by this stage, everybody knew that Rothenstein had edged Brooke out.

'Hendy stated it would absolve Rothenstein of the most severe charge – of which we all know he is guilty – namely, that he is a terrible manager, and that the staff do not trust him.'

'I think Hendy was clutching at straws,' Le Roux suggested.

'When I said I could not possibly help, he opened up and spoke more freely about the problems. He mentioned an incident that occurred before I left the Tate and asked whether I remembered the director declaring a financial interest in a documentary film called *The Fake* that was to be shot at the Tate. I told Hendy that I clearly recalled Rothenstein confirming that he had no interest in the film. Hendy replied, "That is how I remember it too." Can you believe it, Le Roux?'

Le Roux could do nothing but shake his head. 'Well, what I can tell you is that at a recent meeting the trustees corroborated Rothenstein's story. Hendy nodded like the rest of them. Reid even said he wrote a contemporaneous minute confirming it. Then, when he was asked to produce it, he said he'd misplaced it, which was a blatant lie to protect the director.'

Brooke said, 'I've written to Jowitt and Playfair saying that if my name is quoted with regard to confirming Rothenstein's managerial prowess, this is incorrect. I have heard nothing.'

'It's very good of you to fill me in. I feel as though I'm in a swamp of alligators,' Le Roux said.

---

99 Maud Russell was a British socialite and art patron.
100 The British art curator Sir Philip Hendy was a National Gallery trustee from 1946 to 1967, and as such sat on the Tate board.

'That is because you are, my dear fellow. When I recounted Sir Philip Hendy's comments about the director's fee, Ritson said, and I quote, "My mission from the Treasury is to restore order at the Tate on the basic assumption that the director is retained."'

Le Roux put his cup and saucer on Brooke's desk. 'This is a lot to consider, Humphrey. Thank you for warning me.'

'I think a campaign to oust Rothenstein will fail, not because he is worth retaining but because he is there, and the Treasury will see to it that he stays.'

5

Interrogation

1952

Sir Edward Ritson's preliminary report on the management issues at the Tate was completed in record time over the weekend of 22 November 1952. On the following Monday morning, Ritson took a taxi to the Tate to deliver it personally. It suggested that the trustees get rid of Le Roux to resolve the problem. Rothenstein had been 'silly', Ritson said, but Le Roux had shown 'gross disloyalty at all times'. Ritson wrote, 'I find Le Roux completely devoid of any sense of his proper place in a government department's hierarchy. He has shown himself completely unaware of the conduct required from a subordinate civil servant.'

Ritson was, however, confronted with unexpected opposition from the chairman, who made it clear that the trustees preferred Le Roux over Rothenstein, and invited Ritson to meet the trustees at the House of Lords on 12 December to discuss the matter. Ritson later confided to Thomas Padmore, a colleague at the Treasury, 'The trustees seem to apply one set of standards to Le Roux and a much harsher set to Rothenstein.'

Ritson began the meeting at the House of Lords by saying he wanted the trustees' views on three matters: Was Rothenstein technically competent? Had the Tate flourished under his management? And what examples had they in mind of cases where he had not dealt candidly with them?

Padmore addressed the trustees: 'On the matter of Le Roux, as long as he is on probation, you can terminate his employment without fuss or disgrace. But it would be another matter if he were confirmed. Of course, it is for the trustees to decide, but on any ordinary standards, it would be quite wrong to confirm Le Roux without further trial.'

Lord Jowitt responded first, setting the tone of the trustees' response. 'I regret to say that Rothenstein is unreliable, disloyal, dishonest and a bully. Staff relations will never be happy while he is there.'

Henry Moore agreed that Rothenstein was a thoroughly bad manager of staff. He spoke with warmth in favour of Le Roux, whom he regarded as a real acquisition who had done a lot of good. 'I hope we keep Le Roux because if, at the end of all of this, Rothenstein stays and Le Roux goes, it would be the wrong way round.'

William Coldstream[101] agreed that Rothenstein was a disaster as head of staff and wished the trustees could get rid of him. But he did not see how they could sack the director without evidence of gross misconduct. 'Having said that, the suppression of the letter from the Marlborough Gallery showing that the Degas bronze had been offered at a much lower price was a flagrant dereliction of his duty as director,' he added.

On whether Rothenstein had disclosed his financial interest in the film to be shot at the Tate, there was conflicting evidence. The trustees did not think he had, but Reid, who had taken the minutes, confirmed in writing to the chairman that Rothenstein had disclosed the remuneration and that he, Reid, had simply forgotten to include it in the minutes.

The trustees, without exception, disliked and distrusted Rothenstein and thought he was dishonest in his dealings with them and the staff. But when the Treasury asked whether the Tate had declined under his management, the answer was 'No. He has done a good job.' The trustees also agreed that Rothenstein had not tried to make money personally out of the Degas purchase.

All of them liked and trusted Le Roux. They stressed – and Ritson accepted – that he had done excellent work putting the publications department on its feet.

Ritson concluded the meeting: 'Well, thank you, gentlemen, for your candour. The important thing is to avoid dismissals or resignations. I will interview the Tate staff to gauge their mood, and then interview Rothenstein and Le Roux. As far as we can see, there are no grounds at this time to dismiss Rothenstein, and it would be bad for morale if Le Roux resigned. I suggest that Padmore and I have a frank discussion with both men, and tell them that the trustees want them to put the past behind them and work together. In the meantime, they are both on probation for a year.'

---

101 The portrait painter William Coldstream was a trustee of both the National Gallery and the Tate Gallery from 1949 to 1963.

After the Dance

As the meeting broke up, the chairman took Ritson aside and said, 'I'm afraid this is a case of "I do not like thee, Dr Fell".'[102]

⁂

The Treasury officials did not believe a compromise would last very long, but they needed to explore all avenues. Ritson and Padmore duly interviewed various staff members, and then honed in on Le Roux, interviewing him over the course of four different meetings on four different days, to see whether he would resume working under the director. Ritson began the meetings with Le Roux by saying they were all off the record, with no minutes taken.

At their first meeting, Ritson made it clear that he felt it was up to Le Roux to undertake to try to establish working relations with Rothenstein, but he did concede that 'the director should have given us information on important matters'.

Le Roux asked, 'What do you, as spokesmen for the Treasury, believe are those "important matters"?'

'Those incidents that have given the trustees cause for concern, such as the Gabor affair, commercial films being made in the rooms of the Tate, and the purchase price of the Degas *Dancer*.'

'With the greatest respect, Sir Edward, you cannot group those matters,' Le Roux said, impatiently. 'We can agree that the photographing of Miss Gabor and the filming show poor judgement on the part of the director, but *The Little Dancer*, where the Tate paid double the going market price for a piece of art, is surely more than poor judgement. Buying art at market prices is the business of the Tate Gallery. If the director cannot negotiate a realistic price for art, what is his function?'

Ritson spread his hands in a mollifying gesture. 'Mr Le Roux, please hear me out. We are not here to dwell on the past. You have complained that the director is not a good manager. When we interviewed staff, there were no complaints about the director so far as their work was concerned. They did, however, feel a sense of insecurity owing to the dismissal of Brooke, which they thought unfair.'

---

102 In pointing out that there seemed to be a personality clash between Le Roux and Rothenstein, Lord Jowitt alluded to the nursery rhyme attributed to Tom Brown, a Cambridge student in 1680: 'I do not like thee, Doctor Fell. / The reason why, I cannot tell. / But this I know, and know full well: / I do not like thee, Doctor Fell.'

'Sir Edward, you would not have to be Sherlock Holmes to detect that the staff detest the director and blame him for the insecurity at the Tate.' Le Roux was beginning to enjoy giving the Treasury a little outing from their comfort area.

'Mr Le Roux, I warn you, if you go on in this vein, I will terminate the meeting.' Ritson looked at his notes: 'Your own behaviour is not exemplary in this regard. Your letter of 20 June to Mr Hockaday-Dawson is reprehensible.'

'It was utter cheek for a junior accountant to question my transport expenses on the Paris trip.'

'Nonetheless, you threatened a subordinate with dismissal.'

'I overreacted because I believed the director had put him up to it. But I have apologised.'

'Frankly, Mr Le Roux, it seems to us that it was an unbalanced reaction.'

'Well, Sir Edward, if that is your opinion, you will reflect it in your report.'

'Mr Le Roux, I began by saying that this discussion is off the record. As you can see, we are not taking notes. I have emphasised that our review is forward-looking. We assume the director will stay in his post, and the question is whether you can work with him.'

Le Roux looked from one Treasury man to the other. 'Gentlemen, if I may be frank, I have no confidence in the director. He is a disaster for the gallery. When I warned him about the price of the Degas *Dancer*, he ignored it and tried to undermine my position. No, the director's past actions make it impossible for me to work for him. I can give no undertakings for the future.'

Ritson pushed his glasses up on to the bridge of his nose and looked at Le Roux. 'The director has agreed to take advice and guidance —'

'And you believe him?'

'Mr Le Roux, I must insist that you listen to what I have to say, because I have not reached the most important point, and we've been here long enough.' Ritson paused, took a breath, and began again. 'You and the director must agree to do your best to work together in the future. In spite of the fact that you have questioned the director's probity, the director will re-establish harmonious relations. Do you understand?'

Le Roux looked bewildered. 'I never impugned the director's probity. I impugned his competence.'

'Please don't be clever with us, Mr Le Roux. We're trying to fix this unfortunate situation, of which you are one of the architects. Are you going to help us or not?'

After the Dance

'If "help" means accepting without comment your ill-informed judgements on matters with which I am intimately familiar, then, no, I am not going to help.'

Ritson slammed a hand down on the papers on the desk and raised his voice. 'Mr Le Roux, there is only one question. Are you prepared to undertake to establish working relations with the director?'

'No.'

'Well, in that case, Mr Le Roux, the only logical thing you can do is resign. I suggest you consider your position overnight, and we will reconvene at 5 p.m. tomorrow.'

The next two meetings between Le Roux and the Treasury, to the Treasury's exasperation, continued in the same vein.

On the evening of 17 December, Le Roux consulted Lord Jowitt, who advised him to compromise. The trustees were not of a mind to fire Rothenstein, Jowitt told Le Roux, and they agreed that the past would be forgotten and the slate wiped clean for both men.[103]

The final meeting between Le Roux and the two Treasury men began at 12.30 p.m. on Thursday 18 December 1952, and Le Roux surprised them by opening, without prompting, 'I have thought about what you've said. If the position is that the Treasury and the trustees wish Rothenstein to remain as director and me to remain as deputy, I will do my best to work harmoniously with Rothenstein.'

After Le Roux had gone, Padmore closed his notebook. 'I don't understand it. We ask the same question for seven hours, and finally, he answers it.'

Ritson responded, 'Le Roux knows that there's a move among the trustees to get rid of the director, and he thought that if he held out, the trustees would back him. But whoever he saw last night told him they wanted the compromise solution. That is the only way I can explain his behaviour. Come on, we need to see Lord Jowitt with the good news.'

So Ritson and Padmore made their way in a taxi along the Embankment, past Parliament, towards the Tate. The streets were crowded with Christmas shoppers going home, and progress was slow. But when they arrived, they found Lord Jowitt in a thunderous mood.

'I have just had a delegation of three staff members complaining about your enquiry.'

---

103 Letter from Lord Jowitt to Le Roux dated 7 January 1953. The letter refers to advice that Jowitt had given Le Roux during the Treasury interviews in December 1952. Tate Gallery Archive.

Ritson and Padmore looked at each other. 'I don't understand,' said Ritson.

'They complained that your questioning was biased and tendentious, that you cross-examined them like a counsel for the defence, that they could not say what was troubling them, and that they do not believe you will give a true account of their concerns.'

Ritson threw up his hands. 'This is Le Roux up to his tricks again!' he said. 'The staff can write to me if they have something to add.'

'Well, Sir Edward, if that is your response, I will get the relevant staff members here now, and we can ask them together.'

'That will not be necessary. As you know, that would be a breach of protocol, as interviews with staff were conducted in the strictest confidence.'

Lord Jowitt glared at Ritson. 'The trustees are in no mood for games. If this goes on any longer, several trustees will resign.'

'That is what we came to tell you. After considerable discussion, Mr Le Roux has agreed to work with the director.'

'A result, at least. Thank you, gentlemen, and good day.'

As Ritson and Padmore travelled back to Somerset House in the taxi, they discussed the notes they had made of the four meetings with Le Roux, despite their assurances to him that no notes would be taken.

'Well, Ritty, my conclusion is that Le Roux is a shifty, unstable, untrustworthy character of a degree of intellectual dishonesty, of which I do not remember having seen the parallel.'

'Paddy, I would like you to add that to your notes, then put the notes in a sealed envelope in Le Roux's file, only to be opened if Le Roux is to be considered for another senior Civil Service position.'

Sir Edward Ritson added a further note in Le Roux's file, copied to his senior, Sir Edward Playfair: 'As a result of long conversations with Mr Le Roux, I fear he is a difficult man for any director to cope with. Whereas I found the director agreeable to all suggestions made to him, Mr Le Roux has been a most difficult man to bring to an agreement. He seems to ask for freedom and independence inconsistent with his place in the organisation of the Tate.'

So began the truce in which everybody pledged to get on and try harder to make things work.

After the Dance

As 1953 progressed, Le Roux fretted about the precarious state of affairs between himself and his superiors. This was especially true when Lord Jowitt, who had generally supported Le Roux in the arguments with the director and the Treasury, indicated his decision to resign the chairmanship. Although there was no outbreak of hostilities, Le Roux felt frustrated that he had not achieved a decisive victory.

Discreetly, he tried to engage the art world outside the Tate in his war against the director.

In February 1953, he phoned Tony Kloman at the Institute of Contemporary Arts to suggest lunch at the Arts Club to discuss *The Unknown Political Prisoner*, an exhibition curated by the institute to be held at the Tate the following month.[104]

As they got stuck into their steak-and-kidney pies, Le Roux announced, 'I must tell you, in confidence, that it has been difficult to advocate that your exhibition gets appropriate billing at the Tate. The director and the trustees were dead against the project.'

Far from ingratiating himself with Kloman, the comment raised his eyebrows: what Le Roux said was contrary to the discussions he'd had with the director, with several trustees present. But Kloman didn't want to disturb the arrangements with the Tate and merely said, 'Well, I'm very grateful.'

After the exhibition opened, feeling assured of Tony Kloman's support, Le Roux invited him and his wife Theo to dinner at their flat. Philippa outdid herself with the meal, and the wine flowed, and by the time they were drinking coffee in the living room, Le Roux's tongue had been loosened.

'You know, Johnny made our lives a misery when we first arrived,' he told Kloman. 'Philippa let it slip that we had several introductions to the foreign embassies in London from their counterparts in Pretoria, and he forbade us from using them.'

Philippa, sensing that Le Roux was wading into deep water, interrupted him. 'There were plenty of other people who entertained us.'

Le Roux turned to her with a frown. 'No, darling, my point is that Johnny said that we were in a subsidiary position and should behave accordingly.'

---

104 In the early 1950s the Institute of Contemporary Arts organised a worldwide sculpture competition to pay tribute to those who had been imprisoned or lost their lives in the cause of human freedom. It attracted over 3,500 entries and culminated in this exhibition at the Tate.

'Well, he is very conscious of his position,' Kloman said in a conciliatory tone.

'I knew his father, you know,' Le Roux said, missing the cue given by his guest. 'I trained under him at the Royal College of Art. Now, Sir William was a connoisseur. As everyone can see, Johnny knows very little about art, and worse still, he's a terrible administrator.'

Later, after the Klomans had said their goodnights, Le Roux sat on the sofa reading *The Times* while Philippa washed up. 'Is it wise, Le Roux, to talk like that about Rothenstein? I saw the look that Theo gave her husband. I would be careful of him,' she said.

'Oh, rubbish, darling, Tony is a friend, and I am the only person who advocates the institute's interests at the Tate. He knows he needs my support.'

Le Roux had, however, badly misjudged the relationship. Shortly afterwards, Kloman wrote to Rothenstein saying that, after careful consideration, he wanted Rothenstein to know what Le Roux was saying behind his back. He recounted Le Roux's comments, adding, 'Le Roux is dangerous and emotionally unstable.'

Rothenstein immediately forwarded the letter to the Treasury. He drew their attention to the dates of the reported conversations with Le Roux, in that the one in Paris had predated the row in 1952, and the second one, in Le Roux's flat, had taken place after the Treasury settlement.

The Treasury men, who had already made their minds up about Le Roux, waited for the inevitable renewal of hostilities.

6

Royalty and Riches

1953

In June 1953, excitement about the forthcoming coronation of the young Elizabeth II was running high.

'You'll have to make your own arrangements to see the show,' Le Roux told Philippa one evening. 'I've been commissioned to broadcast the whole thing from Westminster Abbey live to South Africa.'

'How absolutely lovely for you,' she exclaimed. 'You'll see the whole coronation first hand! Oh, Le Roux! What an honour!'

She'd resigned herself to remaining at home with Philippe on the big day, when, ten days before the event, a letter arrived. She phoned Le Roux with her wonderful news.

'Can you imagine! I've had a letter from a friend of the Selbys. Do you remember, he was the American press attaché in Pretoria when I was on the *Rand Daily Mail*, and I was very friendly with them? Well, a friend of theirs, Mrs Thomas, is in London, and she says the Selbys asked her to look us up. She has two tickets for the coronation,[105] but they are in different places. She is here alone and wondered if I would care to use the ticket for the Dorchester Hotel!'

Le Roux was impressed. 'I must say, it's a princely offer. Are you going to accept?'

'If I can get a babysitter. I shall phone the service at once.'

---

[105] This was the first televised coronation. Tickets were sold to seats on stands along the processional route, accommodating 96,000 people, while private companies sold tickets to events that included the televised ceremony; and establishments on the processional route offered prime viewing positions.

That evening, a happy Philippa told Le Roux, 'The babysitting service will fetch Philippe the night before, and then I have to walk up to the Dorchester before seven the following morning. The ticket says I can have breakfast and a champagne lunch. Imagine!' She looked at him. 'I can watch the whole abbey service on television there, and then see the entourage pass from a specially built seat overlooking the Park Lane section. Isn't that wonderful?' She rushed into the bedroom to find the ticket to show him. 'I wish you could be with me,' she said wistfully; 'it would be so lovely to share this.' Then she remembered: 'But, of course, your seat in the abbey will be even more spectacular. Shall we meet afterwards?'

'Heavens, no! To begin with, the crowds will be appalling, and I don't know what time I shall be through.'

'But the abbey part is in the morning. Surely you would have plenty of time to —'

'Philippa,' Le Roux interrupted, putting down his knife and fork, and wiping his mouth. 'I'm delighted you have this opportunity to see the coronation, but I cannot meet you. There will be some sort of celebration with the radio people, so I don't know what time I shall be home. Please just make your own arrangements for the evening. By the way, Enslin du Plessis and Frank McEwen[106] want to sleep here the night before, and I've told them they can.'

'Where?'

'On the floor or in Philippe's room. It will be empty.'

It was Le Roux who woke up first on the morning of 2 June 1953. He went to the kitchen and at 4 a.m. brought Philippa a cup of tea. 'I'll get some for the others, and then I think they will be off. Don't worry about food for any of us,' he whispered to her in the dark of the bedroom.

An hour later, the three men left.

Philippa tidied the apartment in the early light of dawn. As she locked the front door behind her, she saw the street full of people walking purposefully towards Westminster Abbey. She joined the throng, and the crowd became thicker as she walked up Sloane Street to Brompton Road.

---

106 Francis Jack McEwen, born in 1907, was an English artist, teacher and administrator who helped found the National Gallery of Rhodesia (Zimbabwe). He also spent some time on the British Council. He died in 1994.

At the Dorchester, she sat down for a delicious breakfast, then was directed to the television rooms. She found several sets in three separate lounges, with deep, comfortable armchairs.

She settled down and, as she watched people arriving at the abbey on the TV, imagined Le Roux giving his broadcast to South Africa, which she had proofread at the weekend.

> I am speaking to you from a wet but jubilant London which, even now as you hear my words, is reverberating with the cheers of the scores of thousands of people who have surged like some great irresistible flood-tide to Buckingham Palace, The Mall and all the area around. A great many of these people have been up all night on the pavements to make certain of their own spot along the route. Some, indeed, have spent their second night there. All of them have most certainly been on their feet since four or five o'clock this morning. Nothing could or would have stopped them or spoiled the colourful excitement of this great day.
>
> To her subjects, the festive joys of this day will only end when the young Queen has made her final appearance on the famous balcony of Buckingham Palace and has switched on the fantastic illuminations of the rejoicing city as a sign for the great display of fireworks to start at the South Bank and the chain of bonfires to be lit which will soon blaze across the whole United Kingdom.
>
> Much of the mood of the service was created by the abbey itself. You need not come to the Coronation Service to become conscious of how the very fabric of this building is impregnated with history. Edward the Confessor began this building in 1045, and next to his grave here, William the Conqueror was crowned, and so for 900 years, the high ancient walls have looked down on the crowning of one sovereign after another, lending a timeless significance to the ritual.[107]

After the service, Philippa found herself splendidly placed with a view of the route the carriages would take. For a short period it rained, but then the sun filtered through.

The cheering commenced from a distance, growing in power until the noise obliterated every other sound as the golden carriage approached and the British cheered their monarch and her consort. There she was,

---

[107] Excerpt from *The London Review* no. 159, broadcast by Le Roux on the SABC on 2 June 1953.

waving, her jewels flashing in the sunlight and her crown glinting as she moved her head.

Philippa followed the carriage as far as she could see, and then, with a sigh, she watched the rest of the dignitaries pass. How beautiful the horses were with their plumes and shining brass accoutrements. How straight the Horse Guards sat on their chargers. There were the grenadiers and their busbies bouncing along in rhythm as they rode the trotting horses.

The seats around her were empty when she finally got up to leave. Idly, she walked along in the direction of home. The sun was lower against the skyline, a huge red ball staining everything with a rose light. She couldn't help wondering where Le Roux was at that moment. Where would he spend his night of celebration? Who was with him?

One morning Philippa couldn't find her gold watch, a present from her parents before she left South Africa. She asked Le Roux but he hadn't seen it.

'It's strange, because I had it here yesterday.'

'I am sure it will turn up,' he said as he put on his hat and coat and left for work.

The Daimler remained with them, and despite the joy it had given her in the summer, Philippa spoke to Le Roux about it one day. 'Darling,' she said hesitantly, 'you know I love this car as much as you, but I do feel awkward using the car of a woman I have never met. Surely by now you should return it to her?'

To her surprise, he agreed with her. 'I quite understand how you feel. Lois is still away, but I'll return it to her solicitors this week.'

A month later, they were dining with Walter and Leila Spicer, when Leila said casually, 'I saw you driving around in the most beautiful old Daimler the other day, Le Roux. Since when have you become so affluent?'

He laughed easily. 'Not me, dear Leila. I wish it were so! What I wouldn't give to own such a car!'

'Ah, but, dear friend, it was you. Nobody could mistake you for anyone else, unless perhaps Orson Welles. Is he in town?'

'He might well be,' Philippa chipped in. The conversation took another turn, but she had lost her appetite.

As they walked to the bus later, it was chilly, with a hint of the cold to come. 'You still have the car,' she said quietly.

'Yes. I'm sorry. I returned it to the solicitors as I promised, and after two weeks they sent me a bill for £20 for garaging it. Lois is still away, as I told you. Before she left, I did assure her I would keep the car until her return, but I'm damned if I will get further into debt over the thing.'

Philippa looked down at her shoes, counting the rhythm of their steps. She knew Le Roux would never introduce her to the Daimler's owner.

On Saturdays, Le Roux sometimes took Philippe to the park. 'I'm not taking the pram,' he told Philippa. 'I think it's a device to prevent children from getting exercise. English children go from pram to prep school.'

'How will you take him?'

'Philippe, you can walk, can't you?'

'C'mon, Daddy, let's go,' laughed the three-year-old.

'If the worst comes to the worst, I will carry him.'

'Be it on your head. But I think you are just vain not wanting to be seen pushing a pram.'

'We'll watch the horses on Rotten Row,' said Le Roux, as they set off.

Rotten Row, the broad track along the south side of Hyde Park, looked splendid as the autumn afternoon sunshine pushed its way through the clouds, producing a diluted light. The huge trees up and down the row were graded from the yellow of autumn to the lingering green of summer, and the surface of the row was covered in a thick patterned carpet of golden fallen leaves, lying so deep along the sides that Philippe waded through them up to his knees.

The horses seemed quite spirited in the fresh wind, but what was so different on this particular afternoon was the stillness of the park. There was no sound of the usual traffic: the petrol strike was taking its toll.[108]

'Why are there no cars, Daddy?' asked Philippe, looking over at the South Carriageway.

Deciding there was no simple answer to the question, Le Roux picked him up and put him on his back. He galloped up Rotten Row towards Hyde Park Corner, until he noticed a crowd staring at him and several

---

108 In October 1953, empty petrol tanks faced London as the result of the unofficial strikes of thousands of petrol-tanker drivers, after oil companies decided that some of their products – paraffin and tractor fuel – should be distributed by agents rather than directly by themselves, using their tanker drivers.

Royalty and Riches

policemen at the ready. He slowed, hearing someone running behind him, and looked round to see a man in a white runner's vest and shorts.

Le Roux stopped to ask a policeman what was going on.

'It's the South African runner, Wally Hayward,[109] who's just broken the Bath-to-London record. We didn't expect him for another hour, and the bigwigs aren't even here to meet him.'

On the long walk home, Philippe asked another unanswerable question. 'What's a South African, Daddy?'

When they arrived home, Le Roux slumped in a chair. While Philippa fussed over their son, removing his warm outer clothes, Le Roux said, 'There's something I've meant to mention. You know I've had to stop my TV work because of Rothenstein's reaction, and so my hopes of increased income have dwindled. I'm a bit overdrawn at the bank, and I wondered if you could help me out?'

Philippa's skin prickled. 'Overdrawn? How much?'

'Oh, not much. A few hundred. But as I have no securities, the bank is badgering me over it.'

'But, Le Roux, you know I have nothing except those few shares that my father gave me. They're for an emergency.'

'This *is* an emergency.' His voice was pleasant, but there was an underlying tenseness in his manner. 'Look, if you feel you can't help me, just say so. I have work to do, so I'll see you later.'

Then he was gone, and she heard the door slam downstairs.

Upstairs, in their bedroom, Philippa took out the only jewellery she had of any value: a fine emerald and diamond pendant on a slender platinum chain. Her father had given it to her mother as an engagement present. 'I would like you to have it, darling. Treasure it as I have done,' her mother had said, pressing it into her hands, shortly before they'd emigrated.

She wrapped the necklace in tissue paper and put it in her bag: she would have to sell it to pay off Le Roux's debt. It wasn't only *his* debt, she reasoned, as she dressed; it was also hers: they would never have had to move if she had not had Philippe. She owed her husband this.

On Monday morning, she put Philippe in his pram and walked to Bond Street to find a respectable jeweller. It was barely ten o'clock, and

---

109 Wally Hayward was a South African endurance athlete with a 60-year career. He became one of the greatest 100-mile runners in history. He won the Comrades Marathon five times and completed the distance of around 90 km for the last time just before his 81st birthday. In 1953 he established records in the London to Brighton Marathon (5:29:40), and in the Bath to London 100-miler (12:20:28).

169

the shop was empty. The man behind the counter was elderly and wore a black suit.

'I wondered if you buy secondhand jewellery?' she asked him, nervously.

The man bent his head and looked keenly at her from under a pair of bushy eyebrows. 'We do, from time to time.'

She drew the little parcel from her bag, unwrapped the pendant and handed it to him.

His hands seemed large and white as he took it and examined it. Then he silently opened a drawer and took out a magnifying glass. Disappearing into a back room, he returned with a younger man, who also examined the pendant.

'Is this your own property?' asked the older man.

'Yes. It was my mother's.'

'It's slightly chipped in the one corner,' observed the younger man.

'I want £700 for it,' she said firmly.

Both men stared at her. 'I'm afraid that's impossible. £300 is as far as we would be prepared to go.'

'£550,' she countered. Her voice sounded over-loud, and she felt as if her legs would give way.

'£450, and that is our last word,' the younger man said.

'Thank you,' she said faintly.

He produced a book and wrote something in it, then pushed it towards her. 'If you will sign here... Shall I make you out a cheque?'

'I want cash, please.'

His eyebrows rose into peaks, but he said nothing and counted out the notes.

She felt empty and sad as she walked home, wondering if she had accepted too little.

After giving Philippe his lunch, she put him back in his pram, left the apartment and hailed a cab. At Coutts Bank, she asked to see Mr Tanner, the man Le Roux had mentioned who was dealing with his account. She was shown into a large, carpeted room with a couple of elegant leather chairs and a deep, broad desk.

A young man, fair, dressed in a black frock-coat and grey striped trousers, greeted her politely and asked her to sit down.

'I've come about my husband's account.'

'Yes?'

'I understand he's £400 overdrawn, and that you wish him to clear the overdraft?'

'That is correct.'

Suddenly she felt antagonistic. This man wasn't even sympathetic. 'I cannot settle it,' she said, surprising herself as much as the bank employee.

'We do not allow overdrafts without security, Mrs Le Roux, you understand that.' Mr Tanner forced a smile. 'Your husband mentioned some shares?'

'I have some shares, but I have no intention of selling them. They are mine.' She looked him in the eye. 'I will pay off his overdraft at the rate of £20 a month. That is the best I can do.' When Mr Tanner said nothing, she added, 'I will not let you down.'

'Will you not allow us to hold the shares against the overdraft?'

'No. They remain with my bank. You may telephone Mr Swanson at Barclays Bank if you wish to verify the facts.'

'That will not be necessary,' Mr Tanner said. 'I have your word, madam?'

'You do.'

When she told Le Roux that she'd undertaken to pay off his overdraft, she couldn't tell if he was pleased or not. He didn't comment beyond saying, 'Tanner must have been surprised.'

'He was,' she said.

She said nothing about the sale of the pendant and Le Roux didn't inquire. Perhaps he thought she was getting the money from her father.

That evening, they employed a babysitter and went to see a film, and later they ate at a Chinese restaurant. Le Roux had been affectionate during the evening and, as they walked home arm in arm in the cold starry night, Philippa ventured to ask a question.

'Le Roux?' she started hesitantly.

'Yes, snooks, what is it?'

It was a long time since she'd heard that loving name, and tears started to her eyes. 'I just wanted to ask you... Do you still love me?'

He didn't change his walking pace, nor did she feel any withdrawal from him, so she continued in step with him, feeling as if her whole life depended on the answer. After a little thought, he answered quietly, 'Yes, darling, I do love you, but as the mother of my child.'

I will show him that he can depend on me in all things, she said to herself later, lying in bed, staring at the ceiling, as Le Roux snored softly at her side. No matter how dejected she felt, she would bear it, because it was her fault that this situation had come about. How could she blame him when she had secretly and deliberately gone against his wishes?

V

The Final Curtain

1

The Worst of Times

1953

At the end of July, Le Roux told Philippa that he was going grouse-shooting. While he was away, Philippa invited Walter and Leila Spicer to dinner.

Over the meal, Walter suggested that Philippa and Le Roux join Leila and him on a holiday to Italy. 'I think we should leave at the end of October,' he said. 'If you agree, I'll book our accommodation, and we can get on with our plans.'

'I'll speak to Le Roux about it when he gets home on Monday,' she said. 'He's gone grouse-shooting for the weekend.'

'Grouse-shooting?' Walter looked uncomfortable.

'Yes! If he brings home anything, I'll let you have a bird.'

'But the season doesn't open —' began Leila.

'We're thinking of finishing up the trip in Paris!' Walter interrupted loudly.

'That will suit us very well,' Philippa said firmly, too distracted by thinking about how nice it would be if she and her husband could get away together to notice Leila's flustered look.

Although she knew he was struggling at work, Le Roux had stopped confiding in her, and lately he was spending less and less time at home. At least one evening a week, he attended a meeting of the Civil Defence Corps,[110] while other evenings were filled with the social aspects of his job, including exhibition openings. He and Philippa had agreed that it

---

110 The Civil Defence Corps was a civilian volunteer organisation established in 1949 to take local control of any affected area in the aftermath of a major national emergency.

wasn't sensible to pay a babysitter for a couple of hours just so Philippa could attend, especially when they were so financially strained. 'I will just pop in to the opening, then come right home,' he would assure her. But he invariably 'met a friend', with whom he would go for a light meal at a pub, or he would 'run into someone' significant from the art world and stay out much later. Sometimes she would try to stay up until he returned, but she was usually so weary from her daily chores that she would fall asleep despite her best efforts.

She wondered when her love for her husband had become such a burden that she was never free of the hurt. She remembered all the lonely nights when he'd been away. Once, he'd left her for several weeks, saying he was going to the Algarve, and she'd had only one postcard from him. It was the first time in all the years they'd known each other that such a thing had happened, and she'd forced herself through those days, waiting for his return and blindly hoping that things would be different when he came back. But nothing had changed. Perhaps he might confide in her if they were in new surroundings, she thought.

Le Roux arrived home on Sunday evening with a brace of grouse. As soon as he sat down, Philippa said, 'I want you to come on this trip. Walter has made all the arrangements and I've found a boarding place for Philippe. So please come!'

He crossed his legs. 'I really don't want to, Philippa. Why are you forcing it?'

'Only because I feel it may give us a chance to have some time free from worries, on our own, away from here. Walter and Leila will leave us alone, and it's a cheap way to get abroad, and anyway, I've never seen Italy,' she finished rather desperately.

He thought for a while. 'Well, if you insist. But I can't afford to pay for it, and if the *pension* is dreadful, which I am sure it will be, I won't stay.'

The first few days of their long-awaited holiday passed quickly and pleasantly enough until they approached Lake Lugano in northern Italy and stopped on an unappealing little street, narrow and suburban.

'Are we here?' She looked around, disconcerted, knowing Le Roux wouldn't like it.

'This way.' Leila shepherded her along the cobbled street and through a hidden side door into a long foyer that widened into a larger hall. There, a short, stout man talked earnestly with Leila.

'He says,' Leila translated as they followed him up a passage to some stairs, 'that they have been overbooked this season, and the people who were leaving have enjoyed themselves so much they have stayed a few days longer. The room he'd hoped to give you overlooking the lake is still occupied, but it will be free in two days. Meanwhile, until your room is free, you will be across the passage.'

The room was bright and inviting, featuring twin beds and a wash-basin. The French doors opened on to a small mock-balcony that overlooked the tram-line, while the mountain loomed above.

After a little while, she heard Le Roux enter with the bags. He put them down in the middle of the room.

She summoned up a smile. 'The man says our lovely room overlooking the lake will be free in two days. Have you seen the lake? It's beautiful, and so big.'

The look on his face stopped her.

Le Roux sat down on one of the beds. 'I'm not staying here,' he said, amusedly.

Philippa felt suddenly enraged. 'You're so selfish,' she said. 'I needed to get away, and I thought we might have a chance to talk, but you don't even try.'

The silence grew for a few moments, then Le Roux leaned forward, speaking quietly. 'Look, snooks, why don't you go home to South Africa for a good holiday? I know it hasn't been easy for you. The change will do you good. Take the boy, and give your mom and dad a treat, some time to play Grandma and Grandad.'

'And who will pay for that little jaunt?'

'You know your father will. He would love you to go.'

Philippa stared coldly at her husband. 'You cannot get rid of me that easily, Le Roux. But let me tell you this: if I leave, I shall never return.'

She marched out of the room and joined the Spicers in the bar.

Le Roux arrived about half an hour later, and the four of them went in to dinner. The food was excellent, and the wine full-bodied. It was only when she'd finished the third glass that she realised she'd been unwise. She felt hot, then icy cold. 'Help me out of here,' she whispered to Le Roux. 'I think I'm going to be sick.'

He got up at once. 'Philippa is a bit tired. I think the day has been too much.' He helped her up from her chair and back to their room, and for the next several hours she was up and down, being sick.

At first, Le Roux did what he could to help her, smiling grimly, but then he curled up and slept, and she had to face the rest of the night alone.

The following day, at breakfast, Le Roux told the Spicers he was leaving. He would meet up with them again at the end of the trip, in Paris, he said.

After he left, Philippa had two strong cups of coffee to clear her head and wandered down to the lakeside, where she found a seat under a willow tree. She sat there, watching the light on the water, trying to fathom what she would do about her marriage when she returned to London.

She continued the holiday with the Spicers, who were very kind to her, but the nearer they drew to Paris, the more tense and silent Philippa became. There was nothing she could do to delay their arrival, however, and in the late afternoon of the following Sunday, they pulled up at the house of Le Roux's friend Frank McEwen.[111]

Walter put the car in low gear as they turned into the curved driveway, and they all looked curiously at the large single-storey house where Le Roux was pacing the outside veranda, a glass in his hand. As soon as he came forward to open the car door, although he was smiling and steady, Philippa knew with a sinking heart that he'd been drinking.

The Spicers had booked accommodation for the night at a nearby hotel and had decided to spend a few days in Paris. As Walter helped Le Roux take Philippa's cases out of the trunk, he suggested they all dine together.

'By all means.' Le Roux was expansive. 'Be my guests. Frank will know of a restaurant around here. Tell me where you are staying and I shall call you to tell you where to meet us.'

Le Roux showed Philippa into a large, comfortable bedroom, with his clothes on the chair and in the cupboard. He put down her cases. He looked worn and tired and was perspiring. 'I have to go out now,' he told her. 'Frank's phone isn't working, and I need to call London.'

Later, at the restaurant, as the alcohol flowed, Le Roux entered into the spirit of the evening. He talked excessively and told stories that Philippa had heard before, making everyone but her laugh. It reminded her of Le Roux's first wife Juanita's reaction to his story at the dinner ten years before, the first time she'd met him. She pushed her food around her plate, mesmerised by this man who could pretend everything was normal.

Finally, to her relief, they rose to leave.

---

111 See n. 106.

Back at Frank's house, she went straight to their bedroom. It led off a patio, and the night was so hot that she pulled open the doors and pushed back the thick curtains, letting in the air. She switched on a lamp and, hearing a noise, turned.

Le Roux loomed in the doorway, watching her. He held a bottle of champagne in one hand and supported himself against the door frame with the other. She could see he was so drunk he could hardly stand.

As she walked towards him, he lurched past her into the bathroom. She followed him and saw him trying to open the champagne over the hand basin. At last, infuriated, he banged the neck of the bottle against the tap and the golden liquid shot out over the walls and floor.

'Champagne! A drink for every occasion!' He stood staring at the liquid pouring away down the drain. 'Finished! Like me.' He turned around, shaking the bottle. 'All gone: empty inside.' He laughed. 'You didn't know that, did you?'

She tried to smile. 'What rubbish. You're a brilliant man. Now, come on, Le Roux, come to bed.'

He pushed her arm away. 'You were right about one thing,' he slurred. 'I should never have given up painting.'

She sat on the edge of the bath. 'Tell me what's wrong. Perhaps I can help?'

'Noel Langley[112] has cited me as one of three men in his divorce – co-respondents.'

Philippa sat still, trying to absorb this latest shocking information from her husband. Finally, she said, referring to Langley's beautiful South African wife, 'I don't understand. You never see Naomi.'

He nodded sleepily. 'I have seen her,' he slurred. 'You refused to have Naomi to the house, remember? I thought you were silly. I've known her for a very long time. I like her, and I thought you would too.' Suddenly, he glared at Philippa with genuine malice. 'If only you had invited her to the flat, none of this would have happened!' he snarled.

She stood up. 'Oh, rubbish, Le Roux!' Her hands trembled with indignation. 'It's not my fault. I told you not to get involved with those people. You knew that Noel was antagonistic towards you, and if he found out about your affair with her, he probably hated you.' She turned away, disgusted by the whole sordid tale.

---

112 Noel Langley: see Part II, section 5, 'Success and a schism'.

Le Roux drew himself up and spoke firmly. 'I'm not going to let him have it all his way, not by a long chalk. But the timing is difficult because of the trouble at the Tate.'

'I'm sick of it, Le Roux,' she said. 'The lies. The hurt. All I am is your housekeeper. I know nothing of your movements or whom you see. I expect a divorce would suit you, and it may also suit me.'

She took some satisfaction in seeing a glimmer of panic in his eyes, but then he revealed why: 'If you leave now, everybody will presume I am guilty, and I will have to leave the Tate,' he said, self-pity in his voice.

His self-centredness made her coldly angry. 'You will find another job easily.'

'Not if I leave under a cloud.'

She'd had enough. 'What's the point of continuing with this charade? You no longer love me. We can't even talk to each other.'

She went into the bedroom and prepared for bed.

2

Broken Trusts

1954

It wasn't clear who was responsible for breaking the truce the Treasury had negotiated at the Tate, but a phone call from Lord Kinnaird to the director on 27 November 1953 triggered the resumption of hostilities. Rothenstein was travelling that day, so the call was transferred to Le Roux.

'I'm speaking in the House of Lords about the forthcoming National Art Collections Bill, and I'm curious how the Tate has spent the money in the Knapping Fund,' the peer told the deputy keeper.

Regarding the Bill, the Tate Gallery would operate independently from the National Gallery, and its trustees would have the authority to sell works of art without having to remit the proceeds to the Treasury. Furthermore, to ensure that 'a clearer conception of the purpose of both these Galleries should be recognised', the Bill suggested that the National Gallery be acknowledged 'as a collection of masterpieces of all kinds and all times from all parts of the world', while the Tate Gallery would be 'the National Collection of British pictures and modern pictures generally'.

'A clause of the Bill concerns the bequest by the artist Miss Margaret Knapping, authorising the purchase of pictures, paintings and sculptures by artists of any nationality who were alive within the previous 25 years to be vested in the Tate Gallery trustees. It's this point that I wish to clarify,' Lord Kinnaird said.

'I'm not familiar with the workings of that fund, but I can certainly look at our records and revert to you,' Le Roux responded.

'It is a rather urgent matter, as I am addressing the Lords about it later this week. I would be most grateful if you could come back to me tomorrow.'

Le Roux postponed lunch with a friend and went to the archives, which he knew well because he had set them up. By the afternoon, he had compiled a longhand list of the Knapping Fund's acquisitions and called the Treasury to obtain clearance to pass the list to Lord Kinnaird, which he did later that evening.

The list showed that the Knapping Trust was being used as a general fund for Tate Gallery acquisitions, whereas the bequest stipulated that it should buy works of art by living artists or those who had died in the preceding 25 years. Of the 191 purchases by the Knapping Fund, several dozen did not comply with the bequest conditions.

When Lord Kinnaird raised the matter of the Knapping Fund in the Lords two days later, the trustees were electrified by the implication that if one fund was being used without reference to the terms of its bequest, it was probable, knowing Rothenstein's poor management, that other funds were being misallocated, too.

There was a mad scramble for information. The trustees learnt that the Courtauld Fund, bequeathed by the family of Mrs R.A. Butler, the chancellor's wife, had also been misused. Rothenstein was told to ask Mrs Butler if she remembered being consulted about the purchases of the Léger and the Giacometti works. She said she could not remember, but she would not have approved of the purchase of the Giacomettis because she did not think her father would have cared for them.

At the board meeting on 17 December, the trustees agreed to repay the Knapping Fund and the Courtauld for the incorrect purchases by borrowing from Coutts Bank against the government's Grant-in-Aid for the next financial year.

Le Roux spoke to Coutts about funding the Courtauld and Knapping funds against next year's grant, but Coutts refused. So Le Roux suggested an alternative arrangement to fund these purchases from the Publications Department funds. Coutts agreed, and Le Roux informed the chairman.

The trustees then discovered that a recent purchase of the Picasso *Femme Assise dans un Fauteuil* (£5,250) was approved a month earlier on the premise that the funds would come from the Cleve Fund. At that time, the trustees had not been informed that Mr Cleve's will expressed a preference for British artists. The trustees requested a copy of the will, which indicated that he left his residuary estate in trust for the Tate trustees 'in the hope that they will purchase pictures by British artists'. As a result, the trustees concluded that they could not use the Cleve Fund, and the deputy chairman, Sir Colin Anderson, went to see Coutts, who agreed to lend the purchase price of the Picasso in good faith.

Dennis Proctor,[113] the new chairman, instructed Rothenstein and Reid to go to the archives over the Christmas break and not return until they had a clear picture of what funds had been misused.

The next trustees' meeting took place on 5 January 1954, by which time it was clear that a major storm was approaching. That morning, before the meeting, Rothenstein submitted his list of funds that were being incorrectly used, but his standing fell further when, during the meeting, he was forced to admit that the list was incomplete.

That month, the arrangements with Coutts were leaked to the press, resulting in a severe reprimand for the trustees from the Comptroller and Auditor General. On 26 January, the trustees published a list of trust fund errors in the hope of stopping speculation.

On 29 January, Graham Sutherland was so fed up with Rothenstein that he posted his resignation as a trustee from his house in the south of France without discussing it with anyone, which caused an uproar.

The *Sunday Times* on 31 January quoted Sutherland as stating that 'the trustees had been misled over funds, several breaches of trust had been committed, and testators' wishes disregarded'. His additional criticisms included the indecisive purchasing policy and the missed chances to acquire artworks at a reasonable price, the article noted.

This, in turn, set off a frenzy of editorials, questions in Parliament, and demands for a public enquiry.

The nine trustees held a meeting on 8 February at the house of Sir Colin Anderson,[114] with the single agenda item of whether to sack the director. In preparation, trustee Professor Lawrence Gowing drafted a letter to Proctor, copied to the other Tate trustees, summarising the situation regarding Rothenstein (and including many other points not related to the clash with Le Roux), and suggesting they get rid of him. In the very long list of infractions by the director, Gowing referred to Rothenstein's 'laxity with the Knapping Fund', 'grave unawareness of a director's fundamental responsibility', and 'grossly incompetent' negotiations for *The Little Dancer*. The letter also noted 'that the most elementary records [were] revealed to be in a state which no process of reorgan-

---

113 Dennis Proctor, who worked for the Treasury as transport secretary until 1950, succeeded Lord Jowitt as chairman of the Tate trustees in 1953; he held the position until 1959.
114 Sir Colin Anderson was a wealthy shipping magnate. He would take over as chairman of the Tate in 1960.

isation can excuse'; that 'temporary labels under his direction [were] deficient and permanent ones haphazard'. It went on that 'his actions to his staff must never again lend colour ... to the impression that he disciplines them with threats of slander; ... that Zsa Zsa Gabor remains unmentioned rather than forgotten by those who have the dignity of the gallery at heart; ... and that he must on no account promote his next recruit over the head of a man whom he has better cause to thank than he is likely to know'.

Everyone agreed that the Tate could not continue to run like this. However, some trustees felt that firing the director would require further investigation. So it was agreed that all the trustees would attend the Tate Gallery on Saturday 13 February, to interview all the staff individually. This would be followed by a formal meeting of the trustees on 18 February to decide on the director's fate.

Proctor recorded that of the 12 staff interviewed by the trustees, only three had a good word to say about Rothenstein.[115]

When Le Roux entered the interview room, he counted five artists present whose support he could usually rely on; but there were others who were more difficult to read. He was asked to explain what he considered were the main problems at the Tate. 'Gentlemen, as you know, I am in my fourth year of probation,' he said. 'I expect my appointment to be confirmed at the end of March because I have adhered to the agreement drawn up by Lord Jowitt a year ago, so anything I say, I do not want to be used against me to delay my confirmation.'

Proctor nodded and waved his hand. 'Speak freely.'

'I have said all I need say about the director's management. I will confine myself to the use of bequests. When Lord Kinnaird asked for the history of the Knapping Fund, and I analysed the result, it was clear to me that the director had ignored the terms of this fund's bequest.'

'Le Roux, we know all that,' said the chairman testily.

'Well, Mr Chairman, the matter does not end there. I have spent some time looking at the archives, and even the second list the director produced for the trustees on 5 January is deficient in several aspects, in terms of both omissions within funds and omissions of funds that are affected.'

The meeting was quiet, and all eyes were on Le Roux.

'The full extent of the misuse is contained in this document,' Le Roux said, handing a file to the chairman. 'If you are asked to make a

---

115 Clark, p.166.

statement to Parliament regarding the funds, I suggest you ignore what the director and Norman Reid have produced and rely on this instead.'

The chairman leafed through the file.

'The director has borrowed against future endowments from the government to finance current purchases without the trustees' approval or the knowledge of the Treasury.'

There was a general commotion in the room.

'That cannot be true,' shouted John Piper. 'I do not believe it.'

'It is true,' Le Roux said loudly, his voice breaking into the hubbub. 'You can examine the documents for yourself. The case in point is the Picasso nude that was purchased at the end of last year, improperly using funds from the Cleve Trust, so money was borrowed from Coutts Bank to reimburse the Trust.' He looked around the table and let his words sink in. 'When Parliament examines what has occurred, their conclusion must be that the director has not behaved professionally in administering the business of the Tate and, if I may say so, the trustees could be considered to have been derelict in their duty of supervision.'

There was another outbreak of angry responses as the trustees denied this.

The chairman glared at Le Roux. Far from solving a problem, he had magnified it. 'Thank you, Mr Le Roux, that will be all.'

After Le Roux left, the deputy chairman, Colin Anderson, spoke up. 'Gentlemen, I did know about the Coutts loan. After the questions in the Lords about the misuse of bequests, the gallery could not use the Cleve Fund to buy the Picasso, as it is designated for the purchase of artworks by British artists, so I went to Coutts with the director to borrow the funds.'

The chairman looked aghast. 'But how could the Tate pledge next year's government endowment, which, as far as I know, has not been agreed, against a loan?'

'I made sure that the language omitted any mention of the endowment, although it is implicit that the money will come from the endowment.'

Sir Philip Hendy said, 'What I don't understand is why Le Roux spends all his time in the archives, digging up all this stuff.'

'Oh, Philip, don't be so obtuse; that is hardly the issue,' said Piper. 'It seems to me that Le Roux is the only competent official of the top three. Reid is the director's puppet, and the less said about the director, the better. My view is, we sack the director.'

'And Le Roux,' said another trustee.

There were several 'hear, hears' from around the table.

Lord Robbins[116] intervened. 'The irregularities themselves are not enough to make a damning indictment of the director. If anybody should resign, it should be the trustees.'

There was silence as everybody considered this.

William Coldstream, who had been scribbling on a pad, looked up. 'It's true. We, the trustees, are in an unfavourable position over these matters,' he said. 'I think we can all see that, and the only way we can manage our way out of this mess is with Treasury support. I suggest the chairman pays a visit to the Treasury with Le Roux's file on the funds and the loan to discuss the options. I recommend he also explore the process for getting rid of one or other of Rothenstein or Le Roux, because we cannot go on like this.'

As nobody else had a suggestion, it was agreed that the chairman would visit the Treasury and report back to the trustees.

---

116 Lord Robbins was the National Gallery representative on the board of the Tate Gallery. He was a distinguished economist.

3

The Langley Divorce Case

1955

While his position was becoming more tenuous at the Tate in the early months of 1954, Le Roux spent his waking hours with his lawyers on the rebuttal of Noel Langley's divorce case.

Philippa tried to avoid her husband as much as possible and busied herself in Philippe's room while Le Roux was in the dining room, eating his meals. She went to bed early and feigned sleep when he joined her.

But at last, one bitterly cold Sunday, Le Roux faced her and asked her to sit down to discuss the matter. 'I've had to engage a good barrister,' he began. 'It will be expensive, so we shall have to put this flat on the market. It has six years of the lease left, so we should get a good price.[117] We shall have to go into lodgings for a time.'

'Where do you suggest?'

'For heaven's sake, Philippa! I have no idea! You will have to look.'

'You look. You are the one who has made the mess!'

Unwilling to deal with his wife's hostility, he announced that he would take Philippe for a walk.

Father and son made their way resolutely towards Harrods, listening out for the sound of the muffin man as he strode along the icy pavements, balancing his double wooden trays of muffins and crumpets on his head with one hand, and ringing his bell with the other.

They bought a couple of muffins, and Le Roux asked him, 'Why are there so few muffin sellers these days?'

---

117 The value of a lease to a buyer will depend on the location of the property, how long the original lease has to run, and the rent.

'A shortage of butter, guv'nor.[118] Next year may be better, once we are out of the austerity.' Ringing his cheerful bell, he walked away along the darkening pavement.

The walk had helped to clear Le Roux's head and given him an idea. When they got home, he asked Philippa, 'Do you keep a diary?'

'Only a day-to-day pocket one,' she answered, uncertainly.

'Could you let me see it? You see, Noel has said I spent every Wednesday night with Naomi. I know that's not true, because sometimes I was ill, or you and I had visitors. My lawyer says that if we can cast doubt on his assertions, it will help me greatly.'

Philippa clearly remembered that her husband told her that on those Wednesday nights, he was attending meetings of the Civil Defence Corps.[119] She said nothing about this, however, but she found her diary and handed it to him. He would read some of her private thoughts, but it couldn't be helped. Perhaps he would understand how awful the last year had been for her.

After two days, however, he returned the little book triumphantly with the news that he had found four different dates when the diary contradicted Langley's claims and showed that Le Roux had been at home or with friends. He never commented if he had noticed his wife's fears, loneliness or bewilderment.

'We'll beat them yet!' he cried.

The next day, after having consulted with his lawyers, Le Roux told Philippa that she had to make a deposition.

'What's that?'

'You have to state what happened officially. The lawyers will write it down and ask you to confirm and sign it. If you do that, you need not give evidence in court.'

'Me! In court? Why?'

Le Roux became impatient. 'Philippa! You know this has to go to court! We're trying to show that Naomi was helping me with my work, that it was just a platonic friendship!'

'So, what am I supposed to say?'

---

118 Although the war had ended in 1945, rationing continued. Because of poor weather conditions, bread was rationed until 1948 and potatoes were also in short supply. Rationing was lifted on various foodstuffs over time: tea in 1952, eggs, cream, sugar and sweets in 1953, and cheese, butter, cooking oil, meat and bacon in 1954.
119 See n. 110.

He was silent for a beat, then he shrugged and said, 'Well, it will not go well for me if you insist on saying that you would not have her in this flat and that I was forced to go out and meet her —'

'Then what must I say? That I knew her? That she was a frequent guest and friend?'

'Of course, you must do as you wish, but if you could do that, it would be very helpful, yes.'

'What you are saying to me is that I must lie to your lawyer that Naomi was our mutual friend, and it was with my full knowledge and consent that you visited her?'

He shrugged. 'Something like that.'

'And I suppose I have to say this under oath?'

The more she thought about what Le Roux expected her to do, the more frightened she became. She knew giving false evidence under oath was perjury and was a punishable offence that might carry a prison sentence. She dared not even think of the shame if that happened, of her parents' reaction. And yet, wasn't this the way to help Le Roux, to clear his name and get things over and done with?

A few nights later, after dinner, she told him she would do it.

His face lit up, and he came across the room to kiss her.

She held up a hand. 'No. Listen to what I have to say. I am prepared to do this only because you say I have been instrumental in bringing about this situation. Perhaps I am guilty to some extent. But by making this deposition, I realise that should I wish to divorce you at a later stage, I am, by this action, throwing away any legal grounds that I might have for taking action against you. So I shall only do this if you swear, on the Bible, that you will never try to take Philippe away from me, should I leave you.'

His face hardened. 'How dare you bargain with me at a time like this? It's monstrous.'

As intimidated as Philippa felt, she stood her ground. 'I want you to swear to me on the Bible.'

'Okay, I swear. But don't expect me to forget this.'

A few days later, without discussing her action with Le Roux, she went in to the lawyer's office and gave the deposition.

> I am Philippa Chatfield Le Roux (born Davis), the wife of Le Roux Smith Le Roux, and we have been happily married since June 1947.

> I have never met the Petitioner (Noel Langley), but my husband has often told me about him. They were good friends before the war, and contact was only broken by the war.
>
> From time to time, we would run into Mrs Langley at exhibitions and the homes of mutual friends. She had separated from her husband and was earning money as a journalist, and offered to help my husband with the broadcasts he made every week to South Africa as there had been some criticism in the South African press that his talks from London had lost their South African angle.
>
> My husband would visit Mrs Langley on Wednesday evenings to discuss the weekly broadcast. I did not go with my husband as these were business meetings, and I would have had to hire a babysitter for our son.
>
> Several dates in the Petitioner's statement about my husband's visits to Mrs Langley are incorrect as a point of accuracy. On none of these dates was my husband visiting Mrs Langley.

When Le Roux came home in the evening, she showed him the deposition. His only response was to say, shortly, 'Whatever you have done is of your own volition. Please remember that!'

The lease on the apartment was sold and Le Roux used the money for his defence. Philippa found a rooming house in Sloane Street, where she took a large double room and a bath for herself and Philippe, with a smaller room across the passage for Le Roux.

The weeks passed tediously as they waited for the Langley case to be heard. Le Roux was sweating under the double strain of the Tate inquiry and the worry of the outcome of the divorce case.

One afternoon early in February, on the day before the court case, the phone rang. Philippa answered and heard a man's voice. 'Is Mr Le Roux there?' he asked.

'I'm afraid he is out. It is his wife speaking. May I take a message?'

'Oh.' The man hesitated, then continued, 'It's about the keys of 13 Chapel Street in Belgravia. He promised to return them to our office last week and hasn't yet done so. We have other people interested in the property, and we need the keys.'

'Chapel Street? I'm afraid there must be some mistake. My husband hasn't mentioned the property.'

'No, madam, I'm not mistaken. Mr Le Roux has the keys and is considering purchasing the property. Kindly ask him to telephone Mr Rogers on his return.'

She put down the telephone carefully. There was no doubt in her mind that it was a mistake: Le Roux had no means to buy a house in one of London's most fashionable residential districts.

That evening, Philippa asked him about it. 'Oh, Lois asked me to find her a house,' he said, dismissively. 'She's tired of living in an apartment. I hung on to the keys because she hasn't had time to look at this place yet. But I think she'll like it.'

'I see.'

Le Roux shrugged on his jacket. 'It will need doing up a bit. She wants me to see to that for her, should she be interested.'

The next day, as they both prepared themselves to face the lawyers, Le Roux came across the corridor to Philippa's room. 'Did you ever find your gold watch?' he asked casually.

'No, I never did. I must have lost it,' she said in a voice she hoped sounded normal; she suspected her husband of selling the watch.

Le Roux took his hand out of his pocket and thrust something into her hand. 'Here you are,' he said.

She opened the small package. It was a tiny gold watch on a thin black strap.

'I'm afraid funds did not run to gold straps, but it is 18 carats, and you can get a proper strap later.' He pushed up her sleeve. 'Let me put it on.'

The court building in Fleet Street looked no different from any other, drab yet imposing. Despite the occasion, Le Roux's geniality and expansiveness filled the courtroom, and Philippa found herself watching him with hope because, despite everything, he still had a unique ability to calm her fears when she was near him, to exude assurance and compelling warmth.

She gazed at the centre of the courtroom and saw Noel Langley, tall and pale, in the witness stand. The advocate was questioning him.

Le Roux was next on the witness stand, and she heard his advocate saying, 'Since it has been proven beyond a reasonable doubt that Mrs Naomi Langley committed adultery with the two co-respondents previously named before this court, I request that the case against my client, Mr Le Roux, be dismissed. This is based on the fact that evidence has only shown he dined with Mrs Langley on several occasions over the past year. There is no evidence to suggest that adultery actually occurred between him and Mrs Langley.'

After the Dance

The judge said some words to the council representing Noel Langley, and after further discussion between the advocates and the judge, there was a silence while various papers were read.

Finally, the judge addressed Le Roux. 'Do you swear under oath, Mr Le Roux, that you did not commit adultery with Mrs Langley at any time?'

'I do so swear, my Lord.' His voice was resonant and compelling as it rang throughout the court.

'You may step down.'

As Philippa left the court with Le Roux, she said, 'Thank goodness that's over.'

'Yes!' Le Roux was smiling. 'Noel looked pretty unhappy.'

'He looked ill and tired.'

Le Roux flagged down a cab and helped her inside. 'Tell the cabbie where you want to go,' he said. Then he walked briskly along into the crowd and was gone.

On Sunday, 28 February 1954, a sunny but freezing day, Philippa and Philippe left London. Philippa had dressed her son in his coat which had pin-checks of pale and dark blue, with a sapphire velvet collar and matching cap. Looking at him, she did not regret her decision to give birth to him at the price of her marriage.

There was a knock at the bedroom door, and Le Roux called, 'We need to go; I'm double-parked.' Philippa opened the door, took her son's hand, and went downstairs to the same old Daimler that had haunted their marriage.

They didn't talk as Le Roux drove to Croydon Airport. When they arrived, Le Roux found a porter and the luggage was piled on to the conveyor. Philippa went to check in. She had chosen KLM because a friend had said it was good with children.

'You change at Schravenhage,' the attendant said, 'but your luggage is booked through to Johannesburg.' Philippa thanked her, took the boarding cards and, turning, saw Le Roux striding towards them with a huge teddy bear in his arms. He knelt beside his son and said, 'This is for you, my boy.' Then he tipped his hat to Philippa and strode off.

So that was the end. How strange after all she had hoped for. But she had her little boy, clutching a teddy that was bigger than he was. When they boarded, Philippa put teddy in the overhead storage bin. 'He is tired, darling, and wants a little snooze. Remember, Pooh Bear always wanted a little snooze. Well, all bears are the same.'

She made sure the boy was comfortable, then settled herself into her seat. Fortunately, the pilot signalled take-off before any more could be said.

Now that she was going home, she allowed herself to imagine the smell of the warm earth after rain and remembered how it would accentuate the scent of the bruised flowers; she could see her mother throwing open the windows after a storm to let in the fresh air. My son will grow up knowing all the wonders of South Africa, she thought: the heat of the merciless sun, the pressure of the grey skies when the clouds build up before the summer rains...

Closing her eyes, she longed for the rains to pour over her and wash away all her bewilderment and guilt. Next time I walk along the white sands of Muizenberg beach, I will have my son at my side, she thought. She visualised him playing on the edge of the surf, absorbed in building sandcastles that were knocked down by the waves. He would run towards her with his arms outstretched and his eyes full of laughter.

4

The End of the Tate Affair

1954

In early March 1954, Dennis Proctor, the chairman of the Tate trustees, visited Sir Edward Ritson in Somerset House. The meeting began with Ritson keen to establish that Proctor – unlike Jowitt who had been chancellor – was merely a minister of state for transport, and worked for the Treasury, not the other way around.

'I understand the Picasso has been funded against the Grant in Aid for 1954–55. You realise that the Grant in Aid for 1954–55 requires a vote in Parliament.'

'Yes, Sir Edward. We specifically made no link between the borrowing and the Grant in Aid.'

'Nonetheless, you would agree that there is an implicit link because how else will Coutts Bank be repaid?'

'Yes.'

'Mr Proctor, I believe we all understand what needs to be done to clear up this sorry mess,' Ritson began. 'There are two options. If the trustees wish to dismiss John Rothenstein, they should consult Prime Minister Churchill because the Prime Minister appoints the Director of the Tate. Regarding Le Roux, it is quite straightforward as he is on probation until 8 March. If the trustees decide to dismiss him, it would be better to do so before then, as after that date, his probationary period will end, and he will have held his Civil Service Commission certificate for two years.'

'Your view, then, is that we should get rid of Le Roux?'

'Our perspective has consistently been that restoring order to the management of the Tate is crucial, which involves supporting the director and providing him with the necessary resources to fulfil his responsibilities. Once Le Roux departs, the Treasury will enforce a reorganisation of the Tate's functions, implementing checks and balances that empower the director to manage effectively while ensuring the trustees maintain proper oversight. Are we clear, Mr Proctor?'

Proctor disliked Ritson's tone, yet he recognised that Ritson was providing a way out. As chairman, he was resolute that the trustees should navigate that narrow opening as swiftly as possible.

Consequently, on 5 March 1954, he handed Le Roux a dismissal letter.

Le Roux read the letter and looked at Proctor. 'Well, I don't know what to say. This seems to be a punishment for something, but I'm not sure what.'

'I suggest you go away and consider this letter, which is confidential, and arrange a meeting for next week to clarify any points. The trustees have agreed to pay you six months' salary in lieu of notice. It's a generous offer. Please consider it.'

'Mr Proctor, it is indeed surprising to me that you are terminating my employment three days before my probationary period ends.'

'An unfortunate coincidence.'

The following day, Le Roux took a lunchtime flight to Nice, then a taxi to Graham Sutherland's house in the hills, arriving in time for sundowner drinks.

Le Roux liked and admired Sutherland. As well as being a great artist, he was clever and had a point of view. They talked for a while about life in the south of France, and then turned to the Tate business.

'I can't say how sorry I am that I resigned when I did,' Sutherland said. 'I was so fed up with Rothenstein that I resigned without thinking of the consequences, certainly as far as you are concerned. It's inconceivable to me how badly Rothenstein manages the Tate. Matching purchases to bequests is such basic stuff.' He paused and refilled their glasses.

'Well, Graham, your resignation and the press comment that followed certainly rattled the cage of the trustees. I've never seen so much activity.'

'I should imagine Proctor is beside himself over the director.'

'He is. If he could, he would have fired him, but I'm afraid the Treasury is in control of the process, and I was sacrificed.'

'All is not lost. I will write to the prime minister and the chancellor to see if one of them is up to intervening.'

'That would be very helpful. But I'm afraid the Treasury seems to be running the show now, and their position is to support the senior civil servant in post,' sighed Le Roux.

By the time Le Roux arrived back in London, several members of staff, including Jane Ryder, had written to the chairman to express their amazement and disappointment that Le Roux had been fired. Also, the press had got hold of the story of his demise.

Le Roux visited Dennis Proctor to demand an explanation. 'You said that the letter was confidential but the story is all over the press. I consider it a breach of trust. How am I to secure another position if the Tate has sacked me after four years on probation?'

Proctor nodded glumly. 'It is an unfortunate set of circumstances.'

'I think it's only fair that I be allowed to resign to avoid further damage to my reputation.'

In the meantime, Sutherland delivered his promised letter to the chancellor, summarising what had happened at the Tate. It stated that the trustees had been 'grossly misled' about the director's use of funds for purposes other than as directed in the bequests, by no means 'a trivial matter'. The letter continued:

> I was unfortunate enough to be a trustee during the acquisition of *The Little Dancer* by Degas. The director did not furnish the trustees with the correspondence of this transaction. The sight of these documents would have made it obvious [to the trustees] that the proposed transaction was open to very serious questions... My considered opinion was, and is, that their non-production was a gross dereliction of duty of the most serious kind.
>
> Mr Le Roux ... expressed to the director his anxiety about certain aspects of this transaction, including the excessive price (on which informed opinion is now agreed) and also the absence of written files of the part played by the gallery in the negotiations of such considerable importance. And not long after, the director intimated to Mr Le Roux that he could count on the director's full support if he wished to obtain a post elsewhere.
>
> Finally, certain threats and accusations (unrelated to the bronze, and afterwards shown to be unwarranted) were launched against Mr Le Roux in such a way that the well-founded misgivings about the Degas purchase came to be submerged, and the affair was gradually given the colour of a mere clash of personalities.
>
> Treasury attention was concentrated less on matters in which the director, in the trustees' opinion, had fallen short of his duty, and more on the fact that it was Mr Le Roux, his deputy, who had drawn the attention of the trustees to these lapses. The issue seems accordingly

to have been transformed into a clash of two personalities who were subject to Civil Service discipline. In such a situation, the strong possibility must remain that the senior official may benefit from any doubt at the expense of his junior.

The Treasury was incandescent. Sutherland had, they said, defamed not only the director but the Treasury. They urged Rothenstein to see Churchill, whose support would be crucial if he were to remain.

This Rothenstein did on 24 March. Churchill, who simply ignored Sutherland's approach, told Rothenstein not to resign.

In May, the chancellor finally agreed to meet with a delegation that included Lord Kinnaird, Lord Jowitt and Graham Sutherland. Lord Kinnaird explained that the deputation arose from the trustees' failure to confirm Mr Le Roux in his appointment as deputy keeper after four years of probation. He believed that Le Roux was a 'scapegoat' for the administration's shortcomings regarding the trust funds.

Le Roux was allowed to stay and attend trustee meetings until 24 May, and then resign. As agreed, he was paid six months' salary, tax-free.

In November 1954, at an exhibition, Douglas Cooper, a collector and critic who had sided with Le Roux, pointed at Rothenstein and said, 'That's the wretched little man who is going to lose his job.'

Rothenstein punched him, to the applause of several onlookers.

The Palace forbade the press from reporting the incident at the time because royalty was present.

5

Loose Ends

Philippa divorced Le Roux in 1955 and remained in South Africa, where she returned to her career as a journalist. That same year, Le Roux married Lois Bilton and they had two children, Ariane and Fabrice.

After leaving the Tate, Le Roux worked as a journalist and continued his weekly broadcasts on SABC. These broadcasts included him recounting his meetings with key figures such as Marilyn Monroe while fishing on the Miramichi River, in Canada.[120] He also tells the story of visiting Pablo Picasso in Vallauris for a TV documentary about him and spending several days watching the great modern master at work.

Lord Beaverbrook, having observed the Tate affair from afar and received regular briefings from Graham Sutherland, promptly hired Le Roux to write for the *Evening Standard* about fluctuations in the prices of artworks. He then asked Le Roux to work for him full-time at a salary of £2,000 per annum, which significantly exceeded what the Tate had paid him.

Le Roux's first task was to compile a list of 20th-century artists for acquisition by the Fredericton Gallery. In June, Le Roux served as an intermediary for Beaverbrook with the dealers, sending around a dozen paintings to Arlington House: a Wilson Steer from Agnew's; a Matthew Smith, a Wadsworth, a Paul Nash ('I believe I can find a better one'); two Stanley Spencers from Tooth's; a Christopher Wood ('a bargain'), and a Wyndham Lewis from the Redfern Gallery; a Ben Nicholson, an Ivon Hitchens, and a Francis Bacon (*Yawning Man* – 'a bargain') from Gimpel; and a Peploe still life from Lefevre. On 28 June, he travelled to Oxford to purchase a Paul Nash landscape from Nash's widow

---

120 *The Contemporary Scene* no. 137, talk on the SABC by Le Roux Smith Le Roux, 29 September 1956.

for £400.[121] Le Roux described this as a busy and chaotic period. He also convinced Beaverbrook to purchase several of the finest pieces on display, including *Hotel Bedroom* by Lucian Freud, which turned out to be one of his most significant works.

Le Roux then travelled to Canada with Beaverbrook to visit the proposed site of the gallery in Saint John, where he persuaded Beaverbrook that the provincial capital of Fredericton was a far superior location. Bob Tweedie,[122] a friend and confidant of Beaverbrook's was tasked with assisting Le Roux in New Brunswick. 'I did everything I could to facilitate Le Roux's work (for Lord Beaverbrook). In between times we had a lot of fun. He was a great companion and a witty conversationalist.'[123]

In the autumn of 1955, Le Roux wrote to Tweedie: 'My senior partner [Beaverbrook] was in an extremely odd mood when I saw him in N.Y., one moment threatening to abandon the whole art gallery scheme, the next to build something more ambitious and complaining throughout that he lacked reliable advice. So I told him that he had too many advisers and, from my point of view, seemed only interested in the advice which agreed with his preconceptions. That cleared the air considerably but may hasten my demise as a member of the Beaverbrook set-up.'

Perhaps the writing was on the wall. In 1956, Le Roux's relationship with Beaverbrook became increasingly strained. Whether through Le Roux or one of the many other advisers, Beaverbrook acquired a Constable painting of Flatford Mill and a Turner titled *View from the Giudecca*. In April 1956, Beaverbrook grew anxious about the provenance of the Constable and the Turner. He did not have the papers and was unable to assist with their whereabouts as his secretary had been taken away and he had not been in the office. On 26 May, Le Roux wrote to Lord Beaverbrook resigning, effective 31 May 1956, as he needed to go to Paris for treatment.

Beaverbrook sent Percy Hoskins, the *Daily Express* crime reporter, to investigate Le Roux. Aside from reporting that Le Roux was 'a ladies' man', there was nothing to spark further inquiry. However, Rothenstein claimed in his memoir that Beaverbrook told him, 'Le Roux had swindled him out of about £40,000. Additionally, Le Roux had

---

121 *Beaverbrook: A Life* by Anne Chisholm & Michael Davie (HIL/Box 1/File 5).
122 Robert Allison (Bob) Tweedie was born and lived most of his life in New Brunswick. For more than half a century he influenced provincial politics.
123 Tweedie, p.173.

been receiving secret commissions from several dealers, including some reputable ones.' Beaverbrook did not pursue Le Roux, which, considering Beaverbrook's litigious nature and the magnitude of the amounts involved (approximately £1.2 million at today's worth), raises doubts about whether Beaverbrook made these remarks to Rothenstein or held Le Roux accountable.

Rothenstein went on to say:[124]

> In May 1960, despite all his past and his minimal proved competence, Le Roux was able to obtain a position at Wildenstein's. In 1965, I met a senior partner of Wildenstein's, and I forewarned him that in my forthcoming autobiography, I should have to characterise one of his late employees as a criminal. "You don't surprise me in the least," he answered. He went on to tell me that from his own firm, too, Le Roux had been dismissed on the grounds of misconduct and that he had been found dead immediately after he had received his notice of dismissal. The misconduct, it was implied, concerned money and also included much trouble-making among staff.

What actually happened was that, in October of that year, while travelling in France on Wildenstein's business with his mistress, Charmian Salmon – who had a daughter with Le Roux, Gabrielle, born on 18 January 1961 – the couple were involved in a serious car accident. Salmon escaped relatively unscathed, but Le Roux's injuries were life-changing.

Lois, Le Roux's wife, chartered a special Air Ambulance to fly him back to England, and he was transferred to the London Clinic.

On 30 January 1961, Lois wrote to Philippa with an update on Le Roux's condition.[125]

> Dear Philippa,
> I am writing to put you in the picture re Le Roux.
> The brain surgeons believe that in breaking his neck, the main artery feeding the brain has been damaged. If they find this for sure, they can't do anything about it, which is another matter. So you see the likelihood of sudden death hangs over L.R. like the Sword of Damocles.
> Le Roux has no money, just an immense pile of doctors' bills. To give you some idea of how much assistance one can expect from

---

124 *Brave Day Hideous Night* by John Rothenstein, published by Hamish Hamilton, 1966.
125 Original letter dated 30 January 1961, from Lois Le Roux to Philippa

Wildenstein's, although Le Roux was travelling on the firm's work when he crashed, George Wildenstein did not write to me even at Christmas time. He must have known that this crash brought dreadful worry and hardship. Le Roux was very much the new boy in the firm and received a nominal salary and 2½% commission once a specific figure in turnover is reached (which so far has not been reached).

Please do not let anyone else know of the news in this letter; although people promise not to talk, they always do and I have kept the horror from his Mama; I want to spare her everything until it is safely over.

Yours sincerely
Lois

As a result of the accident, Le Roux lost his memory and spent much of his two-year recovery period in hospital trying to re-learn information he had known previously. He never returned to work at Wildenstein's and died of a heart attack[126] in August 1963 at the age of 48.

Rothenstein published his autobiography, *Brave Day, Hideous Night*, in 1966, which, among other inaccuracies, claimed that Le Roux had committed suicide. The Atticus column in the *Sunday Times* quoted this. Lois challenged Rothenstein and the *Sunday Times* at the Press Council, which found in her favour. As an apology, Rothenstein wrote a letter in the *Sunday Times*, stating: 'It was part of an account given to me' and 'I felt justified in regarding it as authoritative.'

Rothenstein continued as director of the Tate Gallery until he retired in 1964. He was succeeded by his number two, Norman Reid.

In June 1964, a year after Le Roux's death, Lois wrote to Philippa that the man who had shared their lives 'will always remain a mystery'. 'I must confess that when anyone speaks to me of Le Roux, I feel as though I am on shifting sands,' she admitted. 'It seems that we all knew him and yet did not truly know him. One could laugh if he had not squandered such immense gifts and caused such chaos in others' lives.'

---

[126] The death certificate on file states Le Roux 'died of a coronary occlusion due to atheroma' (natural causes).

Acknowledgements and Thanks

Before embarking on this project, I pursued a diploma in creative non-fiction at the Institute of Continuing Education, Cambridge University, and an MA in Creative Writing at Birkbeck College, University of London. I appreciate the support and encouragement from Derek Niemann at Cambridge and Wes Brown's team at Birkbeck.

Special thanks to my editor, Tracey Hawthorne, for her guidance in bringing this book to its final form, and to Leanne Raymond for her generous insights into my father's and Eleanor Esmonde-White's early life. I also thank my historian and archivist, Gustav Heinrich, for uncovering intriguing facts about my parents, and Susan Bromley-Challenor for her assistance with my father's letters and broadcasts.

I am grateful for the invaluable resources provided by Tate Archive and The National Archives at Kew.

I owe heartfelt thanks to my friends Veronica Metter, Carey Rosenfeldt, Jamie Dunford Wood, Sue Ollemans, Caryn Solomon and Chris Von Christierson for their advice and encouragement throughout this long process.

Lastly, I express my deepest gratitude to my wife and funder, Amanda, for her unwavering patience and support.

Sources and References

Books and journals

Armstrong, H.C. 1937. *Grey Steel: J.C. Smuts: A Study in Arrogance.* Arthur Barker.
Berthoud, R. 1982. *Graham Sutherland: A Biography.* Faber and Faber.
Clark, A. 2018. *Fighting on All Fronts: John Rothenstein in the Art World.* Unicorn Publishing Group.
Dunlop, I. 11 October 1966. 'The Row at the Tate'. *Evening Standard.*
Hansard. 24 November 1953. UK Parliament. National Art Collections Bill. Volume 184.
Le Roux, P. 1978. *Mirage.* (Unpublished.)
Malala, J. 15 April 2001. 'The house of the rising sun'. *Sunday Times Lifestyle.*
Marriott, C. 17 May 1938. *The Times.*
McKever, R. 5 August 2014. 'The Tate Affair: Then and Now'. *Apollo* Magazine.
Muller, C.F.J. 1990. *Sonop in die Suide.* Nasionale Pers.
Raymond, L. 2015. *Eleanor Esmonde-White.* Main Street Publishing.
Richardson, J. 19 July 1997. 'Punch up at the Tate'. *Telegraph.*
Richardson, J. 2001. *The Sorcerer's Apprentice: Picasso, Provence, and Douglas Cooper.* University of Chicago Press.
Rothenstein, J. 1966. *Brave Day, Hideous Night: Autobiography 1939–1965.* Hamish Hamilton.
Shearing, T. and D. 1999. *Commandant Gideon Scheepers and the Search for his Grave.* Privately printed.
Smith, D. 2 January 2005. 'Zsa Zsa's photos shook the Tate to its foundation'. *Guardian.*
Smith, J.A. 1939. *Ek Rebelleer!* Nationale Pers.
Spalding, F. 1999. *The Tate: A History.* Tate Gallery Publications.
Steyn, R. 2018. *Louis Botha: A man apart.* Jonathan Ball Publishers.
Tweedie, R.A. 1986. *On With The Dance.* New Ireland Press.
Sunday Times. 31 January 1954.
The Burlington. September 1947. Editorial.

The Illustrated. 25 October 1952. 'Zsa Zsa Gabor photographed in the Tate Gallery'.
The Listener. 5 July 1951. 'Review of the BBC Third Programme'.

Le Roux's radio broadcasts

3 May 1951. *Opening of the Festival of Britain*, broadcast on SABC.
20 June 1951. *London Review* no. 63, broadcast on SABC.
2 June 1953. *London Review* no. 159, broadcast on SABC.
22 July 1957. *The Contemporary Scene* no. 366, broadcast on SABC.
9 June 1958. *The Contemporary Scene* no. 412, broadcast on SABC.

Archives

National Archive at Kew
Ossewabrandwag Archive, Potchefstroom University
Tate Gallery Archive
Treasury files

Personal diaries and letters

Index

Afrikaner people 62, 74–5, 105
Agnew, Hugh 97, 112, 121, 198
Alfonso XIII, King 46
Alte Pinakothek, Munich 91
American Academy, Rome 46
Anderson, Colin 182–3, 185
Anglo-Boer War *see* Boer War
Anson, Hugo 95
Arezzo, Italy 43
Arts Council 120, 127, 133–4
Ashcroft, Margaret 'Peggy' 97
Athlone, Princess Alice, Countess of 54
Attlee, Clement 92

Baker, Herbert 40, 64
Barnes, Kenneth 95
Barnes, Thomas 152
BBC (British Broadcasting Corporation) 133–4, 135–6
Beaufoy Institute, London 60
Beaverbrook, Max Aitken, Baron 198–200
Benson, Robert 4
Berlin, Germany 41
Bilton, Lois 122, 123–4, 145, 167–8, 191
  marriage to Le Roux 198, 200–201
Boer War 6, 62, 65, 66, 68–75
Bond Street Gallery, London 141
  see also Marlborough Fine Art Gallery, London
British School, Rome 45–6
Brook, Peter 94
Brooke, Humphrey 107, 108, 112, 131, 132–3, 142, 158
  accusations against 100, 138–9, 151
  as Royal Academy secretary 153–5
Bunny, Aunt 27, 30
Burlington, The 132
Butcher, Miss 110
Butler, Rab 151, 182
Butler, Sydney Elizabeth née Courtauld 182
Byam Shaw, Glencairn Alexander 'Glen' 95

Calder, Alexander 121
Caledonian Charity Market 4
Cape Argus 35, 77
Carlton Hotel, Johannesburg 10, 11
Chamberlain, Neville 59

Charles (housemate) 28, 35
Cherrie (model) 50, 51–2
Churchill, Winston 59, 194, 195, 197
Civil Defence Corps 175, 188
Civil Service Commission 133, 194
Cleve Fund 182, 185
Coldstream, William 157, 186
Constable, John, *Flatford Mill* 199
Cooper, Douglas 108, 197
Copenhagen, Denmark 41
Coutts Bank 170–71, 182–3, 185, 194
Craig, Frank Barrington 'Barry' 31, 94
Cranko, John Cyril 127

Daily Express 199
Darwin, Robin 95
Davenport, Nicholas 92
Davenport, Olga née Solomon 92, 97
Davis, Adolf (father-in-law) 8, 14, 89, 105–6, 169, 177
  opposes daughter's marriages 9–11, 16–17, 22
Davis, Blanche (mother-in-law) 2, 8, 9–11, 16, 22, 169, 177
Degas, Edgar, *The Little Dancer* 139–40, 141, 148–9, 152–3, 157, 158–9, 196
Department of Building Research, Watford 53
Department of Education, Pretoria 5, 12–13, 82–3
Die Burger 66
Dinkel, Ernest 34, 39, 48, 52, 53
Dollfuss, Engelbert 42
Dorchester Hotel, London 164–5, 166
Driefontein, South Africa 71–4
Dronsfield, John 77
du Plessis, Enslin 113, 165
du Preez, Hugo 83, 84
Dutch Reformed Church *see* Groote Kerk, Cape Town

Eastern Cape, South Africa 65, 69–74
Edward VII, King 66
Edward VIII, King 36, 37
Egeland, Leif 92
Eivert (Swedish writer) 45, 46–7
Elizabeth II, Queen 164–7

205

Engelbrekt Church, Stockholm 41
Epstein, Jacob 31–2
Esmonde-White, Eleanor
  friendship with Noel Langley 54–5, 57, 59–60
  scholarship 25–7, 29–33, 35
  in Europe 40–47
  South Africa House murals 39–40, 48–56, 57
  remains in England during WWII 59, 64
Evans, Edith 91, 97, 125
Evening Standard 198

Fake, The (film) 152, 154, 157
Festival of Britain (1951) 120
Festival of the First Fruits 50–51
Ffrangcon-Davies, Gwen 1, 90–91, 92, 95, 106, 145
'fig leaf campaign' 45
First World War 41, 58
Fountains, The, Pretoria 3, 5
Fredericton Gallery, Canada 198–9
Freud, Lucian, *Hotel Bedroom* 199
Frost, Honor 132, 138

Gabor, Zsa Zsa 151–2, 158, 184
Gaunt, Dr. 144
George VI, King 134
Giacometti, Alberto 182
Gibbs-Smith, Charles 93
Giotto 43
Goldsbrough, Arnold Wainwright 126
Gowing, Lawrence 183
Graaff-Reinet, South Africa 69–70
Groote Kerk, Cape Town 62–3

Hardy, John 110
Harper, Reginald 'Reggie' 10
Hayward, Wally 169
Hendy, Philip 154–5, 185
Hertzog, J.B.M. 64, 76–7
Hindenburg, Paul von 41
Hitler, Adolf 1, 41, 42, 58–9, 64
Hockaday-Dawson, Mr 141, 147, 151, 159
Holland-Africa Lines 88
Hoskins, Percy 199
House of Lords 156, 181, 182
Hulton, Paul 131–3, 151
Hutchinson, Leslie 'Hutch' 37

Illustrated, The 151
Illustrated London News, The 84
Imperial Institute, London 142
Institute of Contemporary Arts, London 140, 162

James, John Morrice Cairns 18–21
James, Philip 133–4
Johannesburg Art Gallery 83
Johannesburg Municipality 59
Johannesburg Railway Station 29

Jowitt, William Allen Jowitt, Earl (Chairman of Tate Gallery) 147, 151–8, 160–62, 184, 194, 197
Juta, Jan 29–30, 35, 53

Khoisan people 68, 73–4
Kinnaird, Lord 181, 182, 184, 197
Kitchener, Horatio Herbert Kitchener, Earl 68
Kloman, Theo 140, 162–3
Kloman, Tony 140, 162–3
Knapping, Margaret 181–2, 183, 184
Koos (servant) 84, 86, 104
Kruger, Paul 87
Kruger National Park, South Africa 87–8
Krugersdorp, South Africa 68
KwaZulu Natal, South Africa 74

Lake Lugano, Italy 176–8
Lambert, Leonard Constant 126
Langley, Naomi 55, 58, 59–60, 103–4, 112–13
  divorce case 113, 179, 188–9, 190, 191–2
Langley, Noel 54–5, 57–8, 103, 104
  divorce case 113, 179, 187, 188, 190, 191–2
Lawrence, D.H., *Sea and Sardinia* 29
Le Roux, Ariane (daughter) 198
Le Roux, Fabrice (son) 198
Le Roux, Gabrielle (daughter) 200
Le Roux, Gerhardus (great-grandfather) 68
Le Roux, Juanita (wife) 1–7, 12–13, 15–16, 20, 22, 89, 104, 178
Le Roux, Le Roux Smith
  birth of son 125–6
  change of surname 77
  health and death 14, 89, 199, 200–201
  marriages and affairs 200–201
    see also Bilton, Lois; Langley, Naomi; Le Roux, Juanita (wife); Le Roux, Philippa Chatfield née Davis (wife)
  scholarship
    travels to London 25–33
    European tour 40–44
    British School course 45–7
    Royal College of Art course 34–5, 39
  travels
    to Canada 198–9
    to Eastern Cape with father 67–76
    to Europe 40–44, 175–80, 88–9, 195
  work 198–200
    artworks and commissions 57, 61, 76, 88–9, 97, 112
    South Africa House murals 39–40, 48–56, 57, 64
    media 146, 148, 164, 166, 169, 198
    see BBC (British Broadcasting Corporation); SABC (South African Broadcasting Corporation)
    Pretoria Art Centre 2, 5, 81, 88, 104, 105

see also Tate Gallery, Le Roux as Deputy Director
Le Roux, Lois (wife) *see* Bilton, Lois
Le Roux, Philippa Chatfield née Davis (wife)
   marriage to John Russell 8–12
   affair with Le Roux 1–7, 11–14, 15–17, 18, 21–2
   moves to Cape Town 17–18
   relationship with Morrice James 18–21
   married life with Le Roux
     in South Africa 83–6, 87, 88–100
     moves to London 105–6, 108–9, 110–12
   discussion about having children 85, 112, 113–14, 115–16
   during pregnancy and childbirth 121–6
   during The Great Tate Affair 135–6, 137–9, 142, 143–4, 162–71
   holidays 114–17, 145–6, 175–80
   suspicions of his affairs 100–104, 123–4, 127, 139, 145
   see also Bilton, Lois; Langley, Naomi
   Langley divorce case 187–92
   returns to South Africa 192–3
   divorce from Le Roux 198, 200–201
Le Roux, Philippe (son)
   birth and childhood in London 125–6, 135, 137, 145, 165, 168–70, 176, 190
   moves to South Africa 189, 192–3
Life magazine 114, 122
Listener, The 134
Lombard, Jacobus 82–3, 88
London Review 121, 166

MacDonald, Ramsay 54
Malala, Justice 56
Malan, D.F. 92
Malherbe, Diana 114, 116, 117, 122
Manchester Guardian 56
Marchant, Stanley Robert 95
Marlborough Fine Art Gallery, London 148–9, 153, 157
Marriott, Charles 56
Matt (pet dog) 84, 85–6
McEwen, Frank 165, 178
Merwe, Piet van der 72–3
Michaelis, Lilian Elizabeth 81
Michaelis School of Fine Art, Cape Town 25
Michelangelo 45
Milroy, Den 4, 18
Milroy, Lee 4–5
Monroe, Marilyn 198
Moore, Henry 149, 157
Mountbatten of Burma, Edwina Mountbatten, Countess 37
Mountbatten of Burma, Louis 'Dickie' Mountbatten, Earl 36–7
Muizenberg, South Africa 17, 193
Munich, Germany 41–2, 91
Munnings, Alfred 93, 94
Mussolini, Benito 42, 44

Nash, Paul 198–9

National Gallery, London 91, 181
National Party, The, South Africa 105, 122
National Theatre Movement 53
Natives Land Act (1913) 75
Nazism 6, 41–2, 62, 122
Neues Museum, Berlin 41
Nomen, Betty 117, 119
Nomen, Carol 119
Nomen, Coco 116–17, 118–19
Nomen, Jacqueline 119
Nomen, Terence 116, 117

Old Mutual, Cape Town 61, 76
Ons Koerant 69
Oslo, Norway 40–1
Ossewabrandwag 6

Padmore, Thomas 156, 157, 158–61
Padua, Italy 43
Paris, France 114–117, 140–41, 178
Perfect, Mr. 107, 108
Peter (friend) 135–6
Picasso, Pablo 198
   Femme Assise dans un Fauteuil 182–3, 185, 194
Pierneef, Jacob 29–30, 53
Piero della Francesca 43
Piper, John Egerton Christmas 127, 149, 185
Playfair, Edward 153, 154, 161
Press Council 201
Pretoria Art Centre 2, 5, 81, 88, 104, 105
Pretoria Art Gallery 87
Pretoria City Council, Art Collection 81
Pretoria General Hospital 8
Proctor, Dennis (Chairman of Tate Gallery) 183, 184, 185, 194–6
Public Works Department, South Africa 57
Purcell, Henry 126–7

Quaglino's, London 35, 37, 49

Rand Daily Mail 2, 4, 18, 19, 55, 83, 114, 164
Raphael 45, 126
Raymond, Leanne, *Eleanor Esmonde-White* 39, 60
Reid, Norman 107, 109
   during The Great Tate Affair 139, 148, 150, 152, 154, 157, 183, 185
   as Tate Gallery director 201
Rey, Jean 99
Rey, Jill 99, 102, 104
Ric (band leader) 37, 49–50, 51–2
Richardson, Ralph 97
Ridley, Jasper 111–12, 131, 132
Ritson, Edward 153, 155, 156–61, 194–5
RMS *Queen Elizabeth* 57
Robbins, Lionel 186
Roberts, Emmanuel 49–50, 51–2
Roberts, Frederick Sleigh 68
Rome, Italy 44, 45–6
Rose (Philippa's grandmother) 17–18

Rothenstein, Elizabeth 93, 94, 109–10
Rothenstein, John ('Johnny')
  knighthood 134
  as Tate Gallery director 111–12
  visits South Africa 84, 87–8
  invites Le Roux to London 90–92, 94, 100
  hires Le Roux 105–10, 131
  unpopularity 131–4, 138–9, 162–3
  accusations against Le Roux 147–51
  The Great Tate Affair 139–40, 141–2, 151–61, 181–6
  dismissal of Le Roux 194–5
  punches Cooper 197
  retirement 201
  written works 108, 110, 131
  Catalogue of Modern English Painters 133
  inaccuracies in memoirs 199–200, 201
Rothenstein, Lucy 93
Rothenstein, William 39, 43, 93
Royal Academy of Arts, London 93–4, 140, 153
Royal College of Art, London 27, 28, 29, 34, 39, 53, 95, 163
Royal College of Music, London 95
Russell, John 1, 9–12
Russell, Maud 154
Russell, Philippa *see* Le Roux, Philippa Chatfield née Davis (wife)
Ryder, Jane 106–7, 117–18, 139, 140–41, 196

SABC (South African Broadcasting Corporation) 116, 121, 135, 166, 198
Salisbury Art Gallery 142
Salmon, Charmian 200
Scheepers, Gideon 72, 73
Scrovegni Chapel, Padua 43
Second Boer War *see* Boer War
Second World War 10, 58–9, 62, 76–7, 83, 96
Sekoto, Gerard 81–2
Shaw, George Bernard 53–4, 55
Shaw, Mrs 45
Shillingford, Oxfordshire 93, 94–5
Siena, Italy 44
Simon, Jacques de 1–3
Simpson, Wallis 36, 37
Smith, Anna (mother) 63–4, 65, 67, 76
Smith, Annette (sister) 63, 67
Smith, Anthonie (brother) 63, 65
Smith, Johannes Antonie (father)
  political views of 5–6, 48, 62, 64–6, 67, 74–5, 76
  relationship with Le Roux 12, 63–4, 67–76
Smith Le Roux, Le Roux *see* Le Roux, Le Roux Smith
Smuts, Jan 'Oubaas' 20, 64, 65, 77
South Africa House (High Commission), London 27, 28–9, 35, 39–40, 48–56, 57, 64
South African Arts Association 88
Spicer, Leila 114, 127, 167, 175, 176–8

Spicer, Walter 114, 123, 125, 144, 167, 175, 176, 177–8
Stevens, Mr 27, 29
Stewart, Mr 49, 50–51
Stockholm, Sweden 41
Sunday Times 183, 201
Sutherland, Graham 141, 149, 183, 195, 196–8

Tanner, Mr. 170–71
Tate Gallery, London
  exhibitions 82, 83, 87, 88, 120, 162
  funds 181–2, 183, 184, 185, 194
  Le Roux as Deputy Director
    turns down first offer 100
    duties 105–10, 117–19, 120–21
    visits Paris 115–17, 139, 140–41
    The Great Tate Affair 133–4, 138–9, 141–2, 147–51, 181–2, 184–6
  trustees support for 156, 157
  dismissal 194–7
  see also Jowitt, William Allen Jowitt, Earl (Chairman of Tate Gallery); Rothenstein, John ('Johnny')
  Publications Department 107, 109–10, 131, 141, 153, 182
Tempest, Marie 28
te Water, Charles Theodore (High Commissioner) 27, 29, 39–40, 48, 53, 55, 61, 64
Thames, River 107
Thomas, Mrs. 164
Times, The 49, 56, 117, 149
Transvaal, South Africa 68, 83, 84
Treasury Department 107, 108, 110, 132, 138, 150, 181, 182
  handling of The Great Tate Affair 152–3, 155, 156–63, 185–6, 194–7
  see also Padmore, Thomas; Ritson, Edward
Turner, J.M.W., *View from the Giudecca* 199
Tweedie, Robert Allison 'Bob' 199

University of Pretoria 105

Valentin, Curt 149
Vanne, Marda 1, 91
Vatican City 45
Venice, Italy 63
Victor (Spanish painter) 45, 46–7
Vienna, Austria 42
Viljoen, J.H. 105
Vredehoek, Cape Town 62

Welles, Orson 117, 119, 167
Western Cape, South Africa 67–9
Wildenstein, George 200–201
Wildenstein's (private art dealership) 200–201
Wizard of Oz, The (film) 54–5, 57
Wylde, Geoffrey 98

Zulu people 40, 48–52, 55–6, 64